The Confident Writer

Dolly Withrow
West Virginia State College

MIRROR PRESS™
IRWIN

Chicago • Bogotá • Boston • Buenos Aires • Caracas
London • Madrid • Mexico City • Sydney • Toronto

Material on pages 3–4 of this text is taken from *The Oxford Companion to the English Language,* Tom McArthur, ed., 1992. Material is reprinted by permission of Oxford University Press.

Material on page 268 of this text is taken from "The Silver of Imagination," a book review of *The Man Who Thought He Was Messiah,* in *The Charleston Daily Mail,* March 1, 1991, p. 5–A. Reprinted with permission.

©Richard D. Irwin, a Times Mirror Higher Education Group, Inc. company, 1997

Mirror Press:	*David R. Helmstadter*
	Elizabeth R. Deck
Marketing manager:	*Carl Helwing*
Project supervisor:	*Gladys True*
Production supervisor:	*Bob Lange*
Designer:	*Matthew Baldwin*
Prepress Buyer:	*Jon Christopher*
Compositor:	*Electronic Publishing Services, Inc.*
Typeface:	*10/11 New Baskerville*
Printer:	*R. R. Donnelley & Sons Company*

Times Mirror
Higher Education Group

Library of Congress Cataloging-in-Publication Data

Withrow, Dolly.
    The confident writer / Dolly Withrow.
        p.   cm.
    Includes index.
    ISBN 0-256-22034-4
    1. English language—Grammar.   2. English language—Grammar—Problems, exercises, etc.   I. Title.
    PE1112.W58   1997
    428.2—dc20   96–20985

Printed in the United States of America
1 2 3 4 5 6 7 8 9 0 DO 3 2 1 0 9 8 7 6

The Confident Writer

To Bill, my husband and friend

Preface

This book was written for the sole purpose of connecting the rules for writers to actual writing. Created for students—not for linguists—*The Confident Writer* is based on the belief that the reader will need to know how to write grammatical sentences regardless of his or her field of study.

Beginning with information that is easiest to understand and progressing to more difficult material, the text has been developed to enhance classroom instruction. The instructor, however, can begin with any chapter and move either forward or backward. *All* material is expressed in clear, straightforward language with minimal use of jargon.

This book provides flexibility for the instructor and accessibility to the student. It removes much of the tediousness of grammar instruction, leaving more time for the creative and enjoyable part of teaching. *The Confident Writer* has been tailored to meet students' needs, regardless of their current level of competency.

The Confident Writer uses an innovative approach that gives students reasons for learning the rules of grammar—reasons that will help motivate them to read, learn, and apply what they have learned. Each chapter is designed to help students become competent, confident writers. Rather than offering random sample sentences to illustrate concepts, plentiful exercises provide a thread of continuity and a context for the reader's clear understanding of the rules.

A number of exercises contain dialogue among several fictional characters. Two dominant characters, Matt and Annie, often discuss writing. Matt is intelligent but has not mastered the rules of American standard English. Many readers will surely identify with Matt. Most beginning writers are intelligent. Each has an area of expertise, although it may not be in language usage. This book reinforces the point that being unaware of the rules is not at all synonymous with being unintelligent. Precisely because Matt is intelligent, he wants to learn the rules that govern the use of American standard English. Annie is a professional writer. She offers concrete and entertaining comments about the rules of writing. The dialogue between Matt and Annie is designed to capture the reader's attention and encourage learning.

In addition to offering dialogue and humor, each exercise set is unified by a single subject. Some focus on art, authors, and outer space; others center on felines, football, government, and ghost stories. Including many more subjects, the exercises provide the raw material for students to practice their skills in creative sentence-writing and paragraph-editing.

Other features that contribute to the text are class-tested **tips** to help students remember the rules of writing. Each chapter contains a list of **chapter objectives** and a **summary** in addition to the many high-quality exercises. In cases where contradictory rules of grammar and punctuation may cause confusion, both rules are discussed and explained before a recommended usage is given.

To provide the immediate feedback that helps students master concepts, alternate answers are provided in the textbook.

Locations of Answers to Exercises

Answers to **odd-numbered** items within each exercise set appear in the Answers to Exercises at the end of the book. **Answers** to **even-numbered** items are in the *Instructor's Manual.*

Acknowledgments

I am grateful to the many reviewers of my manuscript for their suggestions, support, and encouragement: Eleanor Davidson, Nassau Community College, New York; Thomas A. Mazola, Macomb Community College, Michigan; Mary E. Ray, Indiana Business College, Indiana; Sid Silvester, Bob Jones University, South Carolina; Forrest Williams, Utah Valley State College, Utah; and Alaina Winters, University of Pittsburgh, Pennsylvania.

I appreciate my husband's constant help as I worked on the manuscript. To all the editors who patiently pored over my writing and made valuable suggestions, I extend my gratitude: Bess Deck, Jan Fitter, Rosalyn Sheff, and Gladys True. I am grateful for David Helmstadter's belief in the book and for the title, which he contributed. I appreciate Helen Carper for her support. I thank Don Mellert for reproducing the disks. Finally, I am indebted to Delores Castle, the teacher who ignited my desire to learn more about our language.

Dolly Withrow

Contents

PART 3 : Spelling, Capitalization, Mechanics, and Numbers

Chapter 1

Grammar: A Base for the Confident Writer

◢ OBJECTIVES

In this chapter, you will learn to

- ••• understand the connection between grammar and effective writing
- ••• trace the sources of English and grammar
- ••• approach grammar with confidence

The importance of acquiring excellent writing skills cannot be exaggerated. Whether you are writing fiction or nonfiction, prose or poetry, whether you are writing in a classroom or in an office, you must know the basic rules that govern the use of our language. Knowing the conventions of grammar provides the needed base for constructing any sentence and, therefore, any body of writing. When you know the rules, you write with confidence, sometimes even with power. With precise word choice and effective word combinations, your prose can instruct, enlighten, entertain, amuse, inspire, and persuade. It can move the reader to laughter, to tears, to action.

When people speak English as a second language, they have learned the rules of the language along with the vocabulary. When they speak or write, they work hard to apply the rules that govern usage. Unlike many native speakers of English, they have not formed dialectical speech habits that deviate from the rules. They have learned the language from the outside, but native speakers have learned the language from the inside.

As children, native speakers listen to and imitate the dialect spoken by those around them. Those children soon form the habit of speaking that dialect, a dialect they usually continue speaking and writing when they are adults. For that reason, it is far more difficult for native speakers of nonstandard dialects to break old habits and form new ones.

My mother speaks the Appalachian dialect fluently. I grew up hearing and, in turn, speaking it. For example, many of the people in my area say "unthaw" when they mean "thaw." They say "bedroom suit" when they mean "bedroom suite." They say "poke" when they mean "paper bag." *Don't buy a pig in a poke* makes sense if we know that *poke* means a paper

1

bag. Other regions, of course, have their own deviations in word choices and pronunciations. Many people from Boston pronounce Cuba "Cubar." My daughter's name is Risa, and a former friend of hers from Boston called her "Risar." Natives in New Orleans pronounce their city differently from most of us in the rest of the country. Many speakers may even use a different word order. For example, many people from Louisiana say, "It will do you that." All dialects are valid. They add color, texture, and interest to our linguistic tapestry, but you can understand why regional dialects sometimes cause communication breakdowns.

Some common deviations exist regardless of a speaker's region. For example, irregular verbs give many speakers and writers problems whether they live in the South, North, East, or West. Substituting "poke" for "bag" is one thing, but going outside the boundaries of grammar rules is quite another.

My childhood dialect, as colorful and valid as it is, would not serve me well when writing in college or on the job. It certainly would have been unacceptable when I was a college professor of English. I was able to break old habits and form new ones only by mastering and applying the rules of grammar.

Indeed, *grammar* is a set of rules that will help you combine words and parts of words to construct sentences according to standard American English. Do not be afraid of the word *grammar*. If you have had negative experiences when faced with lists of abstract, complicated rules of grammar, be assured that the language in this book will be as clear and straightforward as possible. When I shared some of these pages with my college students, one said, "It's just like having a tutor in the book." Since then, I have worked even harder to make the rules understandable to you, the reader. I have diligently worked to be sure you have "a tutor in the book."

Usage means the usual, habitual way in which language is actually spoken or written by members in any given community or culture. The language used may or may not adhere to the rules of grammar. While all dialects have validity, this book focuses on the rules for writers, rules you will be expected to apply when writing and speaking in academia and in most workplaces.

Taking the time, then, to *learn* the fundamentals of good writing is giving yourself a valuable, intangible asset that will serve you well throughout your life. Whether you are writing a letter to a close friend, an essay, a technical research paper, or an analysis of a poem, you will write with self-confidence. Knowing how to apply the rules of writing will set you free to concentrate on content, on what you really want to say. The connection is clear between knowing the rules and knowing how to write well.

Most students, indeed most people, dislike grammar, and the reasons for this vary. Many students feel they write well despite their not knowing the rules of grammar. These students often unwittingly make errors. They, therefore, frequently submit written assignments with mistakes of which they are unaware. To avoid such errors, *learn* the rules. Still other students feel that creativity can replace correctly constructed sentences. They feel their creative talent will be enough. They believe they can submit assignments to professors, or even manuscripts to editors, and their talent alone will bring them success. Professors expect college students to know the rules that govern our language. Editors expect manuscripts of professional quality. Talent helps, but it will not replace your knowledge of grammar. You must *learn* the rules, for they provide the base for effective writing.

The word *basics* implies simplicity. Unlike the basics in most other majors or disciplines, however, the basic rules of English are difficult for most people. Indeed, many people dislike grammar because the jargon (the special terminology of grammar) is hard to understand, the rules are often complicated, and exceptions abound. Most writers do not even like the word *grammar*, much less the discipline itself, and much, much less the memorization of rules.

If you detest grammar or feel that it is too difficult, read the following facts about its history. You will soon understand that the source of your problems with grammar is not you, but rather it is the winding, distorted path that grammar has followed to find its way into our language. Following is a brief history, telling how grammar and our language have separate roots.

The Greeks, during their Golden Age, were the first to divide and classify their language for study. With the spread of the Roman Empire, the Romans "borrowed" the Greek grammar and applied it to Latin. As early as the sixteenth century, scholars of English began to borrow the Latin grammar rules and apply them to the English language. In the eighteenth century, with a penchant for all things classical, they stressed in earnest the importance of learning and following the rules of "Latin" grammar. Latin, or prescriptive, grammar can be traced back over the winding paths to the Golden Age of Greece. Our language, however, does not find its source in Latin but rather in Old German. Our grammar, then, gives us problems. Descriptive grammars have since come along but have thus far not proved helpful in teaching students who are not already scholars of the language.

If you feel insecure when studying grammar of any kind, you can now better understand the reason. It is not that you are a slow learner in English; it is that our grammar can be traced to one source and our language to another. Perhaps, that is why grammarians are rare—and they are. The following excerpt from *The Oxford Companion to the English Language*, 1st ed., 1992, supports the notion that grammar is difficult:

Writing was a mystery to the population at large, which associated scrolls with knowledge and power. As a result, in classical and medieval times, grammarians were sometimes taken to be sorcerers, but the craft was so laborious that the sorcerers' apprentices were often frustrated by it. Ancient attitudes to grammar still survive: many people are in awe of it, know little about it, tend to fear it, often find it baffling and boring if exposed to it at school, and yet a minority is fascinated by it: a field in which precise scholarship and nit-picking have coexisted for centuries.

Knowing all this, however, does not mean we can disregard the rules. There is still a system that serves us well, but you need to know why grammar seems so difficult, so fraught with exceptions.

You will sometimes be asked to memorize rules or even lists of words, but never will this text give you "busy" work. When you are asked to memorize anything, understand that the memorization is crucial to your becoming a good writer.

The following essay is as much about you becoming a good sentence builder as it is about a squirrel being a good nest builder.

The Squirrel and the Writer

One unusually warm day in early January, I spent about an hour watching a squirrel flit up and down a large hickory tree in our back yard. At first, I thought it was playing. Then, I noticed that it returned again and again to the same fork high in the tree, where a cluster of dead leaves formed an incomplete nest. Each time it returned to its nest, it carried a small branch with dead leaves attached to the end. Amazed, I watched the intelligent rodent weave both the branch and leaves into the nest. The squirrel then darted farther up the tree and chewed off another small limb. This time, however, the flexible limb had no leaves. The agile squirrel put the 10- to 12-inch branch into its mouth and carried it back to the nest. I watched as it again wove a twig into the base of the structure. Its head and front paws disappeared into the nest, but its tail rapidly quivered to and fro as it worked to weave the twig securely into the base of the structure. The squirrel wove approximately four or five leafless twigs into the bottom of the nest.

Like a dedicated writer, the squirrel had a singularity of purpose. Like a good writer, this intelligent creature knew its purpose. It concentrated fully on the task at hand. Again and again, it scurried up and down the tree, but the focus was always the same, the nest. After each trip, it returned directly to the nest with more material. Its skill at weaving the *support* into the base of its nest was phenomenal.

When writers construct eloquent and grammatical sentences, their skills may seem phenomenal to the beginner. The squirrel knows instinctively that the twigs must be woven in a certain order and governed by a certain method. The writer must also know the rules and methods for constructing grammatical sentences. The ability to write correctly is not a natural gift, an instinct. The writer must learn the rules. Still, the connection is clear between a writer constructing a grammatical sentence and a squirrel building a sturdy nest. We can learn a great deal about writing while watching a squirrel build a nest.

Remember, then, as you read each chapter in this book, you must follow the squirrel's example. Learn each lesson as it is presented so that your construction of grammatical sentences can seem as effortless as the squirrel's construction of a sturdy nest. Indeed, as you progress through

The Confident Writer, you will come to understand that the word *grammar* stands for foundation. Just as the squirrel instinctively knows how to build a solid support at the base of its nest, you will learn to use the rules of grammar to provide a solid foundation for building any effective piece of writing.

Remember that without such a base, your writing will probably not get the results you want, for making mistakes in your prose interrupts the message you are trying to convey to your reader. Whether your prose contains a misplaced comma, a misspelled word, an incorrect verb, or a misused pronoun, you lose credibility with your reader. You may also confuse and irritate your reader. This book will help you to avoid such errors.

1

SUMMARY

You now understand why many people have problems with grammar. You know that although our language can be traced back to Old German, our grammar stems from Latin. You, nonetheless, have discovered the connection between the rules of grammar and the quality of writing. You are ready to begin dividing and classifying your language just as the Greeks did in their Golden Age. After learning the rules and lessons in this book, you will be able to use words correctly and to construct sentences grammatically. You will do both with confidence.

The following exercise gives you an opportunity to express your feelings about grammar. Write freely, and do not worry too much about whether all your sentences are grammatically correct. At the end of this textbook, you will have a chance to write on this subject again, *after* you have studied and practiced the rules that all good writers have learned. ∎

1.1 END-OF-CHAPTER EXERCISE

Instructions: Write a paragraph in which you discuss your attitude toward the study of grammar. Give at least three specific examples of problems you have had trying to learn the rules. To help you get started, you can use one of the two sample sentences. Try to limit the number of sentences to eight. You will have a topic sentence, which contains the topic and your opinion about the topic (see sample sentences). Then give three specific examples, following each one with additional details about the event or example. End your paragraph with a sense of finality—that is, with a reinforcing statement of your topic sentence. Couch it in slightly different language, but it should validate your topic sentence. Remember the squirrel's efforts to find and weave in support at the base of its nest. You, too, must find and weave at least three specific examples, which will provide support for your opinion.

Use one of the following sentences as the first sentence (topic sentence) in your paragraph:

1. I like grammar for several reasons.
2. I dislike grammar for several reasons.

TIP: Be sure to proofread your paragraph several times. Answers may vary, and will not be given in the Answers to Exercises at the end of the book.

Diagnostic Test

The following diagnostic test is just what its name implies. It is designed to help you diagnose the strengths and weaknesses in your writing skills. Although the word *test* implies something unpleasant, this test will not be graded. It is for your eyes only. Answer each question to the best of your ability.

Instructions: Underline the preferred word or words in parentheses.

1. By the time I reach the end of this book, I will make (less/fewer) errors in my writing.

2. Learning the rules for writers will (affect/effect) my writing in a positive way.

3. To (insure/ensure) my learning, I will study and complete all assignments.

4. I am (anxious/eager) to improve my writing skills, for good writers are in great demand.

5. The author has (inferred/implied) that I can succeed if I work.

6. In *The Confident Writer*, (their/there) are easy-to-understand explanations of otherwise difficult grammar rules.

7. By the end of this course, I am (suppose to/supposed to) know more than I do now.

8. I can learn (alot/a lot) by checking my answers to these sentences.

9. (Your/You're) sure to succeed if you study regularly.

10. *The Confident Writer* is a (most unique/unique) book; it is user friendly.

Instructions: Identify the part of speech of each italicized word by writing one of the following in the spaces provided:

noun	adverb
pronoun	preposition
verb	conjunction
adjective	

9

11. In this *book*, I will meet fictional characters that will bring the exercises *to* life.

12. *Matt Murray* is one of *those* characters.

13. Many exercises are *entertaining because* they tell a story.

14. The exercises do their job *well, and* they help me to remain enthusiastic.

15. *By* the end of the semester, I will be a *good* writer.

16. I *will learn* all the *rules* and improve my skills.

17. *This* is a lofty goal for *me*.

18. *Since I* will learn to avoid clichés, my writing will be original.

19. If I study *regularly*, I can avoid at least *some* stress.

20. I am *eager* to read about Matt and Annie, *who* bring life to the exercises.

21. *For* now, I am setting my goals and changing my *attitude*.

22. I know that I will *either* study *or* fail, and I do not intend to fail.

23. The connection *between* grammar rules and writing *makes* sense to me.

24. This *class* will be *enjoyable*.

25. I'll chuckle *when* I *read* that Matt has ended a   _____

sentence with a proposition—not a preposition.   _____

Instructions: Underline the correct words in parentheses.

26. The characters in this book work (good/well) together when they fight a forest fire near Mrs. Rebecca Penwright's house.

27. Annie Penwright told Matt and (I/me) to work for the precise word.

28. My friend and (I/me) look forward to learning.

29. We had (run/ran) several miles before the race began.

30. Matt, instead of running, had (went/gone) into the woods to photograph wildlife.

31. Later, he went home to proofread an essay he had (wrote/written).

32. Matt and (I/myself) attended the annual picnic.

33. Matt saw a fly on his food and threw (it/the food) in the trash.

34. The person (who/whom) Matt really liked had not yet arrived.

35. Matt climbed to the top of the hill, and (you/he) could see three states.

36. Matt (hiself/himself) wanted someone special to arrive at the picnic.

37. Everyone who reads widely increases (their/his or her) knowledge.

38. At the top of the hill, Matt (lay/laid) under a maple tree.

39. He had been (laying/lying) there for an hour when he heard footsteps.

40. As Annie walked closer to Matt, she said, "If I (was/were) you, I would look behind me."

41. A goat turned (it's/its) head toward Matt and Annie and then ran down the hill.

42. Matt's stuffy nose made him feel (badly/bad).

43. After he had (saw/seen) Annie, he began to feel better.

44. The couple spent (a/an) hour as they enjoyed a beautiful sunset.

45. Matt was tall, but Jonathan was the (tallest/taller) of the two.

46. Jonathan was a student in (Matts/Matt's) writing class.

47. They helped Annie when she planted (a/an) herb garden.

48. She used (them/those) herbs when she cooked.

49. Her garden (comprised/was comprised of) many kinds of herbs.

50. Annie's cat was named Elizabeth Tailless because (it's/its) tail had been surgically removed.

51. Running down the hill, (Annie's knee was fractured/Annie fractured her knee).

52. Annie, as well as many of her friends, (like/likes) to write.

53. Annie and Matt (meets/meet) at a local restaurant.

54. Each of Annie's many students (have/has) learned a great deal.

55. At the picnic (was/were) a fireworks display, a sack race, and lots of good food.

56. Neither Annie nor her editors (want/wants) to find errors in the published book.

57. They proofread carefully to avoid (mispelled/misspelled) words.

58. They know that (alright/all right) is frequently spelled incorrectly.

59. Annie has (recieved/received) many awards for her books.

60. Annie enjoys (writting/writing).

Instructions: Insert commas, semicolons, apostrophes, periods, and capital letters where needed.

61. Annie enjoys gardening however she has little time.

62. Annie enjoys gardening she has little time however.

63. She teaches at a local bank and at the college and Matt works at the bank and learns at the college.

64. Annie writes gardens and jogs.

65. Annie and matts favorite meeting place is the Whistle Top Buffet.

66. Its located in goldpage.

67. They discuss nouns verbs and adjectives when they meet.

68. During the long tutoring sessions Matt learns a great deal.

69. Matt who wants to succeed works diligently.

70. Anyone who works diligently can succeed.

71. Because Matt works hard, he will become a confident writer.

72. Matts efforts will pay great dividends.

73. Everyones writing will improve.

74. Matt is a talented photographer therefore he hopes to become a professional photographer.

75. Annies and Matts talents will play a leading role in their destinies.

Now check your answers in the Answers to Exercises in the back of the book.

1

Word Choices

Chapter 2

Commonly Misused Words

2

▶ OBJECTIVES

In this chapter, you will learn to

- ••• distinguish between commonly misused words
- ••• sidestep traps that language sets for us
- ••• understand several seemingly esoteric (little-known) facts about word choices

It is usually easier to combine letters to form words than it is to combine words to form sentences, that is, to construct grammatical sentences. Grammar rules sometimes seem abstract and are definitely difficult for many people, but word choice can sometimes be tricky, too. Precise writing demands the exact word, and choosing the exact word often requires more concentration than you might think.

Our language often sets traps for us because of words that sound alike. Even when two or more words do not sound alike, English has many pairs or groups of words that confuse us. Do you, for instance, ever have problems trying to decide whether to use *affect* or *effect, imply* or *infer?* If you do, you are not alone. These terms are frequently misused, sometimes even by professionals in the field of communications. Obviously, correct word choice—diction—is not a simple matter, but it is a skill that you can master with practice. *Diction* also means clarity of pronunciation.

Correctness in writing means many things, but it certainly means *precision*—choosing the right word, not the *nearly* right word. Precision in writing helps us to say exactly what we mean to say—no small feat (not feet!).

Below are pairs (pears/pares) and sets of words and expressions that cause problems for many communicators. Although some dictionaries treat several of these word pairs as *synonyms* (words that mean the same thing), usage dictionaries make a distinction between them, a distinction the precise writer observes.

The lists of commonly misused words in this chapter have been divided into three groups only to give you an opportunity to reinforce what you have learned before proceeding to the next list.

Confusing Pairs and Other Oddities

See if you can define the frequently misused words listed. A few of the expressions are incorrect and should not be used at all. Can you find them?

1. healthy/healthful
2. nauseous/nauseated
3. fewer/less
4. ensure/insure
5. uninterested/disinterested
6. capitol/capital
7. complement/compliment
8. stationery/stationary
9. anxious/eager
10. affect/effect
11. hung/hanged
12. ignorant/stupid
13. comprised/comprised of
14. regardless/irregardless
15. in behalf of/on behalf of

In the following sentences, the frequently misused words are boldfaced and used correctly. See if you can define each boldfaced word after you read each sentence.

1. healthy/healthful — The students and employees at Goldpage University work in a **healthful** environment; therefore, most of them are **healthy.**

2. nauseous/nauseated — Grammar is a **nauseous** subject for many people; grammar makes them **nauseated.**

3. fewer/less — **Fewer** students at the school hate grammar after attending enjoyable writing classes. Those who did not attend write with **less** confidence.

4. ensure/insure — To **ensure** that the students learned to distinguish between **ensure** and **insure,** the professor told them that to **insure** something was to buy protection against financial loss and to **ensure** was to make certain.

5. uninterested/disinterested

At first, the students were **uninterested** in the instructor's comments, but they soon warmed to the subject. When they evaluated Annie, they were **disinterested** and gave her an outstanding evaluation. (If this one is confusing, stay with me. You will soon be able to use both *uninterested* and *disinterested* precisely.)

6. capitol/capital

Matt Murray, a bank employee and a student, learned that **capitol** (when spelled with an *o* as in *dome*) always refers to the building in the **capital** (the city). He further learned that when not referring to the building, he should use **capital** with an *a*.

7. complement/compliment

Annie Penwright's handout was a **complement** to her lectures. Matt paid Dr. Penwright a **compliment** on her skills as a professor.

8. stationary/stationery

The bank was constructing a new building that would provide **stationary** quarters for its employees. The purchasing director had also ordered **stationery** because of the new address.

9. anxious/eager

Matt was at first **anxious** about attending a writing workshop, but after the first session ended, he was **eager** to attend the next class.

10. effect/affect

The class had a positive **effect** on Matt. He knew the following session would **affect** him in the same way. Attending the writing classes would **effect** (result in) excellent writing skills. Annie Penwright did not **affect** cynicism, a characteristic that must be cultivated.

11. hung/hanged

She winked and pointed to words on the board as she said, "Pictures are **hung,** but people are **hanged** when they misuse these killer words."

12. ignorant/stupid

During the first session, the attentive students may have been **ignorant** about grammar rules, but they certainly were not **stupid.**

13. comprise/comprised of

"The whole **comprises** the parts," said the professor, "not the other way around. Never use the word *of* immediately after **comprise** or **comprised.** The phrase *is comprised of* is *always* an error, but many writers nonetheless make this mistake."

14. regardless/irregardless

Irregardless is not a valid word; instead of **irregardless,** all you need and all you will ever need is *regardless.*

15. in behalf of/on behalf of

Annie said, **"In behalf of** means in support of; **on behalf of** means to represent."

2

It is time now to look more closely at the meanings of the boldfaced words in the preceding examples. Carefully read the following sentences, which contain definitions and tips to help you use these tricky words correctly. If you are still confused after reading the definitions, go back to the sample sentences and read them again.

1. **Healthful** is anything that makes a living organism **healthy.**
2. **Nauseous** is anything that makes you **nauseated.**
3. Use **fewer** with anything you can count (*employees,* for example), but use **less** with anything you cannot count (*gasoline,* for example).
4. **Ensure** means to make sure or certain, and **insure** is to protect against financial loss. Health insurance, car insurance, and home owner's insurance are examples of types of insurance that **insure** against financial loss.
5. **Uninterested** means not interested, but **disinterested** means impartial or fair.
6. **Capitol** refers to the building that houses state government in a state's **capital** (city). **Capital** has a number of meanings: (*a*) a capital letter, (*b*) money or property invested in a business, and (*c*) principal or main.
7. **Complement** means to complete or supplement. It can also mean a completion or supplement. **Compliment** is a comment (written or spoken) that praises a person, animal, or action.
8. **Stationery** (with an *e* as in sh*e*et of paper) means paper used for letters and memos. The stationer sells *stationery.* **Stationary** is the opposite of temporary; it is a descriptive words that means permanent or not movable. A building, for example, might be either stationary or portable (movable).
9. **Anxious** means worried or uneasy; think of the word **anxiety. Eager** means enthusiastic, full of anticipation.

10. **Affect** means to **a**ct on, to **a**lter, to influence. Look at the *a*'s that begin **affect,** *act*, and *alter*. **Affect** can also mean to pretend or feign. In psychology, **affect** means a strong feeling or emotion. **Effect** is a noun meaning the result or the influence. **Effect** can also be a verb that means to bring about or result in.

11. The sample sentences for **hung** and **hanged** are self-explanatory. When we mean someone was executed by hanging, we use **hanged.** When we hang inanimate objects, the past tense is **hung.**

12. **Ignorant** means unaware of, but **stupid** means unable to learn quickly.

13. **Comprise** means to include, to contain, to consist of. You can see that the *of* is already contained in the meaning of the word.

14. **Regardless** means despite or in spite of. Do not ever use the word **irregardless.**

15. Again, the sample sentence is self-explanatory. **In behalf of** means in support of, and **on behalf of** means to represent.

2

2.1 EXERCISE FOR YOUR MENTAL FITNESS

Instructions: Beside each word listed, write a sentence in which you use the word. If you have problems with words not listed, include those words in your exercise. Answers will vary, so they will not be shown in the Answers to Exercises at the end of the book.

1. healthy _____

   _____

2. healthful _____

   _____

3. nauseated _____

   _____

4. ensure _____

   _____

5. disinterested _____

   _____

6. capitol _____

   _____

7. capital _____

_____

8. stationery _____

_____

9. stationary _____

_____

10. anxious _____

_____

11. hanged _____

_____

12. comprised _____

_____

13. in behalf of _____

_____

14. on behalf of _____

_____

Good writers love words, for words are the tools with which they work. This does not mean that you must have an extensive vocabulary to be a good writer, although a good vocabulary helps. Your writing in college requires grammatically constructed sentences that are concise and precise. Regardless of the words you choose, they should be used correctly. As you now know, but it is worth repeating, good writing demands precision in diction, the precise word.

More Confusing Pairs and Other Oddities

Here is a list of additional words that are *commonly* misused. Again, see how many terms you already know. See if you can find any words or groups of words that should never be used.

1. pear/pair/pare
2. pored/poured
3. imply/infer
4. imminent/eminent

5. unusual/unique
6. recurred/reoccurred
7. faze/phase
8. oral/verbal
9. there/their/they're
10. lead/led
11. use/utilize
12. supposed to/suppose to
13. almost/most
14. proceed/precede
15. all right/alright

Following are explanations and sample sentences with definitions that will help you to to know which boldfaced words to use in any situation.

1. pare/pair/pear

Annie uses a paring knife to **pare** her **pair** of **pears** during each break. To **pare** is to peel something. A **pear** is a fruit. Two **pears** make a **pair.**

2. pored/poured

Matt **pored** over the essay until midnight. He later **poured** steaming black coffee into a heavy mug. To **pore** over documents is to read them carefully. To **pour** liquid is to let it flow from its container.

3. imply/infer

Annie said, "To **imply** is to suggest, and to **infer** is to conclude. Notice, then, that the speaker or writer **implies,** and the listener or reader **infers.** Do not use these words interchangeably."

4. imminent/eminent

When a storm is **imminent,** the storm is about to happen (almost immediately). Notice that the word *imminent* begins with the same three letters as *imm*ediately. **Eminent** means standing above the rest. It means outstanding or excellent. **Eminent** begins with *e* as in *e*xcellent. An **eminent** professor is an outstanding professor.

5. unique/unusual

Annie's book is **unique.** She has an **unusual** style. **Unique** means one of a kind; it cannot take a descriptive word, such as *very* or *quite*. **Very unique** and **quite unique** are expressions that are always incorrect. **Unusual** means not ordinary.

6. recurred/reoccurred

The event **recurred** last week. **Recurred** means something happened again or repeatedly. Do not use **reoccurred.**

7. phase/faze

The students are moving to another **phase** in their development as good writers. *Phase* is a word with which you are probably familiar. When a college is enduring a budget-cutting **phase,** it is going through a period of budget cutting. Annie's remarks did not **faze** Matt. You have probably heard the word *faze,* but perhaps you have not seen it in print. **Faze** means to disconcert or negatively affect someone.

8. oral/verbal

Many writers believe that **oral** and **verbal** can be used interchangeably; they cannot. **Oral** means spoken, but **verbal** means written or spoken or even both.

9. there/their/they're

There are two colleges in town. **Their** board members are meeting now. **They're** discussing an expansion of **their** curricula. Look closely at **there, their,** and **they're.** Notice that each word begins with *the.*

There often introduces a sentence. Following are additional tips to help you distinguish between **there** and **their.** Put it **here** (in this place). If you add a **t** in front of **here,** you will create the word **there** (in that place).

Now let us deal with **their.** Notice that if you delete the **t** from **their,** you have the word *heir.* An heir owns something, as in the following sentence: It is **their** property. **Their** means belonging to them.

The final word listed in this group is **they're,** which is a contraction meaning they are.

Remember that all three words begin with *the.*

10. lead/led

Lead (rhyming with seed) is the present tense of the verb meaning to guide or direct. **Lead** (rhyming with seed) can also be a descriptive word (adjective). She is the **lead** singer in the choir. **Lead** in the preceding sentence is describing *singer.* **Lead** (again rhyming with seed) can also be the name of something (noun). She is in the **lead. Lead** in the preceding sentence is the name of the front position.

Lead (when it rhymes with **red**) is a metallic element. **Lead** is used in pencils. **Led** is a verb, the past tense of the verb **lead,** meaning to direct or to guide. He **led** the parade yesterday. He has **led** the parade many times.

11. use/utilize

Use **use,** not *utilize.* Use **use,** not *utilization.* Choose the shorter of two words when meaning is not lost. When students **use** their minds, they make the best **use** of their time.

12. supposed to/suppose to

When the word *to* immediately follows *supposed,* you must always end **supposed** with a *d:* **supposed to**—never **suppose to.** In pronunciation, the *d* sound disappears, which explains the common error of omitting the *d* in writing. The class was **supposed to** meet at the bookstore.

13. almost/most

Almost means nearly. **Most** means greatest in amount, number, or extent. Do not use **almost** when you mean **most. Almost** everyone learned **most** of the material.

14. proceed/precede

Proceed means to continue; **precede** means to go before. The **preceding** sentence in this exercise contains the words *proceed* and *precede.* Now **proceed** to the next item.

15. all right/alright

Many writers misspell **all right** by spelling it as one word, **alright.** Actually, **all right** is two words—always. Leave a space between **all** and **right.** Do not use a hyphen. **All right** is written just like *all wrong*—two words.

2.2 EXERCISE YOUR CREATIVITY

Instructions: Choose ten words from the preceding list, and for each, write a sentence in which you use the word. To get the most from this exercise, you should choose words that give you special problems. Answers will vary, so they will not be shown in the Answers to Exercises at the end of the book.

1. _____

2. _____

3. _____

4. _____

5. _____

6. _____

7. _____

8. _____

9. _____

10. _____

More Confusing Pairs and Other Oddities

As you can see, many words in our language are commonly misused. Not all of them are included here, but one additional list will alert you to potential verbal traps. Moreover, you will know how to avoid such traps.

Scan the following list to see how many terms you already know. Are there any words or groups of words you should never use? This time, two prefixes (beginnings of words) are included.

1. a lot/alot
2. burst/bursted
3. reason is that/reason is because
4. centered on/centered around
5. presently/currently
6. in regard to/in regards to
7. moral/morale
8. a historic/an historic
9. continual/continuous
10. a/an

11. your/you're

12. to/too/two

13. cannot/can not

14. as/like

15. intra-/inter-

| 2.3 | EXERCISE FOR CONFIDENCE |

Instructions: Beside each of the following items, write a sentence in which you use the listed word or prefix. If you are not sure how to use the term correctly, look in a dictionary. If you cannot find the information you need, ask for help, but try to complete the assignment by searching for the answer yourself. Notice that the errors in the preceding list have not been included in the following list. (Answers to all of these questions are provided in the Answers to Exercises at the end of the book.)

1. a lot _____

2. burst _____

3. reason is that _____

4. centered on _____

5. presently _____

6. currently _____

7. in regard to _____

8. moral _____

9. morale _____

10. continual _____

11. continuous _____

12. a _____

13. an _____

14. your _____

15. you're _____

16. to _____

17. too _____

18. two _____

19. cannot _____

20. as _____

21. like _____

22. interdepartmental (Define this word in your sentence.) _____
_____

23. intradepartmental (Define this word, too.) _____
_____

SUMMARY

This chapter was designed to increase your awareness of language traps created by confusing words that are often misused or misspelled by writers in virtually every discipline. This chapter does not contain every commonly misused word in our language. It does, however, provide a sufficient number to alert you to the need for checking words that might be misused.

If you invest in an up-to-date collegiate dictionary, you will have at your fingertips another tool to make your job easier. A thesaurus (a dictionary of synonyms) and a good usage dictionary would also be helpful. *The Harper Dictionary of Contemporary Usage* is one of several usage dictionaries available.

Being aware that similar words can have different meanings will help you to become a precise, effective, and self-confident writer.   ■

2.4 END-OF-CHAPTER EXERCISES

Instructions: Choose the correct word in parentheses in each of the following sentences. Write your word choices in the spaces provided.

1. Theodore Roosevelt, the twenty-sixth President of the United States, was known for his (healthful/healthy) lifestyle. _____

2. To (ensure/insure) improved spelling, Theodore Roosevelt tried to simplify spelling by removing unnecessary letters from words such as *night* (nite) and *through* (thru). _____

3. (Anxious/Eager) to create a suitable title for one of his novels, Stendhal, the French novelist, titled one work *The Red and the Black*. _____

4. Reading widely and listening carefully will (affect/effect) grades in a positive way. _____

5. The test (was comprised of/comprised) 45 questions. _____

6. Jonas Salk, a (disinterested/uninterested) microbiologist, developed the first effective polio vaccine in 1954. _____

7. In Truman Capote's *In Cold Blood*, two cold-blooded killers are (hung/hanged). _____

8. To (imply/infer) is to suggest. _____

9. Teddy Roosevelt's attempts to simplify spelling had no (affect/effect) because even the President of the United States cannot change the rules for writers; only speakers can do that over a long period of time. _____

10. Grammarians are quite (unique/unusual); indeed, they were once thought to be sorcerers. _____

11. That kind of thinking might (recur/reoccur). _____

12. If so, such thinking probably will not (phase/faze) the grammarians. _____

13. They will continue to go (their/there) merry way. _____

14. The successful student is an (eminent/imminent) student. _____

15. Annie (pored/poured) over the manuscript until she found *a cappella* and corrected its spelling. _____

2

16. The student (implies/infers) that *a cappella* is singing without instrumental accompaniment; she says that it is not part cap and part umbrella.   _____

17. College students are (suppose to/supposed to) look up words in the dictionary when they are unsure of their definitions or spellings.   _____

18. (Oral/Verbal) means language that is spoken and written.   _____

19. (Your/You're) on the road to becoming a good writer.   _____

20. Annie (lead/led) the writing sessions on Wednesday evenings.   _____

2

Instructions: Find errors in word usage in the following sentences. Rewrite the sentences correctly. Be sure to copy the punctuation and capital letters correctly. Learn to look closely at sentences. If a sentence contains no errors, just smile.

21. Irregardless of her status as a purchased slave, Phillis Wheatley became a published poet.

   _____

   _____

22. The capitol of New York is Albany.

   _____

   _____

23. The speaker often infers that Latin abbreviations and foreign phrases dropped into written works (like famous names dropped into conversations) can be a nauseating practice.

   _____

   _____

24. Many of the structures built in Franklin D. Roosevelt's New Deal Era were stationery.

   _____

   _____

25. Franklin Roosevelt was a most unique leader; he was, for example, given unprecedented power in peacetime.

   _____

   _____

26. It has been said that less and less students know how to locate even major countries on a world map.

_____

_____

27. Reading both fiction and nonfiction compliments learning in the classroom and succeeding in life.

_____

_____

28. Dr. Penwright assured her students that it was alright to reword a sentence when they were unsure of the rule they were trying to apply.

_____

_____

2

29. Most everybody knows that George Washington was the first President of the United States and, therefore, known as the father of our country.

_____

_____

30. To survive in today's society, you must utilize your brainpower.

_____

_____

31. Pablo Picasso, a Spanish artist, was known for his cubistic and abstract works.

_____

_____

32. Alexander Hamilton met his waterloo in a dual with Aaron Burr, his political rival.

_____

_____

33. The Malthusian theory infers that we may all starve one day.

_____

_____

34. The proceeding sentences have been designed for your enhanced education.

_____

_____

35. The reason is because you deserve the best.

_____

_____

2

C h a p t e r 3

Word Choices for Clarity

OBJECTIVES

In this chapter, you will learn to

••• be aware of connotations and denotations when choosing words

••• use concreteness to anchor ideas

••• write concisely

••• avoid needless jargon and status-symbol expressions

••• alter or avoid clichés

••• recognize and avoid slang

••• avoid biased language

••• avoid euphemisms or use them sparingly and selectively

Connotations and Denotations

Words have both connotations and denotations. Connotations are implied meanings that we need to consider when making word choices. Denotations are the definitions given in dictionaries; these definitions are considered to be more objective. They are the literal meanings of words.

Connotations are more subjective, and they can be either negative or positive. The precise writer is aware of connotations because they can frequently cause strong negative responses from the reader or listener. Look at the expressions in the two lists that follow. You will understand how choice of words can cause your audience to react differently. The expressions on the left are less emotion-charged. Do you think the expressions on the right convey negative connotations?

inexpensive	cheap
elected official	politician
slim	skinny
frugal	stingy
assertive	aggressive

eccentric	strange
full-figured	fat
petite	tiny
police officer	pig/fuzz
woman	broad, gal, girl, old hen
lady	lady of the night?

Our language is often polarizing. We have many pairs of words and expressions that have no middle ground. Look at the following lists. These terms all have connotations, either negative or positive, depending on the reader.

Democrat	Republican
left-wing	right-wing
liberal	conservative
pro-choice	pro-life
animal rights activists	"real people" (beef eaters)
environmentalists	big business

The arrangement of the preceding terms may be misleading. For example, *liberal* has been placed in the same column with *Democrat* and *conservative* with *Republican*. Of course, not all Democrats are liberal, nor are all Republicans conservative. The same can be said for other terms grouped together. We must, then, be careful not only about how we use these terms but also about how we interpret them. Most of us are complex mixtures of all the characteristics the listed terms imply.

Regardless of the kind of writing you do in both your college classes and your career, recognizing the implied meanings of words will help you to choose words effectively. As you read the following lists of words, you will increase your sensitivity to words with negative or emotion-charged implications.

gossipy	informative
nosy	curious
snoopy	inquisitive
foolhardy	courageous
boastful	self-confident

Would you rather be described by the words in the left or right column? When you choose words, be alert to their implied meanings.

Concreteness

Concreteness anchors abstract ideas with specific details. It means that generalities will give way to specifics, to details. Without specifics, writing can become so vague, so abstract that the result can be confusion.

- **Use specific details.** If you are writing about a person, place, object, issue, or problem, generally avoid generic words such as *interesting, beautiful,* and *nice.* Learn how to "show" rather than merely to "tell." In other words, provide details—specific numbers, sizes, and the like.

- **Use concrete language to anchor abstract words.** Words such as *loyalty, courage,* and *patriotism* are all abstract. If you write that someone exhibits loyalty or courage or patriotism, give concrete examples. Give specific incidents that demonstrate the person's loyalty, courage, or patriotism.

- **Use language that draws a word picture.** Suppose you have been asked to describe a place. You might be tempted to say that it is beautiful or gloomy or special. Keeping in mind the point you are trying to make, you should instead draw a word picture by including specific sounds, colors, aromas (odors), tastes (if appropriate to purpose), and feelings. Is the place cold or warm? How do you feel inside? In other words, to draw a word picture, you must use sensory language—that is, appeal to all or any combination of the five senses. In practice, this is more difficult to do than merely using bland words such as *beautiful* and *interesting.*

3.1 EXERCISE FOR PURPOSEFUL WRITING

Instructions: In each of the following sentences, replace the italicized word with a more objective word.

1. The man approaching the teller's window was dressed in *weird* clothing. _____

2. The *aloof* Mr. Bons discovered a mistake when he counted the money the teller had given him. _____

3. *Miserly* Mr. Bons informed the teller of the error. _____

4. Famous for his courtroom style, Mr. Bons remained *subdued* when told he must wait until the teller balanced his cash drawer. _____

5. Usually *stubborn* in his beliefs, Mr. Bons agreed to return at the end of the day. _____

6. A *notorious* attorney, he was a busy man. _____

7. Tall and *skinny*, he was an imposing figure. _____

8. To win cases, he was often able to *manipulate* jury members. _____

9. To relax at the end of the day, he walks home and *dawdles* in the park. _____

10. Mr. Bons is also a *politician*. _____

3.2   EXERCISE FOR CONCRETE WORD CHOICES

Instructions: Rewrite each of the following general statements to make it more specific, more concrete. Replace vague words with concrete details. Do not be afraid to be creative.

Example

The desk was beautiful.

Standing on graceful cabriole legs, the desk was constructed of solid cherry with an intricate pattern of inlaid satinwood.

1. The student is conscientious.

_____

_____

_____

2. My dog is loyal.

_____

_____

_____

3. My friend is interesting.

_____

_____

_____

4. My professor has high standards.

_____

_____

_____

5. The steak was delicious.

_____

_____

_____

6. The desktop was cluttered.

_____

_____

_____

7. The test was long and difficult.

_____

_____

_____

8. The waiting room was crowded.

_____

_____

_____

9. The traffic was noisy.

_____

_____

_____

10. The students were obviously tense just before the professor distributed copies of the test.

_____

_____

_____

Conciseness

Now that you have learned how to make your writing more concrete by supplying supportive details and specific language, you are ready to learn how to avoid unnecessary words in your writing. On the one hand, you will be told to develop your paragraphs. On the other hand, you will be cautioned to be concise. A tension does exist between including sufficient support and eliminating needless words. You should, however, avoid unnecessary repetition and other forms of *wordiness* just as you would avoid "dead corpse."

This section will help you to write concisely if you let the following suggestions guide you.

• **Avoid redundancies.** Because we do not have time to "edit" when we speak, we use redundancies (needless words) in our everyday conversations. When we write, we should eliminate them.

The following expressions are commonly used redundancies:

Easter Sunday	descended down
round circles	red in color

summer month large in size

two twins most favorite

honest truth actual fact

consensus of opinion advanced planning

basic essentials

See how many additional redundancies you can list.

_____

_____

_____

Sometimes, we need to use intensifiers, but most of the time, they add little to our meaning. Form the habit of reading your prose to see if you can eliminate words without sacrificing meaning. All good writers read and edit their writing several times before the final version is submitted or mailed to a reader. Here are additional suggestions to keep in mind as you edit for wordiness.

Avoid overuse of intensifiers, such as *very, quite, basically,* and *really.*

Be cautious about beginning sentences with the subject delayers *there* and *it.* If you must, be sure you check for subject–verb agreement (see Chapter 9).

Be aware of the *I-believe* or *I-think* syndrome. When you express *your* opinion in an essay, you do not need to preface your comment with "I think," "I believe," or "in my opinion." Your name on your work tells your reader that the opinion is yours.

Stick to your topic or thesis. Do not stray from the main idea of a paragraph or from the main topic of your essay.

Delete all unnecessary words and information.

Each of the following sample wordy sentences has been rewritten to avoid wordiness. Since writing styles differ, the rewritten versions (italicized) may be slightly different from what you would do. Some of the rewriting decisions are explained in parentheses.

1. Matt, I would like to take this opportunity to thank you for speaking to the members of our writers' organization, Easy Writers, on June 4, 1995.

1A. *Thank you, Matt, for speaking to members of Easy Writers on June 4, 1995.* Matt's name helps to personalize the message. Also, the date should be included because Matt may have spoken to the same organization at another time.

2. Due to the fact that a majority of our faculty members voted for the new insurance coverage, it will become effective on September 1, 1995.

2A. *Receiving a majority of the votes, the new insurance coverage will become effective on September 1, 1995.*
Due to the fact that is wordy; replace it with *because.*

3. The consensus of opinion of the committee was that at the next meeting, it would present free gifts to each officer of Easy Writers.

3A. *The committee agreed to present gifts to each officer at the next meeting.*
Consensus of opinion is always a redundancy; consensus is all you need.

4. Pursuant to your request, I have enclosed a copy of the famous essay "How to Say Nothing in Five Hundred Words."

4A. *As you requested, enclosed is a copy of "How to Say Nothing in Five Hundred Words."*

5. In my opinion, the essay is very unique.

5A. *The essay is unique.*
You do not need *in my opinion.* Also, *unique* cannot take a qualifier.

3

Notice the difference between the groups of sentences that were expanded in the section "Concreteness" and the preceding sentences (in the section "Conciseness") that were shortened. The first group had to be expanded to enhance communication from the writer to the reader. The second group had to be shortened to eliminate needless words.

3.3 EXERCISE FOR CONCISE WRITING

Instructions: Rewrite the following wordy paragraph to make it less wordy. You may want to discuss your rewritten version with other students.

The Advantages of Concise Prose

When we write, we should use as few words as possible, at least in my opinion. I think that eliminating all the really unnecessary words in our writing has several advantages. When we actually delete needless words, I believe we make our writing very much easier for the reader to understand, and that's the honest truth. Also, I believe that the reader can find the main point because it is not hidden in a big sea of words. Most of our readers do not actually want to twist and turn through our foggy maze of long, long sentences and excessive numbers of words that honestly add nothing to our actual meaning. It is an actual fact that most people do not want to read wordy, wordy prose. We should, therefore, stick to the basic essentials to save a great deal of time and eliminate much frustration.

In the Answers to Exercises there is a rewritten version of the preceding wordy paragraph. Yours will be somewhat different, but be sure you have deleted all redundancies and other forms of wordiness.

3.4   EXERCISE FOR AVOIDING WORDINESS

Instructions: Learning how to edit involves recognizing wordy phrases that we often use in our conversations. In the space provided beside each wordy phrase, write a word or shorter phrase that conveys the same meaning.

1. first of all _____

2. at this point in time _____

3. new innovation _____

4. future prospects _____

5. still remains _____

6. spoke on the subject of verbs _____

7. actual fact _____

8. a period of ten days _____

9. absolutely certain _____

10. necessary requirements _____

11. due to the fact that _____

12. final outcome _____

13. end result _____

14. completely finished _____

15. most unique _____

3.5   EXERCISE FOR YOUR EDITING IMPROVEMENT

Instructions: Rewrite each of the following sentences to reduce wordiness. Be sure to include all necessary information so that you do not change the original meaning.

1. First of all, criminal justice is a very unique field of study.

_____

_____

2. It is absolutely necessary that students who major in criminal justice completely understand the Miranda case.

---

3. The end result of the Supreme Court's 1964 decision was that all accused persons should be read their rights, and Mirandizing accused persons is a necessary requirement of the arrest procedure that still remains.

---

4. I am not sure, but I believe, criminal justice used to be known as law enforcement, at least, in my opinion.

---

5. The professor spoke on the subject of *surveillance*, which means to watch a suspect very, very closely.

---

6. The robber's most favorite weapon of choice was a Smith & Wesson .44 Magnum revolver.

---

7. Reporters are extremely careful to use the word *alleged* when referring to persons accused of breaking any laws.

---

8. Interrogating a suspect in these the post-Miranda days is really quite different from the old coercive interrogating methods in the old days before the significant Supreme Court's really big decision.

---

9. Deciding when to interview a critically injured victim of violence can be a very delicate and sensitive decision due to the fact that the victim should be interviewed without delay if at all possible.

3

10. In my opinion, future prospects for reducing the rate of crime at this point in time are not very good.

_____

_____

3.6 EXERCISE FOR REDUCING WORDINESS

Instructions: Rewrite each of the three following paragraphs to reduce wordiness. Again, you might compare your revisions with a group of your classmates.

Paragraph A

Crime Pays

Crime really pays if you decide to write about it. I know that many of the well-written novels on the bestsellers' lists are really crime novels. If you just think about the large numbers of authors who have made a lot of money writing about crime, you will see what I mean. There are so very many of them, and they prove that writing about crimes pays truly big dividends. There are many, many authors who write crime novels. Some successful authors are James Lee Burke, Mary Higgins Clark, Patricia Cornwell, Elmore Leonard, Ed McBain, and James Patterson. Their best-selling novels have really given them very comfortable lifestyles. In order to make money though, they have to be able to write quite concisely, very correctly, and most creatively. If they can do all that, they can earn a real fortune, tons of prestige, and widespread fame. Of course, it goes without saying, they must really know all the basic and essential rules for writing very, very well. Besides knowing all the rules, I think they must also research and research again to make sure that every single fact in their writing is accurate. If you can do it really, really well, writing novels and stories about crime does pay.

Paragraph B

A Cappella and Other Types of Caps in Humor Writing

Humor writing is really in such great demand simply due to the fact that people need to laugh. Richard Lederer, Andy Rooney, and Art Buchwald are all three humor writers who have already proved that if you can make people laugh, really laugh, you can surely make lots of money. Writers of humorous prose, however, honestly must perform a tremendously high balancing act on a "write" rope. A humor writer really has to watch very closely though due to the fact that what is funny to one reader may not be the least bit funny to another reader, if you know what I mean. Writers who write humor and are very, very successful have learned to perform that most delicate balancing act, and that is the honest truth. For example, Lederer has quoted many, many of his former high school students, and the end results have been quite hilarious. The many quotations in his books, done most anonymously, do not offend anyone at all. Lederer's quoted definitions remind me of the time one of my fellow students defined *a cappella* as part cap and part umbrella. Just perhaps, I could one day write a funny book of humorous quotations because, after all, humor writing really, really pays, at least, in my opinion.

Paragraph C

A Naked Audience and Other Speech-Making Tips

To many, many people (most people, really), only cold, grim death is really more frightening than public speaking. It is second on their list of most-feared things. Even many college students are quite terrified to stand in front of a group of their peers in the classroom and speak. Some public speaking gurus have advised speakers who are very nervous to pretend that members in their audience are naked. Actually, that just never, ever worked for me; indeed, I just found such silly pretense to be quite disconcerting, if you follow me on this. So, my very first tip to you is to completely forget and totally ignore that tip (whatever else you do). Next, you should really get to know your subject thoroughly if you do not already know it. What I mean is that you should research and research until you have found all the information you need to make yourself feel comfortable talking about your topic. Your next step is to write some notes on index cards. You will need to make subtopics in large print at the very top of each and every card, which you should also number. Then make just a few notes that will serve as guides when you are speaking in front of your audience. Remember that you are not going to actually read your speech. You will now want to stand in front of a mirror and practice, practice, practice. You can also tape your speech if you want to. When the day finally arrives, you should dress appropriately, but when you are actually in front of the members of your audience, forget all about how you look. I know that if you are really enthusiastic about your topic, your audience, always fully dressed, will be very enthusiastic, too.

3

Jargon

The term *jargon* refers to technical vocabulary in a particular field or discipline. (*Jargon* can also mean nonsensical, incoherent, or unclear language, which should always be avoided.) Vocabulary used solely in a particular field can be useful, but it can also be confusing, depending on your audience.

When you go to a medical doctor, he or she may use terminology that you do not understand unless you are a medical doctor, too. If I write an explanation in which I use terms such as *anaphora*, *enjambment*, and *onomastics*, you are probably going to be confused, even frustrated. Unless I know that my readers are scholars of literature and linguistics, I should generally avoid specialized terms in those disciplines. Jargon has its validity. It can serve as a kind of linguistic shorthand that persons within a discipline use to communicate. Virtually every field has its jargon. When we write for people outside our field, however, we must be careful to avoid using jargon that will be unclear to our readers.

In-Vogue or Status-Symbol Words

Words that are in vogue or used as status symbols are vague and generally overused. What, for example, are we really doing when we *interface*? If you and I *bond*, are you superglued to me? If you have *internalized* information, have you learned it? Can we no longer say what we mean? Think about the word *relationship*. Today, everyone is having a *relationship*. Several years ago, people did not have relationships. They were married, engaged, going steady, playing the field, or living together. *Having a relationship* is a vague expression when compared to *being engaged*.

Look at the following expressions. Have you heard any of them? You can probably think of many other vague expressions that have become buzzwords. You might try brainstorming with your classmates or friends to see how many similar expressions you can add to this list.

infrastructure	the smoking gun
worst-case scenario	touch base with you
window of opportunity	twisting in the wind
level the playing field	downsize
conceptualize	networking
hidden agenda	give me a break
on a roll	address the issue
smoke and mirrors	posturing
at this point in time	data dumping
(Time does not have points.)	significant other

Clarity—avoiding vague diction—also means avoiding foreign words unless they have become part of our everyday vocabulary. Abbreviations of foreign words are no longer preferred. If, for instance, you write *i. e.* instead of *that is*, you are not writing clearly for many readers. Also, avoid *e. g.* and *et al.* If you mean *for example* (e. g.), write the words; if you mean *and others* (et al.), write the words. Do not assume that everyone has a knowledge of Latin or, for that matter, any other foreign language.

3.7 EXERCISE FOR CLEAR COMMUNICATION

Instructions: Read the following paragraph carefully. Underline each word with which you are not familiar. Look up the underlined words in your dictionary and write both the words and definitions in the spaces provided. Answers will vary, and will not be given in the Answers to Exercises at the end of the book.

The Poet's Tools

Writing poetry requires a thorough knowledge of language structure and a broad vocabulary. Outstanding poets must have insight and talent. In addition, they must know the devices that help them say a great deal with only a few words. Excellent poets, like Emily Dickinson, know how to use onomatopoeia skillfully. They use other devices, such as caesura, enjambment, and anaphora. An explication of a poem may reveal clever use of juxtapositions, alliteration, and assonance. These are all tools in the poet's mental workshop. Writing poetry, indeed, takes a great deal of knowledge and talent.

3

Unknown Word	Definition
_____	_____
_____	_____
_____	_____
_____	_____
_____	_____
_____	_____
_____	_____
_____	_____
_____	_____
_____	_____
_____	_____

Did you find the preceding paragraph difficult to understand? If so, you can now understand the problems jargon can cause when writing to someone outside your major or discipline. If you are writing an essay to be read by an English professor, you can use literary terms. If, however, you are writing an essay for a biology professor, generally avoid using jargon from the field of English.

3.8   EXERCISE FOR SELECTIVE USE OF JARGON

Instructions: List three words that represent jargon from each of the following majors or professions: biology, criminal justice, psychology, business administration, and education. Answers will vary, and will not be given in the Answers to Exercises at the end of the book.

Biology   **Criminal Justice**

_____   _____

_____   _____

_____   _____

Psychology   **Business Administration**

_____   _____

_____   _____

_____   _____

Education

_____

_____

_____

3.9   EXERCISE FOR AVOIDING STATUS-SYMBOL WORDS

Instructions: In the following sentences, underline the status-symbol expressions. Next, write your interpretation of each expression.

1. In the event of a chemical explosion, we must have escape routes for a worst-case scenario.

   _____

2. It is only fair that employers level the playing field in their hiring practices.

   _____

3. Large companies have been downsizing for several years.

   _____

4. The student said that she had bonded to her dorm room.

   _____

5. Data dumping can be part of the writing process.

_____

6. The leader was known to do a great deal of posturing.

_____

7. Networking is a vital part of job searching.

_____

8. The student felt that she had been left twisting in the wind.

_____

9. The student's argument consisted mostly of smoke and mirrors.

_____

10. The club president wants to touch base with me.

_____

3

Clichés Versus Creativity

Clichés: Don't touch them with a ten-foot pole. Make clichés in your writing **as scarce as hen's teeth.** When it comes to avoiding clichés, **be true blue.** You have probably guessed that there's **a method in my madness** here. Every sentence with a cliché will be **as flat as a pancake** and will render the reader as **cold as ice.** If you avoid worn-out expressions, your writing will be **as pure as the newly fallen snow.** It will be **as fresh as a daisy. Take the bull by the horns** and work to create your own expressions. You'll no longer be **as nervous as a cat in a roomful of rockers** if you know how to rid your writing of clichés. **In the final analysis,** your writing will make you seem **as smart as a whip** and **as sharp as a tack** if you avoid expressions like the ones boldfaced in this paragraph.

Of course, all the boldfaced words in the preceding paragraph are clichés (expressions worn out from overuse). See how many additional clichés you can list. You might want to work with classmates to compile your list.

_____

_____

_____

_____

_____

_____

Clichés have a way of creeping into our writing. When we speak, we often use tired and ragged language because we do not have time to revise and change expressions into fresher wording. When we write, we should read our prose to look for trite expressions. Then, we should delete them.

TIP: Do not use awkward wording or words that are unclear just to avoid using a cliché. Using a trite expression is preferable to using unclear language. Still, avoid clichés whenever possible.

Writing creatively requires a special effort and extra time. For example, when I was asked to write for a local telephone company about the Telephone Pioneers of America, I spent an entire day composing the following two sentences: *Who created a cricket without legs, a dog without a bark, and pig without an oink? Who put a beep in a pickle barrel and a buzz in a baseball?* The company wanted an introduction that would grab the reader's attention. (The article helped the reader to understand that technical devices had been made available to the visually impaired by phone company volunteers.)

When you write an essay, you must work hard to avoid boring your reader. You want to grip the reader's attention and hold it to the last word, and knowing some creative techniques can be helpful. The following tips will help you to write creatively. You will not be able to use all tips in all situations. Use them as general guidelines to meet your specific purpose and topic.

- **Use figures of speech creatively.** Trite expressions that are also figures of speech should be avoided. Examples are *out of the frying pan into the fire* and *light at the end of the tunnel.* Since it is often difficult to create new figures of speech, you can sometimes fracture (alter) a worn-out phrase and make it original again. The following altered cliché is an example: *He is every other inch a gentleman.* The addition of *other* has given the the expression new life. Another example was displayed on a billboard that had a picture of a new automobile. Beneath the picture was the following caption: *This is the best make you'll ever move.* The clever writer had fractured the following cliché: *This is the best move you'll ever make.* Transposing *move* and *make* made the expression not only fresh again but also effective and appropriate.

- You can **begin an essay with a provocative question,** as I did when writing about the Telephone Pioneers.

- You can **make a startling statement** if it is consistent with your topic. An example follows: *A man sat on death row because of a misplaced comma.*

- You can **create a narrative introduction.** This means you can use the same devices a fiction writer uses because to narrate means to tell a story. Your narrative can be factual. You can tell about an event that includes a sense of time and place. You can also use dialogue and drama to bring your introduction to life. This technique requires a great deal of creativity, especially if it is to be effective. If you have the talent, try it. Let others read your writing to be sure you have not left gaps in your "story."

- You can **use a quotation** if you give the source of your quoted material. Be sure the quotation (the exact written or spoken words of someone else) is enclosed in quotation marks (see Chapter 11). Do not use a quotation unless the wording is much better than anything you could create. Also, be sure it is appropriate for your topic.

- **Use repetition and rhythm.** These techniques are especially effective, even powerful, in speeches and oral presentations (see Chapter 12). They can, of course, be effective in essays as well if they are used with caution. When writing, we can easily and unknowingly repeat words needlessly. For example, the word *very* is often repeated unknowingly by beginning writers. This, of course, is not the kind of repetition we want to use. Deliberate and skillful repetition creates a rhythm, which is pleasing to readers. More than that, repetition can artistically highlight a main point. Following is an example of deliberate repetition and the accompanying rhythm:

> Caught between darkness and light, order and chaos, flesh and spirit, Nachman begins a spiritual journey in search of self-identity, in search of the real Reb Nachman. The year is 1800. (Dolly Withrow's book review of Curt Leviant's *The Man Who Thought He Was Messiah*, *The Charleston Daily Mail*, March 1, 1991.)

Notice the repetition of the three sets of words connected by *and* in the preceding exerpt. If you read them aloud, you will hear the rhythm the repetition has created. Also, the repetition of "in search of" emphasizes a journey of searching. You will probably notice that the final sentence has emphasis because of its brevity.

The success of any piece of writing lies in the results it gets. The effectiveness of creativity in a well-written essay cannot be exaggerated.

Slang

Slang consists of expressions created by a particular generation. Each generation has its own music, its own clothing styles, and certainly its own pet words. For that reason, slang is fleeting. It quickly dates the user. Although slang expressions, such as *chill out* can be creative and descriptive, listeners and readers do not always understand them. If you want to communicate clearly across the generational boundaries, you will want to avoid slang expressions. Moreover, slang is used in informal writing. Your writing in academia will conform to the rules you will learn in this book. These rules, when applied to actual writing, will produce prose appropriate for any reader.

Slang can be colorful, humorous, exaggerated, and original in its time. Following are examples of slang expressions of several generations:

- nerd (a socially unacceptable person)
- kook (a strange person)
- crashed (became suddenly tired)
- cool (poised)
- square (a person whose beliefs are outdated)
- duh (an expression meaning someone is "duh"—not bright)
- brain is fried (brain has been damaged by drugs)
- burned out (tired from overwork)
- to pig out (to eat too much)
- wired (hyperactive)
- jumping off the walls (hyperactive)
- bombed (drunk, intoxicated)
- wasted (under the influence of drugs)
- later (see you later)
- catch you on the flip side (see you later)
- that's the way the mop flops (that's the way things happen)
- that's the way the cookie crumbles (that's the way things happen)
- burst your bubble (disappoint you)
- rain on your parade (disappoint you)
- put a fork in it, it's done (quit; move on)
- slam back a cool one (drink a cool drink)
- ticked off (angry)
- heavy (serious, deep, insightful)
- on the same wave length (communicating well)
- has a full plate (has many chores)
- get all your ducks in a row (get organized)

As you can see, communication from a person of one generation to a person of another can be blocked by slang expressions. In academic writing, unless you are using slang for special effect or a specific purpose, avoid it altogether.

3.10 EXERCISE TO SHARPEN YOUR AWARENESS OF CLICHÉS

Instructions: Select all the clichés from the following sentences and write them in the spaces provided.

1. Despite his age, the dancer is as fit as a fiddle.

_____

2. He's liked dancing since he was knee-high to a grasshopper.

_____

3. Students should not count their chickens before they hatch.

_____

4. They should not burn their bridges behind them.

_____

5. We know that an ounce of prevention is worth a pound of cure.

_____

6. After receiving her test grade, the student decided it was all water under the bridge.

_____

7. Before final examinations, students burn the midnight oil.

_____

8. After many students receive grades in the mail, their egos become as flat as pancakes.

_____

9. The student was true blue.

_____

10. If students remember that a stitch in time saves nine, they will make high grades on all tests.

_____

_____

3.11 EXERCISE FOR AVOIDING CLICHÉS

Instructions: Read the following ten sentences. Rewrite each sentence, replacing the cliché with the literal meaning or with an altered cliché. If you do not know how to interpret a cliché, write a cliché you do know; then replace it in your sentence.

1. He is in the pink.

_____

_____

2. She was as nervous as a long-tailed cat in a roomful of rockers.

_____

_____

3. Too many cooks spoil the broth.

_____

_____

4. He is as slow as a seven-year itch.

_____

_____

5. Let sleeping dogs lie.

_____

_____

6. It is no skin off my nose if you change jobs.

_____

_____

7. Every dog has its day.

_____

_____

8. Birds of a feather flock together.

_____

_____

9. Little pitchers have big ears.

_____

_____

10. He has one foot in the grave and the other on a banana peel.

_____

_____

3.12   EXERCISE FOR YOUR CURIOSITY

Instructions: Ask someone who is at least ten years older or younger than you to share slang expressions of his or her generation. How many of them can you interpret? Write the slang expressions in the spaces provided and bring your expressions to class and share them. This exercise should demonstrate the obstacles slang can place between the sender and the receiver of a message, either written or oral. Answers will vary and will not be given in the Answers to Exercises at the end of the book.

_____

_____

_____

_____

_____

_____

_____

_____

_____

_____

_____

_____

3

_____

_____

_____

_____

_____

_____

Biased Language and Euphemisms

Certainly, to choose expressions that consider your reader, that are not offensive to your reader, is to write with clarity and courtesy. It is important, then, that you look at word choices in ways you may not have previously looked at them. Biased language is language that can be offensive in certain environments. For example, referring to women as _girls_ or _gals_ and to men as _boys_ can be offensive to many people. To strip people who are not close friends of their professional titles can be offensive. If, for example, your professor wishes to be called Professor X or Dr. X, you should oblige. If an older person wishes to be called by a courtesy title, such as Ms., Mrs., or Mr., you should do so. If you are unsure how to address a new acquaintance, ask.

Do not confuse this kind of sensitivity to audience with politically correct language in the extreme, which has become a topic of nationwide debate. To call a short person _vertically constrained_ is not what this chapter recommends. To use expressions that verge on absurdity is not recommended, especially by those who work for clear communications. Use good judgment, then, when trying to avoid offending your reader.

A euphemism is an expression used as a substitute for a harsher expression. For example, when we say that someone has *expired* or *passed away* instead of *died*, we are using a euphemism to buffer the finality of death. When used wisely, euphemisms can prevent us from offending or embarrassing our audience. Generally, avoid euphemisms. For example, avoid using *terminated* if you mean killed, executed, murdered, or fired. Other common euphemisms are *elderly, senior citizen, golden years, peace-keeping force,* and *visual surveillance.*

Biased language is language that is offensive to certain groups. For example, writers have traditionally used the suffixes *-man* and *-men* when referring to certain professions and titles regardless of the gender makeup of those professions. In other words, *congressmen* was traditionally used even for women members of Congress. The following expression has also been traditionally used even when *everyone* referred to both men and women: *Everyone should read his assignments carefully.* The fact that the readers might consist of both men and women was not viewed as relevant. It was said that *his* was generic and referred to both men and women. Most language scholars agree that such practices have been unfair, and an effort has been launched to change the language to coincide with increased respect for everyone. Today, a savvy writer would write: *Everyone should read his or her assignments.* An even better choice follows: *All students should read their assignments.*

SUMMARY

Choose words wisely by increasing your awareness of connotations, that is, the implied meanings of words. Also, anchor abstract terms by giving specific support and examples. As you write, avoid unnecessary words. They clutter your writing and frustrate your reader. You can use jargon only if your reader shares the vocabulary in your major or profession. Be wary of status-symbol expressions, such as *level the playing field*. Clichés should be avoided, although they can be altered to make them fresh again. Avoid short-lived slang expressions. They not only quickly date you but also make communicating with members of a different generation difficult. Also, do not use biased language that offends your reader. If, on occasion, you must use polarizing language, do so with respect for your reader. Most linguists oppose the use of euphemisms. Generally, avoid them. Again, you must use good judgment. On rare occasions, you may need to use a euphemism. For example, the speaker in the following fictional story probably should have used one:

Three men were fishing when suddenly Mr. Brown died of a heart attack.

Mr. Gomez said to Mr. Johnson, "Which one of us will tell Mrs. Brown?"

Mr. Johnson said, "I'll take care of it. I can be gentle."

Later, when Mrs. Brown answered the knock at the door, she faced the two men who had gone fishing with her husband.

Mr. Johnson asked, "Are you Widow Brown?"

Mrs. Brown said, "I'm not a widow."

Mr. Johnson said, "The heck you're not."

Mr. Johnson thought he had been tactful. When we write, unless we are aware of word choices, we may think we are tactful when, in fact, we are not. In this chapter, you have learned to use euphemisms with constraint and wisdom. You have learned to avoid them when they reach the point of absurdity.

As you read additional chapters, you will learn even more about word choices. You are on your way to becoming a confident writer. ■

3

3.13 END-OF-CHAPTER EXERCISES

Instructions: Replace the following euphemisms and biased expressions with acceptable substitutions:

1. chairman _____

2. Gal Friday _____

3. stewardess _____

4. congressman _____

5. mailman _____

6. fireman _____

7. weatherman _____

8. policeman _____

9. mankind _____

10. female logic _____

11. typical woman driver _____

12. typical male brutality _____

13. man and wife _____

14. workman _____

15. manhole cover _____

Instructions: In the following sentences, you will find italicized examples of jargon, status-symbol words, clichés, biased language, and euphemisms. Improve each sentence by replacing all italicized words with your own creations. When replacing the italicized words, you may use fewer or more words than in the original version. Be creative without changing the meaning.

16. *Freewriting* is a useful prewriting activity.

_____

_____

17. Novelists often refer to *perpetrators* as *perps*.

_____

_____

18. The student has a *hidden agenda.*

_____

_____

19. Annie wanted *to touch base with* Maria.

_____

_____

20. After the final exams, Juan *crashed.*

_____

_____

21. Annie and José *slammed back a cool one.*

_____

_____

22. The *mailman* brought Annie a note from her editor.

_____

_____

23. *Miss* Perez, a *policeman* in our neighborhood, just received a promotion.

_____

_____

24. During World War II, the Nazis *terminated* more than 2 million European Jews, as well as large numbers of Gypsies and others.

_____

_____

25. The use of excessive *alliteration* should be avoided *like the plague.*

_____

_____

Instructions: Rewrite each of the following sentences, replacing wordiness, jargon, status-symbol words, clichés, biased language, and euphemisms. Look up words you do not know in your dictionary.

26. The professor asked the student to submit a hard copy of her essay.

_____

_____

27. The doctor told her patient that he must have a cholecystectomy.

_____

_____

28. Maria's classmate assured her that he could feel her pain.

_____

_____

29. The editor of the student newspaper wants the best man for the job.

_____

_____

30. The previous reporter's grandmother had passed away.

_____

_____

31. Although _jargon_ has several meanings, the department's Gal Friday views it as specialized or technical language used in a particular profession.

_____

_____

32. He had been in the correctional facility for 40 years.

_____

_____

33. At that point in time, I wondered what we had done.

_____

_____

34. The committee interfaced for an hour.

_____

_____

35. The working mother spends quality time with her daughter on the weekends.

_____

_____

PART 2

The Grammar–Writing Connection

Chapter 4

Nouns: Words That Name

4

▶ OBJECTIVES

In this chapter, you will learn to

• • • define and recognize nouns

• • • recognize and use correctly the subclasses of nouns

• • • anchor abstractions with concrete nouns

A noun is a name is a name is a name. Nouns name things seen and unseen. *A noun is the name of a person, place, thing, quality, idea, or animal.*

Nouns are divided into seven subclasses. They are *concrete, abstract, common, proper, collective, count,* and *noncount.* Do not be nervous about these terms; they will become clear as you continue to read, discuss, practice, and engage in exciting exercises for your grammatical fitness.

Keep in mind that each small section in this book is a building block to help you lay a solid foundation for effective—even powerful—writing. When you become a confident writer (and speaker), all this will have been worth your time and effort.

When you finish this chapter, you will know how to distinguish one kind of noun from another. This is an important distinction because nouns and verbs (action words) form the base for building correctly constructed sentences.

Concrete Nouns

Look around you now. If you are in a classroom, at home, or at work, you probably see many of the following, which are examples of concrete nouns:

instructor	students	lamps	walls	doors
ceiling	floor	windows	pencils	paper
pens	books	desks	pictures	telephone
typist	computer	chalk	calendar	printer

Anything you can become aware of through your senses (perceive) is called a concrete noun. In other words, anything you can see, smell, touch, taste, or hear is called a concrete noun.

TIP: Just as you can perceive a **piece of concrete,** you can perceive a **concrete noun.**

A few additional concrete nouns are listed below. See if you can think of a concrete noun that is somehow connected to each one listed. Write your noun in the space provided.

Example

boat	water
boot	_____
car	_____
house	_____
woman	_____
knife	_____
dog	_____
flower	_____
shirt	_____
ring	_____
hat	_____
lamp	_____
computer	_____

Be sure that each noun you listed can be perceived (seen, touched, smelled, tasted, or heard). You must also be sure that each word is a concrete noun and not some other part of speech. For example, if you wrote *sharp* beside *knife*, you have not written a noun; you have written a descriptive word, a word telling something about a knife. *Sharp* is an adjective, a part of speech we have not yet discussed. Look over your list now to change any words that are not concrete nouns.

Abstract Nouns

Everyone knows that there are things you cannot perceive. Still, you know they exist. For example, students often must have *patience, perseverance, resignation, courage,* and *a sense of humor.* Although you cannot see these qualities, you and your peers have undoubtedly demonstrated these qualities many times.

Abstract nouns name things unperceived, things we cannot become aware of through our senses. Because you need *patience* when trying to learn the rules for writers, you know that *patience* exists even if you cannot see it.

Examples of Abstract Nouns

democracy	loyalty	patience	perseverance
love	hatred	greed	intelligence
generosity	freedom	justice	eternity
courage	chaos	catastrophe	wisdom
ambition	infinity	personality	beauty
strength	joy	oversight	liability
happiness	emotion	enthusiasm	eagerness
ugliness	laziness	knowledge	pride
dishonesty	fun	anxiety	

TIP: When you write, be careful to anchor your abstract nouns with concrete examples. Remember that just as abstract paintings are sometimes difficult to interpret, so is abstract writing often difficult to understand.

Read the following sentences. The first sentence in each pair is a general statement that contains an *abstract noun* that is boldfaced. The second sentence in each pair is a rewritten version that provides concrete, specific language. Which of the two sentences in each pair holds your attention more effectively?

Abstract/General:	The student's **dependability** is commendable.
Concrete/Specific:	The student has not missed a class since the semester began.
Abstract/General:	Matt's **honesty** resulted in a reward.
Concrete/Specific:	Because Matt returned the student's lost wallet, he received a reward of $100.
Abstract/General:	Matt especially enjoyed the **beauty** of the fall day as he walked home one evening.
Concrete/Specific:	In high spirits, Matt strolled home and marveled at nature's masterpiece: leaves of burnished gold and copper, a sky as blue as cornflowers. Ah, autumn!

   TIP: Abstract or general sentences are acceptable as purpose statements that give the main point or purpose of your writing. However, they should be followed by concrete, specific examples.

4.1   EXERCISE FOR USE OF CONCRETE AND ABSTRACT NOUNS

Instructions: Underline the abstract nouns in the following sentences. Then rewrite each sentence to include concrete examples of the abstract nouns. Use your imagination to fill in details that make your version more specific and concrete. Answers will vary, and will not be given in the Answers to Exercises at the end of the book.

Example of sentence to illustrate an abstract noun and vague language.

A.   Matt demonstrated <u>courage</u> when he phoned Annie, the famous writer.

Example of revised sentence to illustrate concrete language.

B.   Although Matt's hands trembled, he pick up the receiver, dialed Annie's number, and waited nervously as the phone rang once, twice, and once again.

1.   He needed help with his writing.

_____

_____

_____

2.   He sensed the confidence in her voice as she answered the phone.

_____

_____

_____

3.   She spoke with authority.

_____

_____

_____

4.   Matt's shyness was caused by his inability to communicate with confidence.

_____

_____

_____

5. Annie's writing had captured Matt's attention when he read her first bestseller.

_____

_____

_____

6. Holding the receiver, Matt momentarily lost his courage as Annie waited for him to speak.

_____

_____

_____

7. His admiration for her writing skills gave him the fortitude to ask her to help him.

_____

_____

_____

4

8. Annie's positive response gave Matt encouragement.

_____

_____

_____

9. Later, however, doubt began to creep into his mind.

_____

_____

_____

10. By the end of the work day, he was beginning to feel a great deal of anxiety.

_____

_____

_____

11. Matt's ambition to succeed gave him a desire to learn the rules for writers.

_____

_____

_____

12. Annie had demonstrated her generosity when she agreed to share her time.

_____

_____

_____

13. Attending classes on a part-time basis gave Matt the freedom to work at the local bank.

_____

_____

_____

14. Still, without enthusiasm, he would not do well.

_____

_____

_____

15. The college campus was known for its beauty.

_____

_____

_____

16. Matt took pride in doing a job well, whether at work or at school.

_____

_____

_____

17. Learning to write well, even with Annie's tutoring, would require patience.

_____

_____

_____

18. His strength lay in his willingness to work hard.

_____

_____

_____

19. Matt could not hide his disappointment when Annie called to cancel their first tutoring session.

_____

_____

_____

20. Much to his delight, he found sufficient help in _The Confident Writer._

_____

_____

_____

Common Nouns

Common nouns name persons, places, things, qualities, ideas, or animals that are in a general class. Common nouns refuse to be specific. They cannot be pinned down to a specific person. If you look at the following lists of typical examples, you will discover that common nouns name things generally and that they can also be labeled concrete and abstract.

Examples of Common Nouns

woman	child	book	ceiling	floor
computer	clock	finger	man	ocean
river	page	room	building	county
city	dog	cat	company	ship
astronaut	county	month	day	class
cashier	money	writer	autumn	foliage

TIP: Notice that the classifications of nouns overlap. For example, a concrete noun can also be a common noun. _Desk_ is an example; it is both a common noun and concrete noun. Still, these classifications help us in a number of ways, all of which will become clear as you continue to read.

Proper Nouns

Unlike the common noun that names general categories (examples are _city, woman,_ and _cat_), _proper nouns name specifically._ They tell us the specific city (Boston), the specific woman (Annie), and the specific cat (Elizabeth Tailless).

Of course, since proper nouns tell us the names given to particular persons, places, and things, _proper nouns must be capitalized._

The following two lists will help you to distinguish between common and proper nouns.

Examples of Common Nouns	Examples of Proper Nouns
dog	Bruno
man	Mr. Matthew Murray
author	Ms. Annie Penwright
professor	Professor Long
book	*A Tale of Two Cities*
river	the Mississippi
city	New York
continent	North America
day (of the week)	Friday
month	February
holiday	Thanksgiving
company	Writing Services, Inc.
candy bar	Snickers
cola	Coke

Notice that all the common nouns in the left-hand list are vague, general. The proper nouns, however, tell us specifically the name of the person, place, thing, or animal. Also, notice that, unlike the common nouns, the proper nouns are capitalized. Rare exceptions to this rule have been deliberately made by companies or individuals. (You are probably aware that e. e. cummings, the poet, often wrote his name with no capitalization.) Remember, too, that seasons of the year (spring, summer, winter, and fall/autumn) are not capitalized unless they begin a sentence. Capitalize specific names, however, unless you have seen the written form of a company, bank, or individual name without capitalization. You will find more information on capitalization and some repetition of this information in Chapter 14.

4.2 EXERCISE FOR USE OF COMMON AND PROPER NOUNS

Instructions: In the following sentences, underline all the common nouns once and all the proper nouns twice.

1. Charleston is the capital of West Virginia.

2. Annie Penwright and Matthew Murray live in Goldpage, a small town known for its artists, writers, and friendly people.

3. Matt works at the Goldpage National Bank and attends the local college.

4. Matt and Annie often meet at the Whistle Top Buffet; he gets instruction from Annie that helps him to write well.

5. Saturday is their favorite day because they can relax.

6. In October, the beauty of autumn foliage in the Appalachian Mountains reaches its peak.

7 One fall evening, Annie told Matt that Appalachia would be the next nationwide fad.

8. He doubted her assertion, although he had to admit that Annie usually had her finger on the pulse of society.

9. Annie loved to predict the future and play with language.

10. Indeed, she routinely gave Matt writing tips.

11. She recently told him to capitalize all proper nouns and each word beginning a sentence.

12. Matt liked Annie; Annie liked language.

13. Loyalty is an admirable trait, and the professor has loyalty.

14. New York is the hub of the publishing industry.

15. Annie's editor lives in New York.

Collective Nouns

Like people, nouns sometimes cluster or form into little groups or cliques. *Collective nouns name groups.* The following lists will help you to recognize collective nouns.

Examples of Collective Nouns

band	team
audience	tribe
orchestra	organization
jury	council
assembly	crowd
army	staff
squad	crew
faculty	family
public	company
choir	committee

Because collective nouns can give you problems with verb choice, you must learn how to use them. Verb choice (whether you need a singular or plural verb) will be discussed in Chapter 9. A brief mention of it now, however, will not be too painful.

If you are using a *collective noun* (***choir***, for example) as a single unit, you will need a singular verb, a verb *with* an *-s* on the end of it. (This *-s* is called a *suffix* because the *-s* is placed at the *end of the word*.) *Choir* in the following two sentences means *choir as a single body or unit*.

The *choir sings* beautifully.

The *choir impresses* visitors with its outstanding performances.

If you are using a collective noun (*choir*, for example) as *members within the group*, you will need a *plural verb*, a verb *without* an *-s* on the end. *Choir* in the following two sentences means *choir members*. *Choir* is plural; the verb is plural.

- The *choir have* new robes. (choir members)
- Every Friday evening, the *choir discuss* the program for the next week. (choir members)

TIP: Many writers feel that writing "choir have" is awkward. In other words, they feel insecure when using the collective noun as a plural noun. Although to do so is correct, you can include the word *members* after the collective noun and eliminate any feeling of awkwardness. If you feel insecure about using a collective noun as a plural noun, then you can choose the construction in the following example. You can, in other words, insert the word *members* after the collective noun: *The choir members have new robes.*

Learning to recognize collective nouns will help you to be careful about your verb choice. Just remember that your meaning of the collective noun (whether you mean it to be singular or plural) will help you to decide on a singular or plural verb.

Count and Noncount Nouns

The *count noun* is one of the easiest subclasses of nouns to learn. *If you can count the noun, it is a count noun.* Can you count *calories*? Can you count *pages, books, pens,* and *gallons*? Of course you can, and that means they are count nouns. This book has one page, two pages, three pages. *Page*, then, is a count noun.

Writers do not have problems using these nouns until they try to put a qualifier in front of them. Then, they often make mistakes. Look at the following sentences and see if you can decide which one is correctly written.

Annie now eats meat with *less* calories.

Annie now eats meat with *fewer* calories.

Should you use *less* or *fewer*? You may already know the answer.
You should use *fewer* because you can count calories.

The rule is to *use fewer with all count nouns.* This, of course, is why you need to know about this easy-to-learn type of noun.

A *noncount noun is a noun that is not usually counted.* The noncount noun is referred to as the *mass noun* in many grammar books and handbooks of English.

Can you think of any nouns that we do not usually count? What about *sugar, flour, gasoline,* and *fat*? We do not usually say, "One gasoline, two gasolines. . . ." These nouns are *noncount* nouns.

We should *use less rather than fewer as a modifier of a noncount noun*—for example, *less sugar, less flour, less gasoline,* and *less fat.* We seldom make mistakes with this noun.

Also, we should *use amount with noncount nouns* and *number with count nouns*—for instance, the *amount of fat,* but the *number of calories.* Look at the following example. The **X** marks the incorrect sentence.

X We had a large amount of participants at the workshop.

The word *amount* should be changed to *number* as follows:

We had a large number of participants at the workshop

4.3 EXERCISE FOR COLLECTIVE AWARENESS

Instructions: In each of the following sentences, circle all the collective nouns.

1. The writing class meets every Monday, Wednesday, and Friday.
2. The honor students belong to a literary organization on campus.
3. The council meets every week.
4. Maria plays the flute in the orchestra.
5. The defendant hopes the jury will be impartial.
6. The faculty at the college is outstanding.
7. The public cried for justice.
8. The football team had a perfect season.
9. The crowd outside the star's home became a mob.
10. The faculty values the support staff.

4.4 EXERCISE FOR USE OF FEWER AND LESS

Instructions: Write either **fewer** *or* **less** *in the spaces provided.*

Example

We make _____fewer_____ errors when we learn the basic rules of writing.

1. Matt's red car has _____ gallons of gasoline now.
2. Annie's Jaguar has _____ gasoline now.

3. Since Annie accepted Matt's invitation to dinner, she has had
_____ hours for writing.

4. If she is not careful, she will have _____ buyers for her
books because she will have _____ books.

5. She has _____ sand in her hourglass.

Summary of Noun Types

The seven types of nouns described in this chapter are nouns that, in
some way, might give you problems when you speak or write. The following list will help you to remember them:

Type of Noun	Definition	Examples
1. concrete	the name of anything you can see, smell, hear, taste, or touch	jar, odor, thunder, onion, ice, wind
2. abstract	the name of anything you *cannot* see, smell, hear, taste, or touch	idea, ideal, cowardice, sensitivity, enrichment
3. common	persons, places, things, or animals that are named generally rather than specifically	cat, lake, desk, city, school, ring, bride, groom, county, road
4. proper	the name of specific persons, places, things, or animals (Capitalize proper nouns.)	Annie Penwright, Lake Superior, Pepsi, Fido
5. collective	nouns that name groups (If you are using this type of noun as a single group, use a singular verb. If you are using the noun as members within the group, use a plural verb.)	committee, flock, public, orchestra, herd, class, band, family, choir, staff, assembly, crew, council, crowd, organization
6. count	names anything that can be counted—that is, pluralized (Use *fewer* with this one.)	calorie(s), gram(s), grain(s), gallon(s)
7. noncount (mass)	names anything that cannot be counted or is not pluralized (Use *less* with this one.)	energy, fat, sand, sugar, gasoline, fuel, time, money

SUMMARY

In this chapter, you have learned to define and recognize the subclasses of nouns: concrete, abstract, common, proper, collective, count, and noncount. You have learned to anchor abstract nouns with concrete, specific language. You have learned that proper nouns are capitalized unless they are used in unusual ways for effect. You are now aware of the pitfalls of the collective noun with respect to verb choice. You can distinguish between count and noncount nouns and know the correct qualifiers to use with each type. You are continuing to build a solid base for writing with confidence. ■

4

4.5 END-OF-CHAPTER EXERCISE

Instructions: Make a list of all the nouns you can find in the following sentences.

1. In the Whistle Top Buffet, Annie leaned across the table, smiled, and said, "Remember, Matt, that abstract nouns are most appropriate when they are used in the thesis of an essay."

2. "The remainder of your written assignment will contain specific, concrete examples, illustrations, and explanations that will support your point," added Annie.

3. Matt listened closely, for he wanted to succeed in his college classes. "Tell me more," said Matt.

4. As Annie's brown hair glowed in soft candlelight, she frowned and said, "The count noun can give you trouble. People, for example, often say, 'less employees' when they mean 'fewer employees.' Watch those count nouns, Matt."

5. Matt promised and asked, "Will I learn about pronouns later?"

6. Annie laughed and said, "Yes, Matt, but for now concentrate on this tip: Remember to watch the collective noun for verb choice."

7. Again, leaning toward Matt to emphasize her point, she said, "Always anchor your abstract language with concrete examples. Your writing will improve."

8. She added, "When you write an essay, you want to show, not just tell. You must use specific details, not just general statements."

9. Matt said, "So you're talking about concrete language versus abstract language. It's more than just noun choices."

10. "Right. Also, remember that *January, February, Friday, Thomas Jefferson High School, New Year's Eve, Annie Penwright,* and *Fido* are all proper nouns. They must be capitalized," said Annie.

11. Matt frowned, "Oh, I know that."

12. Annie said, "That's good. Let's change the subject. Your class is sponsoring a picnic next Saturday, isn't it?"

13. "Yes," replied Matt, "will you go with me?

14. She asked, "Will we discuss writing?"

15. "You bet," replied Matt as he motioned to the waiter.

16. They left the Whistle Top Buffet.

17. Dark clouds rolled in the sky, giving promise of an autumn storm.

18. Lightning began to flash in the western sky.

19. The temperature had dropped during the past hour.

20. Matt looked forward to a good book and a cozy fire.

4

Chapter 5

Pronouns: Substitutions for Ease of Writing

▶ OBJECTIVES

In this chapter, you will learn to

- ••• define and recognize personal pronouns and their subclasses
- ••• master pronoun-antecedent agreement in number and gender
- ••• define and correctly apply point of view
- ••• choose the correct pronoun from each of the three pronoun cases
- ••• define and recognize interrogative pronouns
- ••• use indefinite pronouns correctly
- ••• avoid vague demonstrative pronouns
- ••• use reciprocal pronouns correctly
- ••• avoid errors with reflexive and intensive pronouns
- ••• avoid ambiguous pronouns

Pronouns *replace or refer to nouns and other pronouns.* They are substitutions that help you to avoid monotonous repetition when you speak and write. To be a confident writer, you must know how to choose the correct pronoun. For example, you must know when to use *I* (always capitalized) or *me* and when to use *who* or *whom.* Some other pronouns are *he, it, they, those, myself, your, them,* and *their.*

This chapter contains all the information you need for using pronouns correctly and confidently. You are about to take another step on the road to becoming a competent writer. Enjoy the journey.

Because of pronouns, you can avoid boring repetition. Read the following two examples. The first example does not use pronouns; the second example does.

> **Matt** wrote a rough draft of **Matt's** essay, put **Matt's** essay out of sight; then **Matt** wrote a final draft and submitted **Matt's** essay to **Matt's** instructor.

> **Matt** wrote a rough draft of **his** essay, put **it** out of sight; then **he** wrote a final draft and submitted **it** to **his** instructor.

You can readily see the value of pronouns, of which there are eight subclasses:

Subclasses of Pronouns

1. personal (I, you, me)
2. interrogative (who, which)
3. relative (who, that, which)
4. indefinite (someone, anyone)

5. demonstrative (this, these)
6. reciprocal (each other)
7. reflexive (himself, myself)
8. intensive (himself, myself)

If the preceding list seems forbidding, do not be discouraged. This chapter discusses each subclass or type of pronoun in detail. You will soon have enough information on pronouns to guide you along the twisting path toward your goal of becoming a good writer.

Personal Pronouns

Personal pronouns *are called personal because they directly replace or refer to specific persons, places, things, ideas, or animals.* Some examples are *I, you, he, it,* and *they.* They must agree in number (singular or plural) and point of view (person) with the words they replace. You will soon understand the terms *number* and *point of view.*

We must approach personal pronouns with caution. They can be *objective, subjective,* or *possessive.* You will need to keep these three terms in mind. They probably seem confusing now, but by the end of the chapter, you will be able to fit the pieces of the pronoun puzzle together.

In each of the following sample sentences, the personal pronoun and the noun to which it refers are boldfaced. Another term you will want to remember is *antecedent.* The noun or pronoun to which the pronoun refers is called the **antecedent.**

1. **Matt** wants to be a good writer. **He** is learning the rules for writers.
2. **West Virginia** was once part of **Virginia,** but now **they** are two states.
3. Annie's **idea** is workable. **It** will be an asset to her publisher.
4. Matt had several good **plans. They** will be presented at the next meeting.
5. **Elizabeth Tailless** and **Richard Burden** are two beautiful cats; Annie adopted **them** when **they** came to her door.

Pronoun–Antecedent Agreement in Number

Pronouns must agree in number with the words they replace—their **antecedents.** This means if the antecedent is singular, the pronoun referring to the antecedent must also be singular. If the antecedent is plural, the pronoun must also be plural. Look at Examples 3 and 5 in the preceding list of sample sentences. For entry 3, the antecedent, *idea,* is singular, as is the pronoun, *it.* The pronoun, *it,* and the antecedent, *idea,* therefore, agree in number. For entry 5, the two antecedents, *Elizabeth Tailless* and *Richard Burden,* are plural; therefore, they require plural pronouns, *them* and *they.* Look at the following additional examples of pronoun–antecedent agreement in number. The antecedents and the pronouns referring to them are boldfaced.

1. **Biology** is the study of living organisms; that is, **it** is the study of both plant and animal life.

2. **Zoology** is the study of animal life; **it** begins with the word *zoo.*

3. An insect is a small arthropod with six **legs,** and **they** are grouped in two sets of three.

4. People who love to grow flowers probably like **botany** as well; **it** is the study of plant life.

5. **Ornithology** is the study of birds, and **it** is a branch of zoology.

6. **Evening grosbeaks** eat at Annie's feeder occasionally; **they** are black and gold with bits of creamy white.

Pronoun Number and Agreement

Personal pronouns also have number, which means they can be **singular** (*he*) or **plural** (*they*). The pronoun *you* can be either singular or plural, depending on the meaning. You should have few or no problems here. Pronouns must agree with their antecedents in number, which means that a pronoun and its antecedent must both be either singular or plural. You will find repetition of this concept throughout the book for reinforcement.

Pronoun Point of View

As a grammatical term, *point of view* does not mean (as many people believe) someone's opinion. There are only three points of view in grammar: first person, second person, and third person.

First-person point of view means that the writer or speaker is using any of the following personal pronouns: *I, me, my, mine, we, us, our, ours, myself,* or *ourselves.*

When you write essays, you will probably use first-person pronouns. When writing research papers, you should check with your instructor as to his or her preference. The trend in research papers is to use first person, but many instructors still prefer third person because it is more objective. Remember that the big *I,* the big ego, is first person.

Second-person point of view means that the writer or speaker is using any of the following personal pronouns: *you, your, yours, yourself,* or *yourselves.* Remember, then, that the speaker or writer is first person (*I*), and the person to whom the communication is directed is second person (*you*).

Third-person point of view means that the writer or speaker is using any of the following personal pronouns: *he, it, its, she, him, his, her, hers, they, them, their, theirs, herself, himself, itself,* and *themselves.* Remember that all the people or things that **you** (second person) and **I** (first person) talk or write about are referred to as third person (**they**).

Switching point of view illogically is a common error. Look at the following example:

Soon after Matt entered the building, **he** rode the elevator to the top floor; **you** could see the entire city.

Notice that *Matt* is the antecedent of *he*, but the pronoun *you* has no antecedent, which is one reason for changing *you* to *he*.

More important, notice the switch from third person *he* to second person *you*. The switch is illogical because *you* were not on the elevator. The pronoun *you* should, indeed, be changed to *he*. Switching point of view is an easy mistake to make but also easy to catch and change if you are aware of the pitfall.

Once you have learned to match pronouns with their antecedents in number (singular with singular and plural with plural), you then must learn how to choose the correct pronoun in terms of pronoun case. This will become clear as you continue to read and learn. For example, you may have sometimes wondered when to use *I* and when to use *me*.

Pronoun Case

5

The following table will help you to *learn which pronouns are in which cases,* necessary facts for you to know. The table will further reinforce your knowledge of number and point of view.

	Subjective Case	**Objective Case**	**Possessive Case**
	Singular	*Singular*	*Singular*
1st person	I	me	my, mine
2nd person	you	you	your, yours
3rd person	she	her	her, hers
3rd person	it	it	**its***
3rd person	he	him	his
3rd person	who(ever)	whom(ever)	whose
	Subjective Case	**Objective Case**	**Possessive Case**
	Plural	*Plural*	*Plural*
1st person	we	us	our, ours
2nd person	you	you	your, yours
3rd person	they	them	their, theirs
3rd person	who(ever)	whom(ever)	whose

*Although **its** is possessive, **its** when in the possessive case (singular) does not have an apostrophe. The word *its* is, of course, a personal pronoun, and personal pronouns do not require apostrophes in the possessive form. Look at the personal pronouns *hers* and *yours*, for example. No apostrophes are used, but they both indicate possession.

Although pronoun choices often come to you naturally, there are times when you may not be sure of choice unless you take the extra time to memorize the cases and the pronouns that fit into each case. Remember that good writers are in demand, and to be an effective writer, you must be able to choose the correct pronoun every time.

Look at the following sentence and see if you can determine which pronoun to use. If you are not *sure* about your choice, then you will understand the importance of this chapter.

Matt will drive Annie and (I/myself/me) to the party.

Did you guess without knowing the rule? Such random guessing usually leads to an incorrect choice and to a mistake made unknowingly. The correct choice is *me.*

The following tip is for the reader who wants to be confident *most* of the time.

TIP: If you had deleted the words *Annie and,* you would have chosen the correct pronoun, *me.*

You would never say, "Matt will drive *I* to the party."

You would never say, "Matt will drive *myself* to the party."

You would say, "Matt will drive *me* to the party."

If deleting words in this manner helps you to choose the correct pronoun, by all means, do so.

You can see by the example that when we add someone else's name and the word *and,* we can easily become confused as to pronoun choice.

The following tip is for the reader who wants to be confident *all* the time.

TIP: If you want to be sure of choosing the correct pronoun *every* time, memorize the three pronoun cases and the pronouns that fit into each case.

There are only three cases: **subjective** (**subjects** come from this case), **objective** (**objects** come from this case), and **possessive** (**possessive pronouns** come from this case). If you are confused, do not give up. Stay with me, and you will soon see all the pieces of the pronoun puzzle fit together for your benefit.

Speakers and writers often unwittingly make errors in pronoun usage. If you, however, commit yourself to learning—really learning—the information in this chapter, you will not make such errors. Read the following statement several times until you **believe it.**

Learning the three pronoun cases and the pronouns that fit into each case is the *only* way to be sure of choosing the correct pronoun—*every* time.

Now you are going to learn *why* you must learn the cases and their pronouns. Read the following rules several times and learn them. Again, the pronoun has only three cases. Although you do not know yet which pronouns fit into which pronoun cases, you will in time. Now just memorize the rules in the same way you would memorize math formulas in a math class.

Rule 1. Subjective Case: If the pronoun is doing the action or is the **subject** of a weak verb, such as *is*, it must be pulled from the subjective case. (**He** loves grammar. **She** is a writer.)

Rule 2. Objective Case: Objects of the verb and **objects** of prepositions come from this case. (The speaker drove Annie and **me** home. The speaker looked at **us.**)

Rule 3. Possessive Case: Possessive pronouns come from this case. (**Anyone's** guess is as good as mine. The dog ate **its** food.)

As long as we refer to only one person, we do not usually have problems selecting the correct pronoun from the correct case. As soon as we put someone else in the sentence, however, we often veer down the wrong road. Look at the following examples in which the pronouns are boldfaced. An **X** before the sentence indicates that the boldfaced pronoun is incorrect.

    1. Annie gave **me** the report.

X **2.** Annie gave Matt and **I** the report.

X **3.** Annie gave Matt and **myself** the report.

The first sentence is correct. The second and third are not. Just because I decided to include *Matt and* in the second and third sentences does not mean I can change the pronoun from *me* to *I*, or worse, from *me* to *myself.* Look at the cases in the pronoun table. Matt is receiving the action, and so is the pronoun *me. Me* is in the objective case. I must choose the pronoun *me.* I have no other choice.

Again, remember that when a pronoun *receives* the action (even indirectly), it must come from the objective case.

Read the next two examples. Remember that if the pronoun is the object of a preposition, it must also come from the objective case.

    1. Annie gave the books to **me.**

X **2.** Annie gave the books to Matt and **I.**

The second sentence is incorrect because *I* cannot be used in an object-of-the-preposition slot. All objects come from the objective case.

TIP: Now, you can see why *between you and I* is incorrect. *Between* is a preposition. *Between you and me* is correct because *me* is the object of the preposition.

Because choosing the correct pronoun case is also important with interrogative pronouns, you will have ample exercises to reinforce this concept in the following section.

A few cautions are in order with respect to choosing personal pronouns. Look at the following sentences:

This is she.

She renames the subject, that is, the word *this.*

It is I.

I renames the subject here, too.

TIP: If you turn the sentence around, this rule makes more sense. *She is this.* You would never say, "*Her* is this."

The following story will help you to understand that many people dislike this rule:

A woman knocked on the door of a house. The man inside asked, "Who's there?"

"It is I," replied the woman.

"Oh, another English teacher," said the man.

If you feel that such expressions (*this is she* or *it is I*) sound stilted or too formal despite their correctness, you are not alone. You can always use your name instead of the pronoun *she* or *he* (*this is Annie*).

You might also have problems with pronoun choice when you use expressions like *we students* or *us students*. If you delete *students* and then decide whether the pronoun is doing or receiving the action, your choice becomes clear. Look at the following examples:

We [students] enjoy learning how to write well.

The instructor is teaching us [students] how to write well.

If you remove the bracketed words from the preceding sentences, you have no trouble deciding whether to use *we* or *us.*

Look at the following examples of sentences with common errors in pronoun choices. An **X** before the sentence indicates the italicized pronoun is incorrect.

X The college is downsizing, and *their* employees will be fewer in number next year.

The college is downsizing, and its employees will be fewer in number next year.

The singular verb *is* tells you that you must use the singular pronoun *its*, which refers to *college* as a singular noun.

X Matt hurt Annie and *I* with those remarks.

Matt hurt Annie and *me* with those remarks.

If you remember to delete *Annie and,* you will choose *me.* Also, if you remember that *me* is in the objective case and in the sample sentence is the direct object of the verb *hurt,* you will choose *me.*

X The instructor congratulated Matt and *he* because they knew how to spell *all right.*

The instructor congratulated Matt and *him* because they knew how to spell *all right.*

If you remove *Matt and,* the sentence begins as follows: *The instructor congratulated him.*

Comparisons and Pronoun Cases

You have learned how to choose the correct pronoun when the pronoun is doing the action, receiving the action, or serving as the object of a preposition. Now, you must consider pronoun cases when you are making comparisons using *than* or *as.*

First, you must consider the meaning of the sentence. Next, you must remember to complete the sentence by adding the word or words that have been omitted. Examples will help you to understand this. Do not despair.

Annie likes writing better than (he/him).

You must know the meaning of the sentence. If the sentence means that Annie likes writing better than she likes him, then *him* would be the choice in this sentence.

Annie likes writing better than (she likes) *him.*

If, however, the sentence means that Annie likes writing better than he does, then the choice would be *he.*

Annie likes writing better than he (does).

Notice that in both choices, we had to determine the meaning first and add words next to determine the correct pronoun choice.

When you compare by using *as* before a pronoun, you can add words to help you choose the correct pronoun. Look at the following example:

Matt is learning to write as well as *she.*

Adding either *does* or *writes* at the end of the sentence tells you that *she* is correct, not *her.*

Now, look at the following comparison statement:

Matt is taller than *I.*

Again, finish the statement: Matt is taller than *I* am.

A general rule that will help you when writing comparisons with pronouns is to finish the statement by adding words, at least in your mind if not in the sentence itself.

5.1 EXERCISE FOR YOUR MENTAL FITNESS

Instructions: Write in the appropriate spaces the antecedent(s) and word(s) referring to the antecedent(s). Antecedents can also be a pronouns.

Example

Annie Penwright's books have received critical acclaim because of their excellent prose.

antecedent   books

pronoun   their

1. Matt likes to talk with Annie because he learns about the language.

   antecedent _____

   pronoun _____

2. Annie helps Matt to improve his writing.

   antecedent _____

   pronoun _____

3. As a student at the local college, he is committed to becoming an excellent writer.

   antecedent _____

   pronoun _____

4. Matt realizes that he must write error-free essays.

   antecedent _____

   pronoun _____

5. Matt and Annie met on a sunny July day when they attended a picnic.

   antecedent _____

   pronoun _____

5

6. The Ornithology Club held its annual picnic in August.

    antecedent _____

    pronoun _____

7. Annie asked Matt to the picnic, and he accepted.

    antecedent _____

    pronoun _____

8. When Matt asked Annie about pronoun–antecedent agreement, she smiled and told him to listen carefully.

    antecedent _____

    pronoun _____

9. "Matt," said Annie, "a singular antecedent requires a singular pronoun. You cannot mix singular with plural."

    antecedent _____

    pronoun _____

10. Feeling lost, Matt said, "There are too many rules; they are difficult."

    antecedent _____

    pronoun _____

11. Matt and his brother attend a writing class each week, and they are earning high grades.

    antecedent _____

    pronoun _____

12. The brothers share their apartment.

    antecedent _____

    pronoun _____

13. Mark forgot to write his name in his book.

    antecedent _____

    pronoun _____

14. When Mark left the book under the desk, it was not returned.

    antecedent _____

    pronoun _____

15. Mark wrote his name in his new book.

    antecedent _____

    pronoun _____

5.2 EXERCISE FOR EDITING IMPROVEMENT

Instructions: Replace either the pronoun or its antecedent to make each sentence grammatical. Draw a line through the incorrect word and write your replacement above it. If the sentence is correct, just smile.

1. The brown-headed cowbird is fascinating; their song is a thin whistle.

2. The cowbird's "talk" is unique; they can sound like stones falling into water.

3. The cowbird lays their eggs in the nest of another species.

4. After shoving an egg out of the other species' nest, the cowbird replaces the egg with their own egg.

5. Cowbirds beg for food, and its begging is noisy.

6. Also fascinating, hummingbirds are the smallest of the North American birds, but it can be aggressive and pugnacious.

7. The hummingbird has a long slender bill, and they can use that bill in the same way a person uses a straw.

8. The bird's wings beat so rapidly it makes a humming sound.

9. Although the hummingbird is barely larger than my thumb, they can travel thousands of miles.

10. The little creature sometimes hitches a ride on the back of a larger bird; they can be clever.

11. The tiny bird flies south in the fall, but they return to the same bird feeder in the spring.

12. Hummingbirds can be fed with a mixture of four parts water and one part sugar; it should never be fed artificial sweeteners.

13. The sweet-eating ant loves the sugar water, and some people rub cooking oil outside the feeder to keep them away.

14. The male bluebird, like most species, has brighter colors than their female counterpart.

15. The male and female bluebirds mate for life, and together they build a nest and feed its young.

16. In early spring, I watched two phoebes build a nest under the eaves of our back porch; it carried small twigs of grass and weeds throughout the day.

17. After several days of hard work, the female laid her eggs; they waited patiently for the eggs to hatch.

18. After the eggs hatched, the mother and father phoebes hunted for food; it, too, can be fascinating.

19. During a heavy rainstorm, the male phoebe perched on the branch of a nearby chestnut tree; despite the downpour, he would not relinquish his watch over his family.

20. The male phoebe eventually flew under the eaves and perched beside his mate's nest; he was as clever to move out of the rain as the hummingbird is to hitch a ride south.

5.3   EXERCISE FOR PRONOUN CHOICE

Instructions: Underline the correct pronoun in the following sentences. Try deleting confusing words (see example).

Example

The president of the Ornithology Club invited Annie, Jan, and (*I*/ <u>*me*</u>) to join her organization.

(If you delete *Annie, Jan,* and *and*, you will choose the pronoun, *me.*)

1. The diners stared at Annie, Annie's editor, and (he/him).

2. The waiter brought a sheepish grin and drinks to Matt, Annie's editor, and (she/her).

3. Matt would drive Annie's editor and (she/her) to the marketing workshop.

4. Then (her/she) and her editor would attend the workshop without Matt.

5. Annie's editor and (she/her) would learn a great deal.

6. During the workshop, the trainer explained to (we/us) participants that the marketing mix comprises the four *p*'s: product, price, place, and promotion.

7. During the break, the trainer told Annie and (they/them) that would-be poets make a living in advertising careers.

8. Annie, her editor, and (they/them) listened to the trainer's comments on subliminal seduction.

9. (We/Us) trainees learned that appearance and reality are often different.

10. The trainer told the editor and (she/her) that prices of products can sometimes be too low.

11. The editor and (he/him) learned that one company's test market of its new product indicated the price had to be raised.

12. The trainer said to Annie, her editor, and (she/her) that more widgets sold at $1.69 than at $1.49, making $1.69 the optimum price.

13. Ms. Wise emphasized to the group, including Annie and (I/me), the importance of attractive packaging.

14. Ms. Wise told the editor and (I/me) that advertisers often use words like *new, outstanding, natural,* and *innovative.*

15. Annie and (we/us) also learned that excellent products have not sold well because of poor advertising campaigns.

5.4   **EXERCISE FOR CONSISTENCY IN POINT OF VIEW AND PRONOUN CASE**

Instructions: Underline the correct word in parentheses.

1. Many people today do not enjoy poetry, but if (they/you) work to understand it, the rewards are great.

2. Two great poets, Emily Dickinson and Walt Whitman, lived during the Civil War (1861–1865); Dickinson wrote shorter poems than (him/he).

3. Emily Dickinson's brief poems stay with readers; they make an impact on (them/you).

4. Emily Dickinson was known as the private poet, and Walt Whitman was known as the public poet; she was surely a more private person than (him/he).

5. Whitman was more widely known than (her/she).

6. My writing class and I climbed to the top of the hill; (we/you) could see the entire city.

7. We took paper, pens, and tape recorders and noted everything we saw, heard, smelled, and felt; (we/you) could then use such notes to write good descriptive essays.

8. William Shakespeare was one of the great writers of literature, certainly better than (me/I).

9. Most readers must work to interpret all the words in Shakespeare's works, but then (they/you) gain insight.

10. Emily Dickinson wrote her letter to the world; she wrote to you and (I/me).

11. As we read, you and (I/me) shall enrich our lives; we shall never be the same.

12. Education—real education—is the key to the future for you, Annie, Matt, and (he/him).

5

13. Emily Dickinson published only seven works during her life, and Margaret Mitchell published only one; Dickinson was more prolific than (her/she).

14. One editor did not like Dickinson's works; he was less knowledgeable than (her/she).

15. José and Mark liked Annie better than they liked John and (she/her).

Interrogative Pronouns

Interrogative pronouns ask questions, as their label (interrogate) implies. Of course, you must still know when to use *who* and when to use *whom*, no small feat. You will learn a formula for choosing the correct pronoun.

The interrogative pronouns are *who, which, what, whose,* and *whom.* We must also be careful not to write *who's* (which means *who is* or *who has*) when we mean to write *whose,* which is in the possessive case. Look at the following sample questions. Each begins with an interrogative pronoun, which is boldfaced.

Who screamed?

Which reader is sobbing?

What do I do now?

Whom do you love as an instructor?

Whose tear-soaked book is this?

Who's screaming again?

Solving the Who/Whom Mystery in Questions

Since the who/whom mystery is even greater in questions than in statements, let us begin by solving it.

Who and *whoever* are in the subjective case. ***Whom*** and ***whomever*** are in the objective case. You know by this time that subjects come from the subjective case (that's logical), and objects come from the objective case (more logic).

TIP: Following are two steps you can follow should you forget the cases for *who* and *whom* in questions:

1. If you are writing a question in which you must use *who* or *whom,* rewrite the sentence to form a statement.

2. Generally, if you can use *he* or *she,* you can use *who* or *whoever.* If you can use ***her*** or ***him,*** you can use ***whom.***

This concept will become clear if we work our way through an example. Read the following question:

(Who/Whom) will they select as their faculty adviser?

- **First,** rewrite the question, making it a statement.

  They will select (who/whom) as their faculty adviser.

- **Next,** see if you can use *he* or *him* in the *who/whom* slot.

  They will select **him** as their faculty adviser.

- **Finally,** you are ready to select *whom* because *him* makes sense.

  Whom will they select as their faculty adviser?

While this step-by-step process will help you *most* of the time, remember that the surest way to be a precise writer *every time* is to know the pronoun cases and the pronouns that fit into each case. *Whom* is the *object* of the verb *select,* and objects must come from the objective case.

5.5 EXERCISE FOR YOUR ASSURANCE

Instructions: In the following sentences, underline the correct word in parentheses.

1. Between you and (I/me), Matt is learning a great deal.

2. My friends and (I/me) are gaining excellent writing skills.

3. The people elected John Broadgrin, Matt Murray, and (I/me/myself) to represent them.

4. I congratulated Matt, Annie, and (he/him) because they knew how to spell *congratulate.*

5. (Who/Whom) did the accountant believe?

6. (Who/Whom) caused the accident?

7. (Who/Whom) is calling?

8. With (who/whom) did you say you had interfaced?

9. John, whose name we misspelled, is angry at Matt and (I/me).

10. "Memorizing the cases and their pronouns is the best way to know which pronoun to choose," said Annie to John and (he/him).

11. Richard Burden, Annie's cat, does not have an ounce of body fat on him, for (he/him) and a few other cats have been working out at Naughtiness.

12. "Remember, Matt," said Annie, "that objective pronouns are (*I* and *we/me* and *us*)."

13. Smiling sweetly, Annie asked, "(Who/Whom) do you like as a tutor?"

14. "We like you, our English instructor, and (he/him)," said the student.

15. (Who/Whose) book is lost?

5.6   EXERCISE FOR CORRECT USE OF *WHO/WHOM*

Instructions: Try your hand at using who *and* whom *in your own sentences. Write two sentences in which you use* who *and two in which you use* whom. *Check your sentences to be sure that the* who *is doing the action and the* whom *is either receiving the action or is the object of a preposition. Answers will vary, and will not be given in the Answers to Exercises at the end of the book.*

1. _____

    _____

2. _____

    _____

3. _____

    _____

4. _____

    _____

5. _____

    _____

Relative Pronouns

Relative pronouns *are called relative because they introduce groups of words that relate to their antecedents (the nouns or pronouns to which they refer).* For example, study the following sentence:

The man who came for dinner was my cousin.

In this sentence, *who* relates to *man. Who* also introduces the word group *who came for dinner.* Relative pronouns include *who, whom, which, whose,* and *that.*

In each of the following sentences, the relative pronoun is in boldface and the antecedent is underlined. You can see why the two are kissing cousins (relatives).

This is the <u>book</u> **that** Annie wrote.

Matt met a <u>deductress</u> **who** was a writer.

<u>Richard Burden</u>, **which** is Annie's cat, loves people.

Annie's other <u>cat</u>, **whose** tail had to be removed, is beautiful.

The <u>man</u> **whom** they elected is sleeping.

You will notice that some of the interrogative pronouns are also relative pronouns. The classification depends on whether the pronoun is beginning a question (interrogative) or relating to the antecedent (relative).

Solving the Who/Whom Mystery in Relative Clauses

To determine whether to use *who* or *whom* in a relative clause—that is, a word group that forms a sentence within a sentence—you must know whether the pronoun (*who* or *whom*) is doing or receiving the action. As you know, if the pronoun is doing the action, you must use *who;* if it is receiving the action, use *whom.*

The relative clauses are italicized in the following examples:

The man *whom they arrested* was John's neighbor.

In this sentence, turn the clause around (they arrested whom). Notice that *whom* could be replaced with *him. Whom* receives the action.

The volunteer *who works hard* will get more work.

In this sentence, you can leave the word order as is. *Who* can be replaced with *he,* and *who* is doing the action.

Caution with Relative Pronouns (Which, That, and Who)

Although you can use *which* when referring to a person in a question, you should never use *which* as a relative pronoun when referring to a person. Look at these two examples:

Which person slipped through the gate? (Interrogative.)
The man **who** has a sheepish grin slipped through the gate.
(Relative.)

You could replace *who* with *that* in the preceding sentence, but you could **never** use "the *man which*." Again, when using *which* as a *relative* pronoun, never refer to persons. Here are three more examples. The **X** marks the incorrect sentence.

  1. This is the **workshop that** David developed.
  2. This is David's **workshop, which** he developed last summer.
X 3. This is **David, which** developed the workshop.

Notice that in the second example, I use *which* and a comma before *which* because I have added information about a workshop that has already been identified. In the first sentence, however, *that David developed* identifies the workshop. I have, therefore, not used a comma in front of *that.* This is an important rule to learn. Use *which,* preceded by a comma, when you are adding information not necessary to the meaning of the sentence.

Use *that* with information that is essential to the basic meaning of the sentence, and do not place a comma in front of *that*.

If you want to become a writer of precise prose, you will want to use *which* and *that* correctly. *Which* and *that* as relative pronouns introduce *relative clauses*. As you will learn in Chapter 10, a *clause* contains both a subject (actor) and a verb (action). For now, the important thing to recognize is how relative clauses and the presence or absence of commas affect the meaning of sentences. See the following examples:

Annie's new book, which is now available, is excellent.

Her books that focus on local color are bestsellers.

A *Tale of Two Kitties*, which included the antics of

Annie's cats, sold out in the first month.

Indefinite Pronouns

Indefinite pronouns do not refer to definite persons or things. They refer vaguely to persons, places, things, ideas, or animals. They are like many beginning writers, reluctant to be specific. Reading a list of indefinite pronouns will help you understand this idea.

all	each	neither	one
any	either	nobody	some
anybody	everybody	none	somebody
anyone	everyone	no one	someone
anything	everything	nothing	something

Remember that an antecedent is a word to which a pronoun refers. One of the most common errors made when indefinite singular pronouns are used as antecedents is the use of plural pronouns that refer to the singular pronouns (antecedents). For example, the pronoun *everybody* is singular in grammar but plural in meaning. Many writers, therefore, mistakenly use a plural pronoun when referring to *everybody*.

Following is an example:

   X **Everybody** reads **their** assignment because **they** want to learn more about Matt and Annie.

The sentence can be rewritten in the following ways to avoid the disagreement in number between **everybody** (the singular antecedent) and *their/they* (the plural pronouns referring to *everybody*).

  1. **Everybody** reads **his or her** assignment because **he or she** wants to learn more about Matt and Annie.

This sentence is awkward, but it is correct. Remember that to use *his* by itself or *he* by itself would result in sexist language (see Chapter 3).

2. **Everybody** reads **the** assignment because **he or she** wants to learn more about Matt and Annie.

Notice that *his or her* has this time been replaced with *the*. This sentence is still a bit awkward but correct.

3. All the **writers** read **their** assignments because **they** want to learn more about Matt and Annie.

This is the best choice. You can see that when you make a gender-neutral antecedent plural, ease of wording results. *Writers* is the antecedent, and *their* and *they* are the pronouns.

Following are examples of sentences with **indefinite pronouns,** which are boldfaced:

1. When **one** uses *one* in his or her writing, he or she is too formal for me.

You now know how to rewrite this. Change *one* to *writers*. Then use *their* to replace *his or her* and *they* to replace *he or she*. See the next rewritten example.

2. **Nobody** wants to lose **his or her** work on a computer.

One way to make this sentence less awkward is to delete *his or her*. *No one wants to lose work on a computer.* You might also write the sentence as follows: *Writers do not want to lose their work on the computer.*

3. **Neither** of them has completed **his or her** assignment.

Neither [one] has completed the assignment.
Remember to combine singular antecedents with singular pronouns and to combine plural antecedents with plural pronouns when using these indefinite pronouns. All this is quite logical.

5.7 EXERCISE FOR INDEFINITE PRONOUN AGREEMENT

Instructions: In each sentence, replace any italicized word(s) with your own words to make the sentence grammatical and less awkward. If the sentence is already correct, just smile.

1. *Everybody* must be careful about *their* use of language.
2. Neither of the women wants *their* poetry published.
3. Somebody forgot *their* books.
4. All students should remember to write *his or her* names in their textbooks.

5. Neither of the women wore *their* hiking boots.

6. Conscientious writers proofread *their* writing.

7. *Each* of the men liked *their* instructor.

8. *Everyone* in the class had completed *his or her* assignment.

9. *Nobody* in the class has written *his or her* second draft.

10. *Anyone* going to the writing group must take *their* favorite poems.

5.8 EXERCISE FOR *WHO/WHOM* CHOICES

Instructions: Write the preferred pronoun in the space provided.

1. (Who/Whom) did you say would
   attend the birthday party? _____

2. For (who/whom) has the party been planned? _____

3. The party has been planned for Annie
   and (who/whom)? _____

4. Annie, (who/whom) we know, is planning
   a celebration. _____

5. I do not know (who/whom) will be invited. _____

6. (Whoever/Whomever) attends will enjoy
   fine entertainment and good food. _____

7. Annie will welcome (whoever/whomever)
   she has invited. _____

8. Matt, (who/whom) I saw yesterday, will
   certainly attend the party, for it is in his honor. _____

9. (Whoever/Whomever) drops names at the
   party will bore others. _____

10. (Who/Whom) do you think is the man in
    the purple tights? _____

11. He talks to (whoever/whomever) stands
    near him. _____

12. (Who/Whom) will be his next victim? _____

13. With (who/whom) did he arrive? _____

14. The man (who/whom) is dropping names
    and wearing the purple tights arrived alone. _____

15. The man (who/whom) wore the purple
    tights was oblivious to others' stares. _____

5.9 EXERCISE TO RELATE PRONOUNS TO ANTECEDENTS

Instructions: Underline the preferred pronoun in parentheses.

1. The person (who/whom) researches a company before a job interview has an advantage.

2. José, (who's/whose) interview was successful, did his research.

3. The interviewee (who/whom) arrives 15 minutes early arrives on time.

4. The interview (that/which) is successful requires a skilled interviewer and a savvy interviewee.

5. José's interview, (which/that) was successful, lasted almost an hour.

6. The person (who/whom) knows how to dress for an interview makes a good first impression.

7. The person (who's/whose) written a flawless cover letter catches the interviewer's attention.

8. The person for (who/whom) appearance is important will research dress codes for job interviews.

9. Jake is the one (who/whom) I believe lost the job because he chewed gum during the interview.

10. (Whoever/Whomever) rehearses answering questions before the interview gains self-confidence.

11. If you could invite any two living persons to your home for dinner, (who/whom) would you invite?

12. I would invite my parents because they are the ones (who's/whose) support has helped me throughout life.

13. The interview (that/which) lasts an hour or more is stressful.

14. The person (who/whom) reads body language when the interviewer looks repeatedly at the clock will leave promptly when the interview has ended.

15. The person (who/whom) asks for the interviewer's business card and promptly sends a thank-you note makes an outstanding impression.

Demonstrative or Pointing Pronouns

Only four demonstrative pronouns exist in the English language. They are *this, that, these,* and *those.*

Demonstrative pronouns, as their name implies, point or demonstrate. They, too, must be used with caution in our writing lest our readers think we are pointing to one thing when, in fact, we are pointing to something else. *This* and *that* are, of course, singular; *these* and *those* are plural. *This* and *these* imply a closeness to the speaker or writer. *That* and *those* imply distance from the speaker or writer.

When you are speaking, you can actually point as you utter one of the demonstrative pronouns. The gesture makes your meaning clear. When writing, however, you must be careful when using demonstrative pronouns. Your reader cannot see your gestures.

Avoid using pronouns that are vague or unclear. Be sure the reader knows exactly what they refer to, exactly what you mean.

Following are a few sample sentences with demonstrative pronouns. You will notice some vagueness since you cannot see any body language.

This young man was walking through the park.

This is a tub of fun.

That is the book I read.

These are my joys.

Those are your joys.

The rewritten versions clarify the meaning of each sentence.

A young man was walking through the park.

This workshop is a tub of fun.

That book, *The Joys of Grammar*, is the book I read.

These aerobic exercises are my joys.

Those persuasive essays are your joys.

Reciprocal Pronouns

Each other and *one another* are the only reciprocal pronouns in our language. They are "I'll-scratch-your-back-if-you'll-scratch-mine" pronouns. In short, **reciprocal pronouns** *reciprocate* or *give and take*.

Use **each other** when you are discussing only **two;** use **one another** when you are discussing **three or more.**

Examples

John and Annie liked **each other's** ideas. (Two persons.)

John, Annie, and Matt enjoyed **one another's** comments. (Three persons.)

Reflexive Pronouns

Reflexive pronouns are a good reflection on the "actor" or subject of a sentence. Beware of reflexive pronouns. They are SELFish. They often push their way into your speech and prose when they should not. All the reflexive pronouns end with either *-self* (singular) or *-selves* (plural). The **reflexive pronoun** *should be used in only one instance: when it reflects on the* "actor" *or subject of the sentence.* Notice that the subject (actor) and the object (receiver of the action) should be identical, as in the following examples. In these samples, the subject is boldfaced and underlined, and the reflexive pronoun is boldfaced.

1. **<u>The bank president</u>** hurt **himself** with his remarks.

   Hisself and *hiself* are not acceptable spellings—ever.

2. **<u>We</u>** taught **ourselves** to love language.

   If the first part of the pronoun is plural, the last part of the word must be plural. Since *our* is plural, we must use *ourselves.*, ending the word with *-selves* rather than *-self.*

3. **<u>I</u>** just want to be **myself.**

4. **<u>They</u>** taught **themselves** the importance of using correct language.

   Be aware that *theirselves* and *theirself* are always incorrect. Use *themselves.*

Just as it is easy to use the wrong form of some personal pronouns, it is also easy to use one of the *-self* pronouns when you need a personal pronoun. An example of such an error will make this statement clear.

X John and **myself** carry dictionaries.

Delete *John and.* You would never write or say, "Myself carries dictionaries." Again, when we put someone else in the sentence, we can easily become confused. You can see that these *-self* pronouns crowd into sentences where they should not be. The sentence should have been written as follows. The **X** indicates an incorrect sentence.

John and *I* carry dictionaries.

Look at the next error with a *-self* pronoun.

X Give the dictionaries **to** John and **myself.**

"Give the dictionaries to myself" makes no sense.

Give the dictionaries **to** John and **me.**

This sentence is correct; we would say, "Give the dictionaries to me.

Avoid *-self* pronouns when personal pronouns are needed. Also, *remember to check pronoun case.* If the pronoun is doing the action, pull the pronoun from the subjective case. If the pronoun is receiving the action or is the object of a preposition, pull the pronoun from the objective case. Following are examples of reflexive pronouns:

Singular	**Plural**
myself	ourselves
yourself	yourselves
himself	themselves
herself	
itself	
oneself	

Intensive Pronouns

Like the reflexive pronouns, these pronouns end with -*self* or -*selves*. **Intensive pronouns,** *as their name implies, intensify or emphasize.* These pronouns are not used as often as most of the others. They give us no real problems, but you need to know that you can use them to emphasize, and when you do, you do not need to set them off with commas. See the examples that follow:

Singular	**Plural**
I *myself*	we *ourselves*
you *yourself*	you *yourselves*
John *himself*	they *themselves*
the dog *itself*	

Look at the following sample sentences. The subject is boldfaced, as is the intensive pronoun.

Matt himself needs a vacation.

I myself want a vacation.

Matt and **Annie themselves** are learning.

We ourselves learn as we listen to their conversations.

They themselves learn as they discuss business writing.

Ambiguous Pronouns

Ambiguous pronouns are pronouns that do not refer clearly to their antecedents. For instance, a pronoun may have two antecedents that leave the reader guessing as to which antecedent the pronoun is referring. As you read the following sentence, you will not know whether *she* refers to Annie or Maria. It is better to repeat a person's name than to use an ambiguous pronoun. The **X** indicates an incorrect sentence.

X Annie shared the joke with Maria as she laughed.

Sometimes, the pronoun refers to an idea contained in an entire word group, but the pronoun has no antecedent. The result is confusion. Read the following sentence to see if you can find a word that serves as the antecedent for the demonstrative pronoun, *this*.

X The trainer distributes handouts to the participants; this enhances the learning process.

One way to correct the preceding sentence is to insert *practice* after the pronoun, *this*.

When a pronoun's antecedent is not consistent with the meaning in the sentence, confusion results. In the following sample sentence, *writer* is the antecedent of the pronoun, *this*, but *this* should refer to an activity (writing) rather than to the person who engages in an activity (writer).

X Annie is a well-known local writer; this is an activity she enjoys.

In informal conversation, people sometimes begin sentences with pronouns that have no antecedents. Look at the following example:

X They say that lightning never strikes twice in one place, but I know that statement is not true.

The pronoun, *they*, has no antecedent and, therefore, should be replaced with a noun and any necessary qualifiers—for example, *some people*.

Like all pronouns, the pronoun *it* must be used with caution. Look at the following example:

X The squirrel built a nest; it was high in a tree.

Was the squirrel or the nest high in a tree? Generally, when you use *it*, be sure you have a clear antecedent.

There are times, however, when *it* is used without an antecedent because native speakers of English know the meaning regardless of the lack of antecedent. You have probably used and heard statements like the following.

It has been snowing since November. (Reference to weather.)

It is clear that Mother Nature is confused. (Reference to "that clause"—see Chapter 10.)

It is now ten o'clock. (Reference to time.)

It is 25 miles from Charleston to Goldtown. (Reference to distance.)

Each time you use pronouns, be sure their antecedents are clear to your reader.

5.10   EXERCISE FOR POINTING CLEARLY

Instructions: Write in the space provided the correct words in parentheses.

1. All (them/those) folks born from 1946 through 1964 are known as Baby Boomers.   _____

2. Many in (this/these) kind of group have already reached their fiftieth birthday.   _____

3. Some Boomers have admitted to finding themselves on common ground with—of all people—their parents; (them/those) Boomers are closing the generation gap.   _____

4. An age difference of a decade or more creates communication obstacles; (them/these) obstacles, in turn, help to create the famous generation gap.   _____

5. Baby Boomers are stereotyped as the "me generation"; (that/those) kind of stereotyping is often unfair and inaccurate.   _____

6. Many Boomers have careers that demand both hard work and decision-making skills; (those/those Boomers) can inspire us.   _____

7. Many have chosen responsibility over dependence on others, and (this/those) kind of choice is admirable.   _____

8. Some people from every generation have decided to travel the path of irresponsibility; (those/that decision) should never be blamed on society.   _____

9. One Boomer told me that drugs cannot be abused, but drugs can surely abuse the mind and body; (this/these) Boomer's viewpoint is unusual, given the repetition of the expression "drug abuse."   _____

10. I like (them/those) Boomers.   _____

11. I like many of (them/those) Boomers.   _____

12. Sometimes, writers need qualifying words to make their statements accurate; (those/that) kind of facts should be ingrained.   _____

13. (This Boomer/One Boomer) I know resents the stereotyping his group suffers.   _____

14. He declares, however, he is not a victim;
(that/that philosophy) works well for him. _____

15. Many Boomers in the 1960s were also known
as Yippies and Flower Children; many Boomers believe (those/those days) were ideal. _____

5.11 EXERCISE FOR REFLECTING AND INTENSIFYING

*Instructions: Edit the following paragraph by correcting all misused reflexive
and intensive pronouns, some of which should be replaced with other types of
pronouns.*

An Appalachian Uncle

When I was a child, my Uncle Alfred was influential in my life. He
hisself had not even gone through elementary school, much less
college. Still, he placed a high value on education. One cold winter
day, the snow was two feet deep. I did not want to go to school, but
my uncle insisted. He upset my mother and myself when he told her
I should go despite the weather. My uncle and mother theirselves
discussed the matter on the phone. Soon, I was on my way to my first-
grade class. Years later, as I reached for my college diploma, my mother,
father, and uncle sat on the front row. We were proud of ourself. They
were proud because they had not let me give up. During my school
years, I had learned much. Education is not an end in itself; it is an
ongoing process. I knew it would enrich the lives of my classmates and
myself. My parents and myself are still grateful to my Uncle Alfred, my
uncle from the hills of Appalachia.

5.12 EXERCISE FOR AVOIDING AMBIGUOUS PRONOUNS

*Instructions: Most of the following sentences have unclear pronouns. Rewrite
unclear sentences to make their meanings clear. If the sentence is correct, do
nothing.*

1. They say you will have bad luck if a black cat crosses your path.

_____

_____

5

2. If you break a mirror, you will have seven years' bad luck, but that is just a superstition.

_____

_____

3. Annie dropped the paperweight on the glass-topped desk and broke it.

_____

_____

4. Mother Nature has made several attempts to kill us this winter by dropping several feet of snow on us; it has been terrible.

_____

_____

5. It has been a terrible winter.

_____

_____

6. Matt read the instructions twice before beginning the test; that was a good idea.

_____

_____

7. Garcia and John like poetry and drama; they are entertaining.

_____

_____

8. Annie observes wildlife and human nature every day; it is fascinating.

_____

_____

9. When Annie added a page to her book, it contained many references to wildlife.

_____

_____

10. Matt is a teller at a local bank; it is his part-time career because he is also a part-time college student.

_____

_____

Review of Pronouns

The eight subclasses of pronouns are listed once again for reinforcement. Unless you are confident when using pronouns, you should spend time reviewing the entire chapter.

Type of Pronoun	Definition	Examples
1. personal pronouns	refer specifically to persons or things	I, you, he, them, we, us, our, it
2. interrogative pronouns	form questions	who, which, what, whose
3. relative pronouns	introduce groups of words that relate to their antecedents	who, which, that
4. indefinite pronouns	refer to general or nonspecific persons or things	anybody, anyone, one, none, everyone
5. demonstrative pronouns	point or demonstrate	this, that, these, those
6. reciprocal pronouns	reciprocate or give and take	each other (for only two) one another (for three or more)
7. reflexive pronouns	reflect on preceding noun or pronoun	himself, themselves, ourselves, itself, herself, oneself
8. intensive pronouns	intensify or emphasize a noun or pronoun	himself, themselves, ourselves, itself, herself

Now that you have reviewed the types of pronouns, test yourself on the following pages. If you find that you have weak areas, continue to read and review until you are confident using all types of pronouns.

SUMMARY

You have learned the eight subclasses of pronouns:

1. personal (I/me/us/they/them)
2. interrogative (who?/whom?which?)
3. relative (who/whose/that)
4. indefinite (someone/anyone)
5. demonstrative (this/that/these/those)
6. reciprocal (each other/one another)
7. reflexive (myself/ourselves)
8. intensive (himself/themselves)

You know that an *antecedent* is a grammatical term that means a word to which a pronoun refers. The antecedent and the pronoun must agree in number; that is, both must be singular, or both must be plural. Also, remember there are three points of view and that you cannot shift from one to the other illogically:

1. first person (I, me, us, we, our, my)
2. second person (you, your)
3. third person (he, she, they, them, it)

You know that there are only three pronoun cases: **subjective** (from which all subjects or "actors" are pulled, **objective** (from which all objects are pulled), and **possessive** (from which all possessive pronouns are pulled). Remember that when you have a compound subject or object, such as *Annie and I*, you can often delete the *Annie and* to determine whether to use *I* or *me*. If you are still unsure, check the pronoun cases. You have learned how to use interrogative and relative pronouns, and you have solved the who/whom mystery when using both types. You have learned the special caution that must be taken with the indefinite pronoun so that the antecedent and pronoun agree in number and gender. Remember to use the four pointing or demonstrative pronouns (*this*, *that*, *these*, and *those*) with clear antecedents. Be sure your reader knows what you are pointing at; otherwise, you will confuse your audience. While there are only four demonstrative pronouns, there are just two pairs of reciprocal pronouns: *each other* and *one another*.

The -*self* pronouns are reflexive and intensive. Do not permit the SELFish -*self* pronouns to crowd in where they should not be. Use them only when you wish to reflect on the subject or intensify as in the following sentences:

I like myself when I learn more about pronouns. (Reflexive.)

I myself need to learn more about pronouns. (Intensive.)

Be sure that the antecedent for each pronoun is clear to the reader.

You now have information necessary to use pronouns correctly. Review this chapter often until you feel confident using even the *who/whom* pronouns. Learning how to choose pronouns correctly helps to build excellent writing skills. Learning how to use the language can give you power in your writing. Indeed, you will have a treasure trove of positive power on which to draw when the need arises. ∎

5.13 END-OF-CHAPTER EXERCISES

Instructions: To make each sentence clear, replace the pronoun or its antecedent with your own words. Draw a line through the unclear wording; then write your words just above it.

1. The *United States Congress* refers to our nation's governing body, which is located in Washington, D. C.; each state is represented in Washington by their members of Congress.

2. Each state has a legislature; they are located in the state's capital.

3. Each legislature comprises two bodies, a senate and a house of delegates; their members' offices are located in the state's capitol.

4. Citizens often visit the legislative sessions; you can learn a great deal during the sessions.

5. The governor of each state gives a state-of-the-state address in which he discusses accomplishments of the preceding year and budget allocations for the next year.

6. State governments make state laws, but Congress makes laws that affect all of we citizens.

7. Governors meet at least once a year; it is a meeting that focuses on the governors' main concerns.

8. One legislator wanted to know whom had written *writing* with two *t*'s.

9. Everybody knows *writing* has one *t*, but *written* has two *t*'s; at least, they should know that.

10. The man who John referred to as a politician is angry.

11. The man whom was called a politician became angry.

12. The senator whose been called a politician is resentful.

13. The senator introduced a bill to increase punishment for persons convicted of driving under the influence of alcohol (DUI), and it was a good idea.

5

14. Legislators, as you know, introduce and pass the bills for you and I.

15. The three branches of government are the legislative, the judicial, and the executive; legislators, who the people elect, write the bills that become laws.

16. Bills which are signed by the governor become laws.

17. You and me are expected to obey those laws.

18. A governor (whom, as you know, can veto a bill) belongs to the executive branch.

19. Members of a state supreme court belong to the judicial branch; the three branches provide a system of checks and balances for we citizens.

20. The capital of New York is Albany, although many people, who's knowledge of geography is limited, think the capital is New York City.

21. West Virginia's capital is Charleston, and it is not part of Virginia.

22. Louisiana, that operates under the Napoleonic code, boasts the city that care forgot, New Orleans.

23. Each of the states has their own brand of politics.

24. Elected officials, who comedians frequently satirize, represent their constituents.

25. United States citizens have the privilege of voting for their representatives, and if you do not vote, you are not a part of the democratic process.

Instructions: Rewrite the sentences to make the meaning clear. You may need to replace, add, repeat, delete, or rearrange words. Look up definitions of words with which you are unfamiliar. If the sentence contains no errors, do nothing.

26. Diction involves word choices; this is important for writers.

_____

_____

27. The members of Congress were in caucus; that is why they arrived early.

_____

_____

28. This libretto will help you to follow the opera's story line.

_____

_____

29. The musician's opus has already become a classic; that pleased the audience.

_____

_____

30. The two decorators' debate with one another resulted in eclectic furnishings.

_____

_____

31. The two diners discussed the meaning of *circumlocution* with one another, and one said, "*Circumlocution* occurs when a dog goes around and around in a circle before it lies down."

_____

_____

_____

32. *Circumlocution* is the opposite of conciseness; and that should be avoided in writing.

_____

_____

33. Ordering prime rib a la carte, the two diners argued with one another over the definition of Cameroon; one said, "Cameroon is not a cookie, but it is an African country."

_____

_____

_____

34. Most college students tell theirselves they should learn the meanings of unfamiliar words.

_____

_____

35. Matt hisself knows that keeping abreast of topical issues is an important part of his ongoing education.

_____

_____

36. Annie amused herself by remembering one friend's definition of *paradox*; the friend defined *paradox* as two doctors.

_____

_____

37. Back at the Whistle Top Buffet, the two diners accused one another of being quixotic.

_____

_____

38. *Quixotic* is derived from Don Quixote, a character in Miguel Cervantes' satirical novel.

_____

_____

39. Don Quixote hisself is quixotic; that is, he tries to reach impossible goals and becomes the target of ridicule.

_____

_____

40. Quixotic persons often tell theirselves they can transform a dystopian society into a utopian society.

_____

_____

41. Proper names from which words are derived are known as eponyms; this is fascinating.

_____

_____

42. Degas often reminds hisself that cynicism is not an innate trait; cynicism must be nurtured.

_____

_____

43. Hearing a mort, Degas knew this deer had been fatally shot.

_____

_____

44. An hour later, the two hunters faced one another; one carried a camera, and the other carried a gun.

_____

_____

45. Samuel Clemens hisself chose the pseudonym _Mark Twain; pseudo_ means false, and _nym_ means name.

_____

_____

Instructions: Write the correct pronoun in the space provided. If you do not know the rule, scan the chapter, find the rule, and read it again.

46. The report's title sounded interesting, but when Matt read (it/the report)_____, he found it boring.

47. Send copies of the memo to (whoever/whomever) _____ you wish.

48. Send copies of the memo to (whoever/whomever) _____ needs the information.

49. With (whom/who) _____ did you say Matt had talked?

50. "Memorizing the pronoun cases is the best way to know which pronoun to choose," said the instructor to Matt and (us/we) _____ participants.

51. (Who/Whom) _____ did the manager believe?

52. (Who/Whom) _____ did Annie blame for the misuse of the pronoun?

53. Matt played with Bob, his five-year-old nephew, and he laughed at (him/Matt) _____.

54. We have taught (ourselves/us) _____ a great deal about pronouns; we can now use them with confidence.

55. Annie was to meet Matt and (he/him) _____ at the Whistle Top Buffet.

56. "Just let me be (myself/I/me)_____," said Annie.

57. Matt and (she/her) _____ looked at the report in stony silence.

58. (Who's/Whose) _____ been writing the word _judgment_ with two _e_'s?

59. (We/Us) _____ readers learned that the whole comprises the parts.

60. The trainer told (we/us) _____ participants not to use _comprised of._

5

61. The clever squirrel jumped from (its/it's) _____ nest onto the squirrel-proof bird feeder.

62. Every squirrel can overcome obstacles on a bird feeder because (they are/it is) _____ an intelligent creature.

63. I watched a squirrel as it hung upside down from a metal feeder; (you/I) _____ could see the squirrel eat as it hung by its back feet.

64. Many creatures live in the woods surrounding my country home; the wildlife provides hours of entertainment for my three cats and (I/me)_____.

65. Between you and (he/him) _____, you should create a popular book on wildlife.

66. Matt is a better photographer than Annie, but she is a better writer than (him/he) _____.

67. Rose Marie, (who/whom) _____ I was telling you about, has been promoted; she is now an editor.

68. (Who/Whom) _____ did you think would get the promotion?

69. Rose Marie, (who/whom) _____ will serve as Annie's editor, is a grammarian.

70. She is as good a worker under pressure as (him/he) _____.

71. Everyone in the woods during hunting season should wear (their/his or her) _____ bright orange clothing.

72. Each of the two women readied (their cameras/her camera) _____.

73. (They/Many people) _____ say that when a person walks under a ladder, he or she will have bad luck.

74. *Live* spelled backwards is *evil,* and *lived* spelled backwards is *devil;* (these/such facts) _____ are fascinating.

75. *Grammar* and *success* are somehow connected; do not try to spell (it/*grammar* and *success*) _____ backwards because they do not spell anything.

Chapter 6

Verbs: Where the Action Is

◗ OBJECTIVES

In this chapter, you will learn to

- ••• define and recognize the verb
- ••• identify the subclasses of verbs
- ••• use tenses correctly
- ••• master irregular verbs
- ••• conjugate verbs
- ••• use the progressive form correctly
- ••• conquer the subjunctive mood
- ••• use passive and active voices appropriately
- ••• discover the uniqueness of the verb *be*
- ••• avoid special pitfalls

An Overview of Verbs

Verbs give life to most sentences. The verb is the throbbing heartbeat, the core around which everything else revolves. Look at the following sentence:

Help!

You can see that, in this case, a word is worth a thousand pictures. Unless you are writing dialogue, every sentence you write will contain at least one verb. *A **verb** expresses action (be it ever so weak) or establishes a state of being.*

Despite the verb's constant use, no part of speech is more misused than the irregular verb. For that reason, a great deal of time will be spent on the irregular verb. Be patient. In time, you will know exactly what an irregular verb is.

Like pronouns, verbs are divided into subclasses. Verbs have tenses, some of which are formed with the help of additional words such as **has,**

have, had, is, are, am, and **been.** It is little wonder that such words are called **helping (auxiliary) verbs.**

According to prescriptive grammarians, verbs have six tenses. You will learn each tense and how to use it in a sentence. Verbs also have moods, but only one mood causes problems. You will learn to recognize this cantankerous mood and how to use it correctly. By the time you finish this chapter, you will know how to use verbs correctly, despite their irregularities, tenses, and moods.

Since a verb provides life to the sentence, you should try to find as specific a verb as possible when writing. Specific verbs can transform weak, vague sentences into vivid, concrete writing. Look at the following sentences in which the verbs have been boldfaced:

> Examples of actual verbs in sentences **are** far better for teaching verb recognition than the rather stilted formal definition of a verb.

> Examples of actual verbs in sentences **capture** the students' attention and **clarify** the abstract definition of the verb.

In the first sentence, the weak verb *are* falls short when compared to the verbs in the next sentence. Learn to use a specific verb if doing so will make your writing clearer or more vivid. For example, *saunter* is more vivid than *walk.* More effort is required to search for a specific verb, but the results are worth the effort.

The six tenses of verbs include those tenses that require the addition of words, such as *has, had,* and *will.* Look at the six sample sentences that follow. Each sentence offers a different example of one of the six tenses. The verbs illustrating the tenses are boldfaced.

1. Annie's smile **sizzles** with underlying meaning. (**Present tense.**)
2. Matt **sauntered** past the bank and toward the park. (**Past tense.**)
3. Matt and Annie **will sashay** out of the Whistle Top Buffet. (**Future tense.**)
4. The student **has muttered** something about the deadline for the lab report. (**Present-perfect tense.**)
5. Annie's stolen Jaguar **had careened** around Route 21's hairpin curve by the time the trooper arrived. (**Past-perfect tense.**)
6. In another few minutes, the driver **will have wrapped** Annie's car around the old oak tree. (**Future-perfect tense.**)

Now that you have only a winking acquaintance with verbs and their six tenses, you need a winking acquaintance with subclasses of verbs. In the following list, types of verbs are accompanied by brief definitions and comments. If you are confused when you finish reading the list, be assured that all will become clear as you continue to read *and* study.

Subclasses of Verbs

1. Regular verbs in their past and past-perfect tenses end with *-d* or *-ed*. These verbs generally give us no problems. (Do not be concerned about the terms *past* and *past perfect*. Soon you will not only know the definitions of these terms, but you will also know how to explain them to someone else. Be patient.)

2. Irregular verbs are all the other verbs, those that do not end with *-d* or *-ed* in past and past-perfect tenses. These verbs cause many intelligent people to make errors in both their speech and writing. They are "demon verbs." If you study them, you will use them correctly and confidently. A great deal of time and space will be spent on these verbs.

3. Transitive verbs are verbs that have objects, that is, words in the sentence that receive action from the verb, either directly or indirectly.

4. Intransitive verbs are verbs that have no objects. You can translate *intransitive* as *not transitive*, meaning no action is transmitted from the verb to an object. There is nothing in the sentence that receives action from the verb.

5. Linking verbs link or connect the subject (actor) in a sentence to either a noun, pronoun, or adjective (descriptive word) that follows the linking verb.

By now, you are probably getting frustrated. Stay with me. You are learning the secrets of grammarians. As you progress through this chapter, all these terms will be explained fully, and you will have ample examples and exercises to help you remember the material.

The Six Verb Tenses

Before you look at lists of irregular verbs, take a closer look at the six tenses to see exactly what is meant by *tense*. First, you must understand that sometimes grammatical tense has little in common with actual time as we know it. For example, when I say a verb is present tense, I am referring to the spelling or form of the verb. The verb may indicate time, but it may not. Look at the following sentence:

Annie **likes** to write.

The verb *likes* is in the present tense because it does not end with a *-d*. The grammatical tense of the verb (present tense), then, does not always mean that something is taking place in the present time. The sample sentence obviously means that Annie likes to write continually—not just in the present. Thus, the present tense expresses not only the present time, but it can also express a condition or ongoing action. Be aware that tense means just grammatical tense, that is, how a verb is spelled in a certain tense.

1. Present-tense verbs indicate a condition (*he is ill*), a routinely performed action (*he walks every day*), and an opinion (*easy reading means hard writing*). Also, when writing about action in a work of fiction, use the present tense. Present-tense verbs end with no additional letters (suffixes) or with the addition of an *-s*. See the following:

Matt and Annie **meet** frequently at their favorite restaurant.

The present-tense verb here does not end in *-s*. Notice how the addition of the word *frequently* in the sentence further reinforces that the grammatical present tense does not mean at the present time.

In the next sentence, the verb must have an *-s*.

Matt often **meets** Annie at their favorite restaurant.

The present-tense verb in the preceding sentence must have an *-s* for four reasons:

A. The subject (Matt) is **singular.**

B. The subject (Matt) is **third person.**

C. The verb (meets) is in **present tense.**

D. There are **no helping verbs.**

Anytime these four criteria are met in a present-tense verb, the verb must end with an *-s*. There are *no exceptions,* so anyone whose dialect omits the *-s* from the present-tense verb must learn this rule for standard written English. In other words, we could never write, "He meet Annie."

2. Past tense means that an action has occurred in the past. Past-tense verbs cannot have helping verbs ride alongside them. Past tense also means that **regular verbs** will end in *-d* or *-ed*. Irregular past-tense verbs refer to the past, but again, without helping verbs. They may be spelled in a variety of ways. Sometimes only the context will give the tense with irregular verbs. For example, the verb *cost* remains the same in all tenses except the present tense, which may require the suffix *-s,* as explained in the discussion of the Present Tense.

The following verbs are all verbs in past tense:

I **read** yesterday.

She **led** the parade yesterday.

I **wrote** to Matt.

I **saw** you at the party.

The dogs **barked** all night.

The dress **cost** $30.

3. Future tense means an action will happen in the future. The future-tense verbs are preceded by either *will* or *shall. Will* and *shall* themselves need to be explained. During the eighteenth century, a language scholar sat down and made up a rule: *Shall* must be used with the first person (I/we) and *will* with the second (you) and third persons (he/they/she). Fortunately, the rule has collapsed with one reasonable exception. If we are asking a question in the first person (I/we), we still use *shall,* as in the following: *Shall I help you?* You can see that the question is different in meaning from the following: *Will I help you?*

Except for the first-person question with *shall,* the distinction between the two words has collapsed. When you use future tense, you no longer need be concerned about whether to choose *will* or *shall* (except in first person when asking a question). In other words, you may write the following: *I will* learn (first person). *You will* learn (second person). *He will* learn (third person). *Shall* is used with second and third persons to indicate determination. Legal documents, for example, contain *shall* with second and third persons.

4. Present-perfect tense means that the verb is preceded by the **present-tense helping verbs** *has* or *have.* This tense indicates an action that began in the past—an action that may have been completed in the past, or it may continue into the present.

Look at the following examples:

He **has been** a faithful learner. (Present perfect.)

They **have gone** for a walk. (Present perfect.)

Matt and Annie **have played** Scrabble for hours. (Present perfect.)

If the present-perfect verb has a singular subject, the helping verb has an *-s: He has gone.*

5. Past-perfect tense indicates that an action has occurred prior to a certain time in the past. The past-perfect verb is preceded by the **past-tense helping verb** *had.* Look at the following examples:

I **had waited** ten minutes when the doorbell rang. (Past perfect.)

He **had written** the letter before I arrived. (Past perfect.)

He **had mailed** it before I could stop him. (Past perfect.)

6. Future-perfect tense means that something will be completed by a certain time in the future. The verb will be preceded by *will* or *shall* and *have* or *has.* If you are confused, take heart. This construction is seldom used. See the following samples:

In two more months, Annie **will have completed** her manuscript.

When she completes her next session, she **will have given** 155 writing workshops.

Regular Verbs

A **regular verb** *ends with -ed in its past, present-perfect, and past-perfect tenses.* Look at the following examples for clarification:

Matt *talked* with the police officer. (Past tense.)

Annie *has talked* with the officers many times regarding her stolen Jaguar. (Present perfect tense.)

Matt *had talked* with her on Wednesday. (Past perfect tense.)

Because regular verbs do not change their spellings when they move from simple past tense to present perfect or past perfect—that is, when we use *has,* have, or *had* with them—they usually give us no problems when we speak or write. We can, for example, write the following sentences without worrying about verb spellings because the spellings do not change:

I **played** yesterday. (Past tense.)

I **have played** every day. (Present perfect tense.)

He **has played** every day, too. (Present perfect tense.)

I **had played** for an hour when you called. (Past perfect tense.)

Look closely at the preceding sample sentences. First, notice that the verb *play* meets the requirement to be a regular verb because it ends with *-ed.* Next, notice that the past tense of *play* (*played*) has no helping verbs; that is, *played* is not preceded by *has, have,* or *had.* Now, notice that the present-perfect tense of the verb is preceded by either *have* or *has.* This meets the requirement for present-perfect tense. Finally, notice that the past-perfect tense is preceded by *had,* which meets the requirement for past perfect.

TIP: The **present-perfect tense always begins with the present tense of have** (with either *have* or *has*). The **past-perfect tense always begins with the past tense of have** (*had*).

Now that you know how simple it is to understand what a regular verb is, you are ready to learn what an irregular verb is.

Irregular Verbs

*All the verbs in the English language that are not regular verbs are called **irregular verbs.*** In other words, they are verbs that form their past and perfect tenses in some way other than adding *-ed.* Look at the following examples, and you will immediately understand the difference:

I **saw** you at the beach yesterday. (Past tense.)

I **have seen** you at the beach many times. (Present-perfect tense.)

I **had seen** the book previously (Past-perfect tense.)

Notice that the verb *see* does not end with *-ed;* therefore, it is an irregular verb. It is one of the verbs, then, for which we must learn the correct forms. For instance, have you ever heard anyone say, "I seen" or "I have saw"? Have you ever heard anyone say, "I runned," "I have went," or "I have ran"? Not one of these expressions is grammatical. Mastering the irregular verbs is obviously essential to successful writing.

Remember that irregular verbs are all the verbs that do not end with -ed in past-tense form and past-participial form.

TIP: The lists of irregular verbs on the following pages hold the key to your successful use of these verbs. If your dialect varies from American edited English, you must work hard to break old habits with respect to the use of some of the verbs listed. These lists are as important as any pages in this book. You must understand what each column of words means.

Look at the following lists of verbs and notice how they change spellings or stay the same as you read across the page. You can see that most of these verbs do not end with -ed. When they do, they become regular verbs. The spelling of each verb often changes when we place helping verbs with it. Notice the verbs that change spellings as they move from past to past participle.

Instructions In the spaces provided above *the middle column* on each page, write: *I cannot use helping verbs with words in this column.* Underline the word *cannot*. Your copying of my words into these blank spaces will help you know how to use these lists effectively as references when you are unsure of which verb form to use. Read your writing on each page and glance at the words in the middle column. Know, then, that you can never write or say, "I have wrote" or "I have went" or "I have ran." Look at the lists again and think about these kinds of mistakes. It takes a great deal of practice and commitment to overcome such errors if you have formed a lifelong habit of making them. In the spaces provided above *the third column* on each page, write the following: *I must use helping verbs with the words in this column.* Underline the word *must.*

6

Irregular "Demon" Verbs

Present-Tense or Base Spelling	Past-Tense Spelling	Past-Participle Spelling (not tense)
	_____	_____
	_____	_____
	_____	_____
	_____	_____
arise	arose	arisen
awake	awoke/awaked	awoken/awaked/awoke
be (is/am/are)	was/were	been
bear	bore	born/borne

Present-Tense or Base Spelling	Past-Tense Spelling	Past-Participle Spelling (not tense)
	_____	_____
	_____	_____
	_____	_____
	_____	_____
beat	beat	beat/beaten
become	became	become
begin	began	begun
bend	bent	bent
bet	bet	bet
bind	bound	bound
bite	bit	bit/bitten
bleed	bled	bled
blow	blew	blown
break	broke	broken
bring	brought	brought
build	built	built
burst	burst	burst
buy	bought	bought
catch	caught	caught
choose	chose	chosen
cling	clung	clung
come	came	come
cost	cost	cost
creep	crept	crept
cut	cut	cut
deal	dealt	dealt
dig	dug	dug
dive	dove	dived
do (does)	did	done
draw	drew	drawn
drink	drank	drunk
drive	drove	driven
eat	ate	eaten

6

Present-Tense or Base Spelling	Past-Tense Spelling	Past-Participle Spelling (not tense)
	_____	_____
	_____	_____
	_____	_____
	_____	_____
fall	fell	fallen
feed	fed	fed
feel	felt	felt
fight	fought	fought
find	found	found
flee	fled	fled
fling	flung	flung
fly	flew	flown
forbid	forbade/forbad	forbidden
forget	forgot	forgot/forgotten
freeze	froze	frozen
get	got	got/gotten
give	gave	given
go	went	gone
grow	grew	grown
hang (an object)	hung	hung (Note: _Hanged_ is used to indicate a person has been executed by hanging.)
have/has	had	had
hear	heard	heard
hide	hid	hidden
hit	hit	hit
hold	held	held
hurt	hurt	hurt
keep	kept	kept
know	knew	known
lay (put or place)	laid	laid
lead	led	led
leave	left	left

6

Present-Tense or Base Spelling	Past-Tense Spelling	Past-Participle Spelling (not tense)
	_____	_____
	_____	_____
	_____	_____
	_____	
lend	lent	lent (Note: *Loaned* is fast becoming acceptable in both past and past-participial spellings.)
let	let	let
lie (to recline)	lay	lain
light	lit/lighted	lit/lighted
lose	lost	lost
make	made	made
mean	meant	meant
meet	met	met
mistake	mistook	mistaken
pay	paid	paid
put	put	put
read	read	read
ride	rode	ridden
ring	rang	rung
rise	rose	risen
run	ran	run
say	said	said
seek	sought	sought
sell	sold	sold
send	sent	sent
set	set	set
shake	shook	shaken
shine	shone	shone (Note: Shined is used to indicate something has been polished. *Shone* is used to indicate something was shining on its own.)

Present-Tense or Base Spelling	**Past-Tense Spelling**	**Past-Participle Spelling (not tense)**
	_____	_____
	_____	_____
	_____	_____
	_____	_____
shoot	shot	shot
show	showed	shown
shut	shut	shut
sing	sang	sung
sink	sank	sunk
sit	sat	sat
sleep	slept	slept
sling	slung	slung
speak	spoke	spoken
spend	spent	spent
stand	stood	stood
steal	stole	stolen
stick	stuck	stuck
stink	stunk/stank	stunk
strike	struck	struck
swear	swore	sworn
swim	swam	swum
take	took	taken
teach	taught	taught
tear	tore	torn
tell	told	told
think	thought	thought
throw	threw	thrown
understand	understood	understood
upset	upset	upset
wake	woke/waked	woken/waked/woke
wear	wore	worn
wind	wound	wound
wring	wrung	wrung
write	wrote	written

6

This chapter will teach you how to conjugate verbs. *A **verb conjugation** is a table that includes number, person, and the forms of a verb in its six tenses.* Teaching conjugations of verbs has come in and gone out of style a number of times over the years. When I was introduced to grammar, my classmates and I were *forced* to conjugate verbs because teaching conjugations was favored then. Living in a home in which only the Appalachian dialect was spoken had made the standard dialect (such as some of these verb forms) sound strange to me. Years later, when I became a professor, many of my own students said again and again, "But that doesn't sound right." I knew what they meant; I had been there. Conjugating verbs, as tedious as the work was, helped open a heavy, reluctant door that one day would permit me to step into the world of correct writing, and, therefore, into a world of increased opportunities. That is my wish for you. That is why I am going to "show" you how to conjugate verbs by giving you an example.

The following conjugation will present a "picture" of the verb's three points of view (first, second, and third persons). It will give you the verb's number (singular and plural). It will, of course, "show" you specifically how to use the six tenses every time you use the verb *go*.

Conjugation of the Verb *Go*

Present Tense

	Singular	*Plural*
1st person	I go	we go
2nd person	you go	you go
3rd person	she/it/Fido/Ann/he goes	they go

Note: There is an *-s* on the singular verb in third person and present tense with no helping verbs.

Past Tense

	Singular	*Plural*
1st person	I went	we went
2nd person	you went	you went
3rd person	she/Mary/it/John went	they went

Future Tense

	Singular	*Plural*
1st person	I will go	we will go
2nd person	you will go	you will go
3rd person	he/my dog/it will go	they will go

Note: In formal writing, you may use *shall* with first person, but remember that the distinction has collapsed except when using the first person in a question: *Shall I go with you?*

Present-Perfect Tense

	Singular	Plural
1st person	I have gone	we have gone
2nd person	you have gone	you have gone
3rd person	Mr. Jones/he has gone	they have gone

Note: When the subject is singular, there is also an -s on the helping verb in the present-perfect tense, third person—*has gone*—because the first word in the verb phrase always carries the tense.

Past-Perfect Tense

	Singular	Plural
1st person	I had gone	we had gone
2nd person	you had gone	you had gone
3rd person	Penny/it/he had gone	they had gone

Future-Perfect Tense

	Singular	Plural
1st person	I will have gone	we will have gone
2nd person	you will have gone	you will have gone
3rd person	it/John's cat will have gone	they will have gone

6

Pitfalls in Choices of Verb Tenses

Direct and Indirect Quotations   A present-tense verb in directly quoted words changes to past tense in an indirect quotation. See the examples.

Matt **said,** "I **understand.** (Direct quotation.)

Look what happens in the following indirect quotation.

Matt **said** that he **understood.** (Indirect quotation.)

When the speaker's exact words contain a verb in the past tense or present-perfect tense, the verb changes to a past-perfect verb. Examples will clarify this.

Matt **said,** "I **wanted** to make an *A* on the test." (Direct quotation.)
Matt **said** that he **had wanted** to make an *A* on the test. (Indirect quotation.)

Annie said, "I **have wanted** to write all morning." (Direct quotation.)
Annie said that she **had wanted** to write all morning." (Indirect quotation.)

If a verb within directly quoted words is in the past-perfect tense, it remains past perfect.

Annie **said,** "I **had wanted** to see the movie *Sense and Sensibility.*" (Direct quotation.)

Annie **said** that she **had wanted** to see the movie *Sense and Sensibility.*" (Indirect quotation.)

Conditional Statements   When a word group begins with *if,* do not use *would* in that word group. Use *would* only in the main word group (clause) in the sentence. (See Chapter 10.) The following examples will make this clear:

X If students **would learn** the rules, they **would become** confident writers.

If students **learned** the rules, they **would become** confident writers.

X If they **would have learned** the rules, they **would have become** confident writers.

If they **had learned** the rules, they **would have become** confident writers.

Recurring Events and Universal Truths   Use the present tense when referring to recurring events and universal truths.

Examples

The Milky Way **is** the galaxy that **contains** our solar system.

Opossums **are** marsupials; they **have** pouches in which they **carry** their young.

Literary Present Tense   When writing essays about literature, use the present tense. Always proofread your literary papers for consistent verb tenses. Shifting tenses in these papers is a common error.

Examples

In Virginia Woolf's *Mrs. Dalloway,* Mrs. Dalloway's thoughts (like a child's slinky) **move** forward and backward from present to past to the future. Such **is** the steam-of-consciousness technique.

In Homer's *Odysseus,* Odysseus **spans** the vast spectrum of human emotions.

Consistency in Verb Tenses   Avoid *illogical* shifts in verb tenses. Your writing will have a controlling or governing tense, and you must sometimes shift tenses because of logic, for example, *I work hard today so that I will have a secure future tomorrow.* The following sentences have illogical shifts.

Examples

X When Matt **met** Annie, she **notices** his plaid tie.

When Matt **met** Annie, she **noticed** his plaid tie.

X The phoebes **build** their nests under eaves and bridges; in this way, they **protected** their nests from heavy rains.

The phoebes **build** their nests under eaves and bridges; in this way, they **protect** their nests from heavy rains.

6.1   EXERCISE FOR RELIEF OF TENSE STRUCTURES

Instructions: Underline the correct verb in parentheses.

1. A few years ago, Annie first (visited/visits) Topsail Island Beach.

2. Located in North Carolina, the beach (was/is) flanked on one side by Onslow Bay and on the other side by inlet water.

3. Annie watched as three gulls (fly/flew) against a bright blue sky.

4. Annie thought that the names adorning some of the houses on the island (reflect/reflected) the islanders' imagination and sense of humor.

5. As Annie walked along the beach, she (appreciates/appreciated) names like "Keene's Kradle," "Yakety-Yak," and "Sea-Duction."

6. The sea at Topsail Island, like the sea the world over, (is/was) seductive.

7. One morning, Annie watched as a woman leisurely (searches/searched) for seashells.

8. Farther along the beach, Annie noticed a white-haired man as he (sits/sat) motionless, staring at the sea.

9. Smoking his pipe, he (seems/seemed) to Annie to be as timeless as the ocean itself.

10. As Annie continued to stroll along the beach, she saw a young man and woman jogging; a black puppy, keeping pace, (yaps/yapped) at their heels.

11. Near a pier, a movement in the sand caught Annie's attention, and she looked in time to watch a crab as it (scuttles/scuttled) sideways across the sand.

12. When she later returned to the pier, the crab (has disappeared/had disappeared) into the sand.

13. For many years, the tourists (enjoyed/have enjoyed) watching the graceful sailboats glide over the inlet water.

6

14. Every day, the boats' bright sails of yellow, blue, and green (bulge/bulged) in obedience to the wind.

15. Annie said to Matt one day, "Each time I visit Topsail, I (met/meet) new friends."

16. Annie told Matt that each time she visited Topsail, she (met/meets) new friends.

17. Annie said, "Through the years, I (met/have met) many exciting people at Topsail."

18. Annie said that through the years, she (has met/had met) many exciting people at Topsail.

19. She (has talked/had talked) about the island since her first visit years ago.

20. She (has talked/had talked) about Topsail even before her first visit.

6.2   EXERCISE FOR CORRECT VERB CHOICE

Instructions: In the space provided, write the correct form of the verb. If necessary, add helping verbs.

1. One cold winter night many years ago, a deep snow (cover) _____ the ground.

2. My aunt was sleeping when around midnight she was (awake) _____ by the sound of someone walking through the snow.

3. As she sat up in bed and listened, she (hear) _____ someone approaching the back porch and climbing the wooden stairs.

4. She then (hear) _____ someone knocking loudly on the back door.

5. The knocking (awake) _____ my uncle, who arose and walked into the kitchen where the back door was located.

6. Turning on the porch light and seeing no one through the glass in the upper part of the door, he (open) _____ the door and looked outside.

7. No one was there, and there (be) _____ no footprints in the snow.

8. By one o'clock that morning, my aunt and uncle (return) _____ to bed.

9. They (lie) _____ awake for a long time as they discussed the strange event.

10. Early the next morning, they (sit) _____ at the breakfast table.

11. Again, they (begin) _____ to hear footsteps.

12. They heard the same sounds they (hear) _____ at midnight.

13. The loud knocking once again (startle) _____ them.

14. They looked through the door's glass, and to their relief, they (see) _____ the silhouette of a large man etched against a winter sun that gave no warmth.

15. My uncle (open) _____ the door.

16. The man asked, "Does Ocie Penwright (live) _____ here?"

17. After telling the sheriff that she did live in the house, my uncle (ask) _____ my aunt to come to the door.

18. The sheriff said, "I'm afraid I have bad news. Your brother (be) _____ fatally shot last night around midnight."

19. In West Virginia, this type of ghost story is (know) _____ as a "token" ghost story.

20. Each autumn, during the week of Halloween, the creative writing instructor (share) _____ this story with her students; she tells her students that it is a true story.

Progressive Form of Verbs

The progressive spelling of a verb is simply the verb with *-ing* as a suffix (ending). For instance, the progressive form of *go* is *going*. This spelling, like the past participle, is not a tense but simply a spelling or form. Other examples of progressive forms of verbs are *arising, becoming, beginning, biting, writing, shining, winning,* and *ridding*. To function as the main verb in a sentence, the progressive verb (*-ing* verb) must have one or more helping verbs. The complete verb is underlined in the examples.

Examples

I <u>am having</u> fun. (Present tense, progressive form.)

I <u>was running</u> when I met a friend. (Past tense, progressive form.)

I <u>will be running</u> in the race tomorrow. (Future tense, progressive form.)

Matt <u>has been running</u> every day. (Present-perfect tense, progressive form.)

Matt <u>had been running</u> an hour when I joined him. (Past-perfect tense, progressive form.)

In another hour, Matt <u>will have been running</u> for two hours. (Future-perfect tense, progressive form.)

6.3 EXERCISE FOR YOUR MENTAL FITNESS

Instructions: Read the lists of irregular verbs shown earlier in this chapter and choose five that you or someone you know misuses. If you have never heard any of the verbs misused, choose five anyway. Conjugate all five of the verbs you have chosen. Use my conjugation of the verb go *as a guide. Follow it carefully, tense by tense. You can begin now, as tedious as the work is, to start pushing open your own heavy, reluctant door to greater opportunities.*

Moody Verbs

Like people, verbs have more than one mood. They have three moods: the indicative, the imperative, and the subjunctive. We can tolerate the first two with ease, but watch the third. It is cantankerous.

The **indicative mood** is used for statements of fact and questions. (*You are frustrated. Are you frustrated?*) That was easy.

The **imperative mood** says that it is imperative that you do something; this mood is used for commands. (*Have a nice day. Sit down. Enjoy your meal. Shut up.*) Did you know that when people tell you to have a nice day, they are issuing a command?

Beware the verb's worst mood, the **subjunctive mood.** The subjunctive mood is used for conditions that are contrary to fact. Such contrary-to-fact statements may be contained in "*if* clauses," "*as if* or *as though* clauses," and in "*that* clauses." (See Chapter 10 for definition of *clause.*)

If Maria **were** [not *was*] here, she would help us. (The *were* tells you that Maria is not here.)

If I **were** [not *was*] you, I would work hard to break the habit of using *was* in statements contrary to fact. (Again, the *were* tells you that I am not—cannot—be you.)

He acted as if he **were** [not *was*] the boss.

Many people make mistakes when they wander into the subjunctive-mood territory. When you have a *that* clause following a wish, command, request, or recommendation, you need the subjunctive mood. See the following examples:

Annie wishes **that** she **were** [not *was*] on vacation.

The trainer commanded **that** there **be** [not *is*] silence.

She asked **that** the woman **be** [not *is]* silenced.

Matt asked **that** the trainer **repeat** [not *repeats*] her last statement.

TIP: If a statement could be a fact, use the indicative mood. See the following examples:

If John **was** trying to deceive us, he should be ashamed. (John may have been trying to deceive us; the statement, then, may not be contrary to fact.)

A few structures familiar to native speakers (idioms) remain:

Be that as it may.

Come what may.

Suffice it to say.

You can now see that the subjunctive mood is the one to watch. We use the verb in an unusual way when we are making statements contrary to fact or expressing a wish.

Transitive Verbs with Two Voices

Transitive verbs have two voices: active and passive. **Active voice** means that the subject comes first in the sentence and is doing the action. The verb comes next and must have an object, something receiving the action or benefiting from the action. The object follows the verb. Passive voice means that the object has been pulled to the front of the sentence and that the subject is acted on rather than doing the action. Examples and a formula for transforming active voice into passive will make this clear. Before a sentence can be rewritten in passive voice, the sentence must first have a transitive verb. Recall that a transitive verb is a verb that has an object; it has a victim that receives the action. You might say that the transitive verb is from Transylvania. Look at the following sentences, all of which have transitive verbs and are written in the active voice:

Active voice

The Count bit her neck.

The dog ate its bone.

Matt wrote the report.

Annie wrote the book on writing.

The reason the preceding four sentences are in active voice is that the subject (actor) does the action and is first in the sentence. The verb is next, and the object is last. If these sentences do not have objects, we cannot rewrite them into passive constructions.

TIP: The order of subject (actor) + verb (action) + object (receiver of action) indicates active voice.

Look at the following sentences that have been rewritten into passive voice.

Passive Voice

Her neck was bitten (by the count).

Its bone was eaten (by the dog)

The report was written (by Matt).

The book was written (by Annie).

TIP: The formula for transforming a sentence into passive voice follows:

1. Pull the object to the front of the sentence.

2. Add a helping verb.

3. Change the main verb to the past participle.

4. Place a preposition (usually *by*) in front of the subject.

If you reread the first set of sentences (those in active voice), then the second set, you will understand the formula more clearly.

Notice that the passive voice requires more words and puts emphasis on the object that has been placed at the beginning of the sentence. Also, notice that the words in parentheses in the sample passive-voice sentences could be deleted. Therefore, if you want to hide the subject or emphasize the object, you can use passive voice.

Most of the time, you should use the active voice because it requires fewer words. It is more direct. However, there are times when you need the passive voice. For example, if someone (let's say Richard) was using the copier in the college library when it stopped working, we would not want the librarian to write on a report that Richard broke the copier. The librarian would use the passive voice: *The copier has been broken.* The passive voice can hide the subject (actor). Also, if we want to focus on the object rather than the subject, we use the passive voice. For example:

Jynx Copiers are used by many college libraries.

Generally, avoid passive constructions. Notice how the following weak, wordy sample sentences become stronger in active voice.

The exam was written on the weekend by the instructor. (Weak Passive.)

The instructor wrote the exam on the weekend. (Active.)

The instructor's makeups are appreciated by us students. (Weak Passive.)

We students appreciate the instructor's makeups. (Active.)

No makeups are given by our instructor. (Weak Passive.)
Our instructor gives no makeups. (Active.)

The lowest grade is dropped by Jean's instructor. (Weak Passive.)
Jean's instructor drops the lowest grade. (Active.)

Intransitive Verbs

Now that you know what a transitive verb is (a verb with an object), you are ready to learn more about the intransitive verb (a verb without an object). Look at the following sentences.

1. Matt read the report. (The report was read by Matt.) (Transitive.)
2. Matt read all afternoon. (**Intransitive.**)
3. Annie took Matt to lunch. (Matt was taken to lunch by Annie.) (Transitive.)
4. They ate at the Whistle Top Buffet. (**Intransitive.**)
5. They ate dinner at six o'clock. (Dinner was eaten by them at six o'clock.) (Transitive.)
6. Elizabeth Tailless, Annie's cat, lay on the windowsill all afternoon. (**Intransitive.**)
7. Annie enjoyed Matt's comments. (Matt's comments were enjoyed by Annie.) (Transitive.)

Notice that all the sentences with transitive verbs can be rewritten in the passive voice; that is not so for sentences with intransitive verbs.

Intransitive verbs can be followed by nothing, adverbs of place, adverbs of time, adverbs of frequency, or adverbs of manner. Read the sample sentences with intransitive verbs once more. You will understand this more clearly after studying adverbs. For now, you know the difference between active and passive voices. That is important.

Linking Verbs

Linking verbs link the subject (actor) in a sentence with a noun, pronoun, or adjective (descriptive word). Look at the following sentences, all of which have linking verbs. Notice the words that follow them. They will be one of the three parts of speech: noun, pronoun, adjective. I have bold-faced the word following the linking verb and have placed the part of speech in parentheses to help you.

1. Matt is a tall **man** (noun).
2. Matt is a part-time **student** (noun) at the local college.
3. He is **tall** (adjective).

4. Answering the phone, Annie said, "It is **I**" (pronoun).

5. She is a famous local **writer** (noun).

6. That is **she** (pronoun) in the red coat.

7. Matt appears **angry** (adjective).

8. Matt and Annie seem **happy** (adjective).

You can see that with the linking verbs, the subject is either renamed or described. Now you have a better knowledge of the three types of verbs:

1. transitive (verbs with objects)

2. intransitive (verbs with no objects)

3. linking (verbs that link subjects to noun, pronouns, or adjectives)

6.4 EXERCISE FOR GETTING IN GOOD MOODS

Instructions: Underline the correct verb in parentheses.

1. The football coach insists that each player (is/be) on time for practice.

2. The players sometimes wish that the coach (was/were) not so strict.

3. Coach Whinning said, "If I (was/were) you, I'd be on time for practice."

4. It is his desire that his team (win/wins) every game.

5. If the quarterback (was/were) more motivated, Coach Whinning would be pleased.

6. If the player (was/were) really deceiving the team, he should be ashamed.

7. The coach demanded that every player (get/gets) at least eight hours of sleep each night.

8. If I (were/was) the coach, I would have the same rules.

9. Sometimes, the senior player acts as if he (was/were) the coach.

10. The coach said that if the quarterback (was/were) perfecting his writing skills he would need to practice, practice, practice.

6.5 EXERCISE FOR CLASSIFYING VERBS

Instruction: Identify the type of verb (italicized) by writing one of the following: transitive, intransitive, or linking.

1. Sitting around a campfire while telling ghost stories *is* fun. _____

6

2. Annie *tells* a ghost story to her writing class each fall. _____

3. She, then, *asks* each student to write a story. _____

4. The students *work* many hours on their stories. _____

5. The story *can be* fact or fiction. _____

6. Rewriting *is* a vital part of the writing process. _____

7. Annie *told* her students and him to revise their stories. _____

8. One student *wrote* a story about a white dog. _____

9. Late one Halloween night, a woman *was walking* along a dark, deserted road. _____

10. Just as she approached a cemetery on her left, she *saw* a large white dog. _____

11. The dog *followed* the woman. _____

12. She *walked* faster and faster. _____

13. As the frightened woman began to run, the dog *ran,* too. _____

14. Never panting and never barking, the dog *looked* eerie. _____

15. After the woman *passed* the cemetery, she looked behind her; the dog had disappeared. _____

6.6 EXERCISE FOR AVOIDING THE DIVINE PASSIVE

Instructions: Using the active voice, rewrite any sentences that are awkward.

1. It is first tantalized by a cat before killing a mouse.

_____

2. Their independence is shown by cats.

_____

3. An artificial rabbit will never be chased around a track by a cat.

_____

4. Its tail will never be wagged in gratitude by a cat.

_____

5. Tricks will not usually be performed for treats by cats.

_____

6. Its master's call is usually ignored by a cat.

_____

7. Another cat is never ignored by a cat.

_____

8. A sled will never be pulled over frozen snow by a team of cats.

_____

9. As an attention-getter, a silent meow is used by a cat.

_____

10. Themselves are bathed by cats.

_____

11. Litter boxes are used by cats.

_____

12. Cats are usually frightened by strangers in the house.

_____

13. Catnip-treated scratching pads are used by cats.

_____

14. Furniture is not destroyed by cats if they have scratching pads.

_____

15. Their intelligence and independence are demonstrated by cats in a number of ways.

_____

To Be: A Unique Verb

Unique means one of a kind. Indeed, one verb in the English language stands apart from all the others. Unlike any other verb, _be_ has eight forms: _be, being, been, am, is, are, was,_ and _were._

This verb can cause special problems for many native speakers of English. The best way to learn how to choose the correct form of the verb _be_ is to look closely at the following conjugation. Even if you have already conjugated this verb, a second look at the verb in its many forms will serve as reinforcement.

Conjugation of the Verb *Be*

Present Tense

	Singular	Plural
1st person	**I** am	**we** are
2nd person	**you** are	**you** are
3rd person	**he/it/John** is	**they** are

Past Tense

	Singular	Plural
1st person	**I** was	**we** were
2nd person	**you** were	**you** were
3rd person	**he/it/Mr. Smith** was	**they** were

Future Tense

	Singular	Plural
1st person	**I** will/shall be	**we** will/shall be
2nd person	**you** will be	**you** will be
3rd person	**he/it/she/Max** will be	**they** will be

Present-Perfect Tense

	Singular	Plural
1st person	**I** have been	**we** have been
2nd person	**you** have been	**you** have been
3rd person	**she/Annie/he** has been	**they** have been

Past-Perfect Tense

	Singular	Plural
1st person	**I** had been	**we** had been
2nd person	**you** had been	**you** had been
3rd person	**she/Matt/it** had been	**they** had been

Future-Present Tense

	Singular	Plural
1st person	**I** shall/will have been	**we** shall/will have been
2nd person	**you** will have been	**you** will have been
3rd person	**he/it** will have been	**they** will have been

6

If you conjugate the verb *be* several times, you will be able to use it with confidence, knowing that you are using the correct form.

Additional Pitfalls

When you use the contraction *don't* with a singular, third-person subject, you are using the incorrect verb form. The following ungrammatical sentences represent common errors:

X It don't matter to me.

X He don't tell me where he is going.

X The assignment don't seem hard to me.

If the contraction is replaced with the contracted words, you will see the problem.

X It do not matter to me.

You know that the verb must have an *-s* ending.

It doesn't (does not) matter to me.

X He do not tell me where he is going.

He doesn't (does not) tell me where he is going.

X The assignment do not seem hard to me.

The assignment doesn't (does not) seem hard to me.

The misuse of *don't* is common among many native users of English.

Two additional words cause problems when they are followed by the word *to*. When the words *use* and *suppose* are followed by *to*, they must end with a *-d*. When we say *used to* or *supposed to*, the *-d* sound disappears. For that reason, many writers forget to include the *-d* when they write these words. Always remember to include the *-d*, as in the following examples:

I use*d* to run.

Annie use*d* to run with me.

We were suppose*d* to run in the race.

He was suppose*d* to be here by now.

SUMMARY

You now know how to define and recognize verbs in sentences. You have learned the subclasses of verbs: regular, irregular, transitive, intransitive, and linking. You know how to conjugate a verb if you have problems using the verb in any of the six tenses. You also have a reference list of irregular verbs to help you when you are in doubt about usage of a verb form. You know to beware of the subjunctive mood. You know how to write sentences in both active and passive voices. You are now aware of special pitfalls when using the contraction *don't*, as well as the words *used* and *supposed* when followed by *to*. Review this chapter often. Remember that verbs provide life to sentences. Use them with confidence, even the irregular verbs like **go, see,** and **be.** ∎

6.7 END-OF-CHAPTER EXERCISES

Instructions: Correct any errors in verb choices by writing the correct verb in the space provided. If a sentence is correct, write correct *in the space.*

1. If I was you, I would study this section.   _____

2. Yesterday, my cat looked as if it was going
   to die.   _____

3. Matt wishes he was on the beach.   _____

4. Matt wishes he were on the beach.   _____

5. If he was trying to impress us, he succeeded.   _____

6. The leader requested that each member
   is present.   _____

7. If Maria was in the writing class, she would
   write compelling essays.   _____

8. Be that as it may, she is still a writer of
   fair prose.   _____

9. Maria has requested that she is admitted
   to the class.   _____ _____

10. Yes, but if she was in our writing class, she
    would be an even better writer.   _____

Instructions: Beside each verb listed, write a sentence using the verb according to further instructions in parentheses. Remember that past tense *means you use no helping verbs. See Examples A, B, and C. Underline the verb, including any helping verbs. Proofread your sentences. Correct any errors in your writing.*

Examples

A. write (with *have*). The engineers <u>have written</u> the report.

B. bring (past tense). Annie <u>brought</u> the error to Matt's attention.

C. choose (present tense with *He* as actor/subject). He <u>chooses</u> to
   learn.

11. become (with *has*)

   _____

   _____

12. burst (past tense)

   _____

   _____

13. run (with *has*)

_____

_____

14. choose (with *have*)

_____

_____

15. eat (with has)

_____

_____

16. do (present tense with *He* as actor/subject)

_____

_____

17. go (with *have*)

_____

_____

18. lay—to place (past tense)

_____

_____

19. lie—to recline (past tense)

_____

_____

20. fly (with *has*)

_____

_____

21. write (with *has*)

_____

_____

22. drink (with *has*)

_____

_____

23. see (with *have*)

_____

_____

24. eat (no helping verbs)

_____

_____

25. freeze (with _has_)

_____

_____

Instructions: Now that you have practiced writing sentences with the correct verb forms, see if you can write the correct verbs in the spaces provided. The present-tense spelling is given in parentheses. You choose the correct verb form, which may or may not be the spelling in parentheses.

(suppose)   **26.** Annie was _____ to lead the workshop last week.

(be)   **27.** If I _____ you, I would watch the subjunctive mood.

(lay)   **28.** Annie _____ the handouts on the desks.

(use)   **29.** She _____ to teach every day.

(go)   **30.** The bank president has already _____ to lunch.

(see)   **31.** Matt _____ Annie at the picnic yesterday.

(see)   **32.** He had _____ her there before.

(become)   **33.** The employee had _____ careless in his speech habits because he said, "It don't matter."

(do)   **34.** He should have said, "It _____n't matter."

(drink)   **35.** By the end of the picnic, Matt and Annie had each _____ three glasses of lemonade.

(ride)   **36.** They had _____ the horses, too.

(lie)   **37.** Annie's cats had been _____ in the sun.

(lie)   **38.** They had _____ in the sun all day while Annie was at the bank picnic.

(hang)   **39.** "The bank executive was _____ for misusing an irregular verb."

(be)   **40.** Annie's friend said, "I want to _____ a writer, but I don't want to study grammar."

6

Chapter 7

Adjectives and Adverbs: Words That Gossip

OBJECTIVES

In this chapter, you will learn to

- ••• define and recognize adjectives
- ••• master usage of comparative and superlative adjectives
- ••• recognize and use adverbs correctly
- ••• distinguish between adjectives and adverbs
- ••• master usage of comparative and superlative adverbs
- ••• use articles *a* and *an* correctly
- ••• identify demonstrative pronouns as adjectives
- ••• recognize other parts of speech as adjectives
- ••• position adjectives and adverbs to modify the appropriate words

Adjectives

Adjectives *are words that describe or modify nouns and pronouns.* You remember that nouns are names of persons, places, things, ideas, or animals. Adjectives, then, tell a great deal about persons, places, things, ideas, or animals. For example, adjectives (italicized) can describe people as *tall, short, intelligent, ambitious, lazy, hungry,* or *svelte.* Adjectives can describe a city as *large, busy, hectic, chaotic,* or *cold.* They can describe a desk as *expensive, cheap, cluttered,* or *organized.* Adjectives can describe ideas as *feasible, great, good,* or *bad.* They can tell us that animals are *docile, frisky, aggressive, angry,* or *dangerous.* You can see that adjectives are, indeed, gossipy. They sometimes tell more about us than we want people to know.

Following are sample sentences with the adjectives boldfaced and the nouns or pronouns being described underlined:

1. You are a **good** <u>writer</u>. (*Good* is an adjective because it tells something about <u>writer</u>, a noun.)

143

2. <u>Fido</u> is **large, mean,** and **hungry.** (Do you remember that adjectives, nouns, or pronouns follow linking verbs? In this sentence, three adjectives follow the linking verb *is.*)

3. Fido is a **mean junkyard** <u>dog</u>. (*Mean* and *junkyard* are adjectives because they describe <u>dog</u>.)

4. Quality is a **tremendous** <u>idea</u> whose time has come.

5. Mr. Jones's **large brick** <u>house</u> is on the hill.

6. The Joneses' **smaller** <u>house</u> is at the beach.

Comparisons with Adjectives

Look at the lists of adjectives that follow this paragraph. The three columns have special significance for choosing the correct form of the adjective. Pay close attention to the words in parentheses under **Comparative** and **Superlative.** The **comparative** form of the adjective should be used when you compare *only two* persons, places, things, ideas, or animals. The **superlative** form should be used when you are comparing *three or more.* Remember and apply these rules each time you use adjectives for comparison. Notice that if the word is awkward to pronounce when *-er* or *-est* is added, then you can use *more* to replace *-er*. **Never use both** *-er* **and** *more.* Replace *-est* with *most.* Remember that *-er* or *more* is added to compare only two, and *-est* or *most* is added to the adjective to compare three or more.

Positive (Base or Dictionary Listing)	Comparative (Form for comparing only two)	Superlative (Form for comparing three or more)
alluring	more alluring	most alluring
angry	angrier	angriest
bad	worse	worst
beautiful	more beautiful	most beautiful
big	bigger	biggest
cold	colder	coldest
eager	more eager	most eager
easy	easier	easiest
enthusiastic	more enthusiastic	most eager
enticing	more enticing	most enticing
fast	faster	fastest
friendly (See **TIP** that follows this list)	friendlier	friendliest
good	better	best

Positive (Base or Dictionary Listing)	Comparative (Form for comparing only two)	Superlative (Form for comparing three or more)
handsome	more handsome	most handsome
important	more important	most important
large	larger	largest
short	shorter	shortest
small	smaller	smallest
some (many/much)	more	most
tall	taller	tallest
quick	quicker	quickest
quiet	quieter	quietest

TIP: You cannot add *-er* or *-est* to *worse* or *worst*, nor can you add *more* or *most* to these adjectives. Also, when an adjective (such as *friendly*) ends in *-y* and the *-y* is preceded by a consonant, you must drop the *-y* and add *-ier* to form the comparative and *-iest* to form the superlative.

Adverbs

Remember that *an adjective modifies or describes nouns and pronouns.* Both adjectives and adverbs are descriptive words. Unlike adjectives, however, **adverbs** *describe verbs, adjectives, and other adverbs.* Read the preceding italicized words until you have memorized them. If you do not understand that the real distinction between the adjective and adverb is in the parts of speech they modify or describe, you will not be able to determine when to use an adjective and when to use an adverb. In other words, you will make mistakes when you speak or write.

Adverbs *tell how we do something,* **where** *we do it,* **when** *we do it, and* **how often.** Sometimes, they even tell **why** (see how gossipy they are). Look at the following lists. Notice how the adjective *sometimes* changes its spelling to become an adverb. Sometimes adjectives end in *-ly*, and sometimes adverbs do not end in *-ly*. At other times, adverbs and adjectives have the same spellings. Often, the adjective or adverb has no counterpart, in which cases you will find blank spaces in the following lists. The point is, of course, that you must know which part of speech the descriptive word is modifying in a sentence. For example, you cannot believe that every word ending in *-ly* is an adverb; it is an adverb only when it describes a verb, an adjective, or another adverb.

Adjectives	Adverbs
_____	already
_____	always
_____	altogether

7

Adjectives	Adverbs
angry	angrily
bad	badly
beautiful	beautifully
big	_____
bright	brightly
complete	completely
brown	_____
desperate	desperately
eager	eagerly
early	early
easy	easily
enthusiastic	enthusiastically
extreme	extremely
fast	fast
frequent	frequently
friendly	_____
good	well
handsome	handsomely
happy	happily
important	_____
late	late (She arrived late.)
late	lately
lonely	_____
_____	manly
loud	loudly
_____	never
_____	not
_____	now
_____	often
_____	only
_____	please
present (means *current*)	presently (means *soon*)
rapid	rapidly
_____	seldom
_____	saintly
short (not tall)	shortly (means *soon*)
slow	slowly
_____	sometimes

7

Adjectives	**Adverbs**
sluggish	sluggishly
swift	swiftly
terrible	terribly
_____	tomorrow
_____	too
quick	quickly
_____	quite
_____	very
well (All is well.)	well (Annie writes well.)
_____	womanly
_____	yesterday

TIP: Do not confuse *already* with *all ready*. *Already* means before or at a specified time. *All ready* means completely ready.

In the following sentences, the adverb is boldfaced and the word it is describing is underlined. Sometimes, prepositional phrases (see Chapter 8) function as adverbs and adjectives—good information for you to know.

1. Matt <u>slept</u> **well.** (Here, the adverb *well* tells how Matt slept. *Well* is describing the verb *slept*. It is an adverb of manner.)

2. At the meeting, the manager <u>snored</u> **loudly.** (Notice that we could not use the adjective *loud* because <u>snored</u> is a verb, and only adverbs modify verbs. See how important it is that you memorize the definitions of both adjectives and adverbs.)

3. The manager <u>snored</u> **there.** (*There* is an adverb because it tells where the manager snored. *There* is an adverb of place and should not be confused with the possessive pronoun *their*.)

4. The manager <u>snored</u> **during the meeting.** (Although *during the meeting* is a prepositional phrase, it tells when and modifies the verb <u>snored</u>. The phrase, then, is functioning as an adverb of time.)

5. The manager <u>came</u> **aboard yesterday.** (Both *aboard* and *yesterday* are adverbs. First, they modify the verb <u>came</u>. Then, we notice that *aboard* tells where, at least figuratively, and *yesterday* tells when.)

6. He <u>does</u> **not** <u>snore</u> **frequently.** (Notice here that *not* is not part of the verb. *Not is always an adverb; not* modifies the verb by making it negative. *Frequently* tells how often; it is an adverb of frequency.)

7. Annie said, "You <u>can</u> **usually** <u>avoid</u> *very* in your writing."

8. She laughed and added, "<u>Use</u> it **very sparingly.**" (*Sparingly* modifies the verb <u>use</u>. *Sparingly* tells how, but *very* modifies the adverb *sparingly*.)

7

You can see that identifying the word in the sentence that is being described is important. Knowing the parts of speech and their functions in sentences is also of the utmost importance. Let no one deceive you about this.

TIP: Remember that **well** is an **adverb** of manner; it tells how. **Good** is an **adjective** that describes a noun or pronoun.

Comparisons with Adverbs

Just as adjectives have comparative and superlative forms, so do adverbs. As with adjectives, when *only two* are being compared, use the suffix *-er* or *more* or *less* before the adverb. When *three or more* are being compared, use *-est* as a suffix or add *most* or *least* before the adverb. Notice that some of the adjectives follow linking verbs. Although such adjectives are called *predicate adjectives*, they are nonetheless adjectives. In fact, when an adjective follows a verb, we know the verb is a linking verb. Examples follow:

1. Matt runs **faster** than his brother.
2. Matt is **more** eager to learn now that he is a part-time employee.
3. Matt was **less** likely to interrupt Annie during the workshop than his manager.
4. Because of his commitment, Matt was the **quickest** to grasp the material in Annie's workshops.
5. Matt is the **most** ambitious student in his writing workshop.
6. He was, therefore, the **least** likely to miss a workshop.

TIP: Do not write *importantly* as an adverb. Can you think of something you can do importantly? Also, avoid using *firstly*, *secondly*, and *thusly*. Use *first* (meaning in the first place) and *second* (meaning in the second place), use *thus* without the *-ly*.

Look at the following sentence:

You must make a commitment to learn how to write confidently, **and more important,** you must work hard to learn all the rules.

The boldfaced words in the preceding sentence really mean "and what is more important." Clearly, *important* is an adjective following a linking verb. Do not be confused when I tell you that the boldfaced words are elliptical; that is, words have been omitted. *What is more important* includes the omitted words *what is*, an inclusion that shows an adjective is the correct choice. I have found it helpful to insert such deleted words into the sentence. You will, too.

Use all modifiers and qualifiers sparingly. In most writing, you must learn to cut needless words. Unlike the specific, concrete verb, adjectives and adverbs can clutter a sentence. Like red pepper, a little goes a long way. If, then, you are not sure whether to use an adjective or an adverb, use neither if the sentence sense is not affected.

Troublesome Adjectives and Adverbs

Remember that nouns, pronouns, or adjectives follow linking verbs. The common linking verbs are *appear, become, remain, seem,* and forms of the verb *be* (*am, is, are, was, were, being,* and *been*). The five senses (taste, smell, see, hear, and feel) are also treated like linking verbs and are, therefore, followed by adjectives.

When you enter the house on Thanksgiving and smell the turkey and pumpkin pies, you never say, "Oh, that smells well." When you begin eating, you never say, "This food tastes well." The food smells good and tastes delicious. You can see that we almost instinctively apply the rule of using an adjective after one of the five senses. When we describe our health, however, we might go astray, as you will see in time.

Look at the following sentences and the comments in parentheses:

1. Matt is **angry.**

2. I am **jolly.**

3. You are **frustrated.**   See how adjectives are following linking verbs in sentences 1 to 3.

4. Annie felt **happy.**   *Happy* follows a linking verb, one of the five senses, and describes Annie, *happy Annie.* We must, therefore, use a predicate adjective.

5. The manager grew **restless.**   *Grew* is a linking verb and must be followed by an adjective.

6. The participants remained **calm.**   *Remained* is a linking verb.

7. By the end of the session, they had become **giddy.**   *Become* is a linking verb and must be followed in this sentence by the adjective, *giddy.*

8. Annie looked **glum.**   *Looked* is a linking verb, and *glum* must be used, *glum Annie.*

9. She felt **bad.**   *Felt* is one of the five senses and should be followed by the adjective *bad* rather than the adverb *badly.*

Now, you must feel **good** after learning all these wonderful tips about using adjectives and adverbs correctly.

7

Some scholars disagree with using *good* when *good* follows the verb *feel* to describe our health. Many feel that we should use *well*. Therefore, you might want to avoid it altogether if you can. Most people do not want to hear how we feel anyway; we must not kid ourselves about this!

I do not hesitate to use any of the following statements:

I feel **fine.**

I feel **great.**

I feel **fantastic.**

I feel **wonderful.**

If, then, I can use such adjectives when discussing how I feel, I can also use *good* when describing my health. You can see which side of this raging controversy I support. I feel **good.**

7.1   EXERCISE FOR YOUR MENTAL FITNESS

Instructions: Underline the adjectives and other modifiers that modify nouns or pronouns in the following sentences.

1. Matt and Annie ate hurriedly at the quaint restaurant.
2. They walked quickly to Annie's expensive car.
3. Matt was eager to return to Annie's exciting writing class.
4. One student in the class had attended a birthday party; he wore purple tights and a lime-green shirt.
5. Annie noticed that the smiling man was the tallest student in the class.
6. Annie's classes were always enjoyable and informative.
7. Organized and ambitious, Matt will surely succeed.
8. The tall man with the broad grin attended the workshops regularly.
9. He seemed anxious during the first session.
10. By the third workshop, he appeared calm and assured.
11. At the last session, he wore an expensive suit and a confident smile.
12. The classroom was quiet, and the students were tense.
13. The assignment was hard, and more important, the nervous participants had little time.
14. They felt confident, however.
15. After the grueling assignment, Annie served refreshments, which tasted delicious.

7.2 EXERCISE FOR YOUR ACCURATE COMPARISONS

Instructions: First, complete Sentences A and B. Then, write in the space provided the correct form of the adjective or adverb as indicated in parentheses. Check to be sure your adjectives and adverbs are spelled correctly.

Examples

A. The comparative form of the adjective or adverb is used when we compare _____.

B. The superlative form of the adjective or adverb is used when we compare _____.

1. bright (comparative adjective) _____

2. pretty (superlative adjective) _____

3. bravely (comparative adverb) _____

4. expensively (superlative adjective) _____

5. efficient (superlative adjective) _____

6. dependable (comparative adjective) _____

7. beautiful (comparative adverb) _____

8. fast (superlative adjective or adverb) _____

9. intelligent (comparative adjective) _____

10. handsome (superlative adjective) _____

7

7.3 EXERCISE FOR YOUR DESCRIPTIVE SKILLS

Instructions: Write six sentences in which you use the adjective or adverb in parentheses. Answers will vary, and will not be given in the Answers to Exercises at the end of the book.

1. (brighter)

_____

_____

2. (prettiest)

_____

_____

3. (more bravely)

_____

_____

4. (most expensive)

_____

_____

5. (most efficient)

_____

_____

6. (more dependable)

_____

_____

7. (more beautifully)

_____

_____

8. (fastest)

_____

_____

9. (more intelligent)

_____

_____

10. (most handsome)

_____

_____

7.4 EXERCISE FOR YOUR MENTAL FITNESS

Instructions: Choose the preferred word in parentheses and write it in the space provided.

1. Learning to write (good/well) _____ prose means making a commitment to learning rules, and more (important/ importantly), _____ it means applying those rules to actual writing.

2. (First/Firstly) _____, we must endure the often boring chore of reading and memorizing rules.

3. Next, we must apply what we have learned. (Third/Thirdly) _____, we must form the habit of proofreading.

4. Annie was the (better/best) _____ of the two trainers the bank had hired because she stressed these facts.

5. Later, a third trainer was hired, but Annie was still the (better/best) _____ of the three.

6. Knowing which words the descriptive word is modifying in a sentence is the (best/better) _____ method of choosing between the adjective and the adverb.

7. The man in the front row is the (most/more) _____ intelligent of the two brothers.

8. He is also the (more/most) _____ conservatively dressed student in the class.

9. Annie chose between the (least/lesser) _____ of the two evils.

10. She felt (really/real) _____ good about the assignment.

11. She was looking (calm/calmly) _____ when Matt asked her to dine with him at the Whistle Top Buffet.

12. Although Annie was the (better/best) _____ writer of the two, Matt could be more persuasive.

13. (Thus/Thusly) _____, she accepted his invitation.

14. When they entered the restaurant, she felt (warm/warmly) _____.

15. The food smelled (delicious/deliciously) _____.

7

Use of Articles

Our language has only three articles: *a, an,* and *the. A* and *an* are indefinite or unspecified articles. *The* is called a definite or specified article. Do not let the terms confuse you. If you learn the following material on articles, you should be able to use them with confidence. That is all that matters.

Correct Use of the Articles A and An

The articles *a* and *an* present special problems. Learn two rules that will guide you every time you must choose between these articles.

Rule 1. You must use **an** when the word immediately following the article begins with a **vowel** *sound.* The vowels are *a, e, i, o, u,* and sometimes *y.* The *y* is usually a vowel when it falls within or at the end of a word. The remaining letters are **consonants.**

Rule 2. You must use **a** when the word immediately following the article begins with a **consonant** *sound.*

In the preceding rules, notice the word *sound. It is not necessarily the beginning letter* of the word that determines whether you should use *a* or *an,* but rather the sound at the beginning of the word. Look at the following examples and you will soon understand.

an herb	an immediate problem	an eminent scholar
an hour	an ambitious person	an employee
an honest person	an ogre	an utter disaster
an eager learner	an umbrella	an aching heart
an unusual book	an eerie feeling	an ice storm

The reason *an* is used before a word beginning with a vowel sound is for ease of pronunciation. If you try to pronounce *a apple,* for example, you will find the pronunciation more difficult than the pronunciation of *an apple.*

In the following examples, some of the words begin with vowels, but they do not begin with vowel *sounds* and must, therefore, be preceded by *a.*

a uniform	a historic event	a book
a European tour	a caring teacher	a desk
a history book	a Queen Anne chair	a character
a decision	a final draft	a hysterical person

TIP: Scholars, as you are now aware, disagree in several areas of usage. Some, for instance, declare that we should say *an historic* because the accent is not on the first syllable; others believe we should follow the rule without regard to accents. I vote for *a historic* but do not condemn those who disagree. I support the authors who believe we should have as few exceptions to rules as possible. Without regard to accents, then, I follow the rule of letting the **beginning sound** of a word govern the use of *a* or *an.* Otherwise, we would be required to say, "an hysterical person."

Other Qualifying Words

Do you remember the four demonstrative pronouns in our language, those pronouns that point or demonstrate? They are **this, that, these,** and **those** (see Chapter 5). The demonstrative pronouns often function as adjectives. The one time you might have problems with them, however, is when you use a plural demonstrative pronoun before a singular noun—

for example, *these kind*—so be sure to use a plural noun following a plural demonstrative pronoun and a singular noun after a singular demonstrative pronoun, as in the following examples.

These kinds of sentences serve us well.

This kind of example does a good job, too.

That kind of session was valuable.

Those examples helped me a great deal.

Also, avoid using *them* when you need *these* or *those. Those books* should never be written as *them books.*

Nouns and other kinds of pronouns can also function as adjectives. Here are some examples:

Christmas party	house warming	his book
anyone's guess	New York traffic	Matt's writing
its food	their party	my chance

TIP: Remember that **too** is an adverb that means *very* or *also.* Like *zoo, too* has two *o*'s and rhymes with *zoo.*

The Well-Placed Modifier

Switching a modifier from one place to another in a sentence can change the meaning. It is, therefore, important that you read each sentence you write to be sure it is saying exactly what you want it to say. Look at the following examples and notice how the meaning changes by just the shifting of the boldfaced word.

Only the manager attended the out-of-state meeting this year.

The manager attended the **only** out-of-state meeting this year.

The manager **only** attended the out-of-state meeting this year.

The manager attended the out-of-state meeting **only** this year.

Annie won **almost** $2 million in the lottery.

Annie **almost** won $2 million in the lottery.

Notice how the modifiers in the following sentences could be modifying either the word preceding them or the word following them; such modifiers are called **squinting modifiers.** Squinting modifiers make sentences unclear to the reader.

X The woman who began her speech enthusiastically made several thought-provoking comments. (Did she begin her speech enthusiastically, or did she enthusiastically make thought-provoking comments?)

The woman who enthusiastically began her speech made several thought-provoking comments.

X The student who had been writing hurriedly left the classroom. (Had the student been writing hurriedly, or did the student leave the room hurriedly?)

The student who had been writing left the classroom hurriedly.

Be cautious every time you use adjectives and adverbs. In the next chapter, you will learn to be especially careful with the verbals, those forms of verbs that function as adjectives and adverbs. Beware of misplaced and unclear modifiers.

SUMMARY

You now understand that an adjective modifies a noun or pronoun. An adverb modifies an adjective, a verb, or another adverb. When comparing only two, you must use *-er* as a suffix on the adjective or precede it with *more* if pronunciation is awkward with the addition of *-er*. When comparing three or more, you must use *-est* or *most*. The same rule applies to the adverb. The article *an* is used before words that begin with vowel *sounds,* and *a* is used before words that begin with consonant *sounds*. You are now aware that other parts of speech can function as adjectives. Be sure to use a plural noun when you use *these* or *those* to refer to the noun. Also, match *this* and *that* with a singular noun. Avoid *them* as a substitute for *these* or *those*. Be sure to place qualifying words close to the words they describe.

It is important to know parts of speech and how they function in sentences. In the next chapter, you will learn to recognize how phrases and verbals fill the modifying role of adjectives and adverbs. ■

7

7.5 END-OF-CHAPTER EXERCISES

Instructions: Correct each incorrect boldfaced word by drawing a line through it and writing the correction above the word. Not all boldfaced words are necessarily incorrect.

1. Annie worked **to** hard this afternoon; she was **all ready** tired when she began to work.

2. She had stopped for a **fast** lunch and was now driving **quick** to get home before the impending storm arrived.

3. Annie taught as **good** as she wrote; students liked her **alot.**

4. Despite her fatigue, she felt **well** about her work.

5. One of the students had told her that her voice projected **good** at the writing workshops.

6. Annie is not just a **good** teacher; she also writes **good.**

7. Well-rounded, she grows **a** herb garden.

8. Occasionally, she visits **an** historic site.

9. She especially enjoys **them** historic mansions in the South.

10. **Those** kind of history is appealing to Annie.

11. One year, she took **an** European tour.

12. She visited **an** art museum that especially impressed her.

13. Of all her friends, Annie is the **more** widely traveled.

14. She found a traveling companion last year; they travel **good** together.

15. Alice, her traveling companion, is **a** honest person.

Instructions: The following sentences contain either redundancies or misplaced modifiers. Rewrite each sentence, making necessary corrections.

16. The man in the front row submitted a most unique essay.

_____

_____

17. The student who was writing rapidly walked to the front of the room.

_____

_____

18. When the student won the lottery, he almost won $2 million.

_____

_____

19. He nearly danced all night.

_____

_____

20. Known to the local diners as the WTB, the Whistle Top Buffet almost stays open around the clock.

_____

_____

21. Its hours nearly run from noon to midnight.

_____

_____

22. Most people only eat three meals a day.

_____

_____

23. The WTB's competition almost stays open until midnight.

_____

_____

24. A few patrons only dine that late.

_____

_____

25. The Whistle Top has very perfect hours for its diners.

_____

_____

Instructions: Correct all misused adjectives and adverbs in the following draft of a speech given by Annie Penwright at a writing conference. Proofread and edit carefully. Use a caret (∧) to indicate correct placements of adjectives and adverbs.

How to Become an Effective Writer

Many people say that they could write a book based on **there** lives. Someday, they plan to write "that book." Most people, however, have not learned the rules necessary for successful writing. They believe they can already write **good** enough. More **importantly,** many who know they make mistakes **easily** believe those mistakes do not matter. **There** writing, then, is often riddled with mistakes that have euphemistically been called surface errors. The problem with so-called surface errors is that they can block the message **an** writer is trying to convey.

These potential writers could write more **effective** if they understood that editors have neither the time nor the inclination to clean up grammar, replace misused words, and correct faulty punctuation. **Only this** kinds of mistakes get manuscripts rejected **more quicker** than anything else, boring writing excluded.

Firstly, you must learn the basics. In recent years, the basics have been downplayed. Many still feel that **almost** teaching rules is tantamount to destroying creativity. Writing, however, is more than creating, although it is that, **to.** Writing is **an** skill that demands knowledge and **a** apprenticeship.

Secondly, to become a writer, you must make a commitment. You must decide if you want to succeed in life or if **only** you want to slide by. **Only** you can decide if you want your work published or if you want to receive rejection slip after rejection slip. You can **only** make **an** commitment to do **good** in life and climb the ladder of success.

Thirdly, and just as **importantly,** you must be a reader. If you are moved by **an** powerful sentence, you have the potential to become a writer. If you savor words that have been carefully chosen and skillfully combined, if you can be touched by the **well**-turned phrase, then you, my friend, do have the potential to become **an** writer in the true sense of the word. Continue to be **a** eager learner. As you begin to feel **well** about yourself, I wish you **well.**

7

Chapter 8

Prepositions and Verbals: Phrases as Parts of Speech

▶ OBJECTIVES

In this chapter, you will learn to

- ••• define and use various kinds of phrases
- ••• recognize prepositions and prepositional phrases and use them effectively
- ••• avoid pitfalls when using prepositions
- ••• recognize two-word or compound verbs formed with prepositions
- ••• recognize verbals and verbal phrases and use them effectively
- ••• recognize and use absolute and appositive phrases correctly
- ••• avoid inaccurate or confusing placement of modifying phrases

Definition of a Phrase

A **phrase** *is a group of words that does not contain both a subject (actor) and a verb (action).* The English language has many kinds of phrases. Some act as adjectives that modify nouns or pronouns. Some act as adverbs that modify verbs, adjectives, or other adverbs. Some phrases function as nouns, forming the subject of the verb, the object of the verb, or the object of a preposition. A phrase is made up of two or more closely related words. A main verb along with its helping verbs is a verb phrase: *has been writing.*

In this chapter, you will learn about prepositions and verbals and how they are used in phrases that add variety and clarity to writing. You will also learn to recognize and use correctly absolute and appositive phrases.

Prepositions

Before we begin our discussion of prepositions, you probably want to know if a discussion is even necessary. Following are the three main reasons you should learn how to identify prepositional phrases:

1. Knowing how to identify a preposition and its phrase in a sentence is essential if you are to know whether to use a singular or plural verb.

2. Being able to identify prepositions, in general, is necessary if you are to know which words in a title to capitalize.

3. Learning that a prepositional phrase is made up of the preposition, any modifiers, and the object of the preposition will help you to choose the correct pronoun if a pronoun is the object (pronouns are discussed in Chapter 5).

Thus, recognizing prepositions and their phrases will help you apply the grammar rules that can build your skills and, therefore, your self-confidence as a writer.

A **preposition** usually implies direction or gives a sense of time or place (figurative or literal). Most authors define a **preposition** as a word that shows a relationship with a noun or pronoun in the sentence.

In the following sentence, you will see how a preposition works to form a relationship between two words. The preposition and related words are boldfaced. The preposition is also underlined.

The **appearance <u>of</u>** the **man** was surprising.

The preposition *of* relates the *appearance* to the *man*. Still, the definition did not help me when I was trying to master the rules for writers. My guess is that it will not help you either. Therefore, do not cheat yourself: Read and reread the following lists of prepositions until they become familiar to you.

In addition, a mnemonic (memory-assisting) definition of the "direction" prepositions may help you. All the prepositions are **boldfaced** in the following paragraph.

A preposition can go anywhere a squirrel can go. It can go **up, down, around, through, over, under, beneath, by, to, toward, in, in front of, behind, between,** and **among.**

The following lists of prepositions and prepositional phrases will help to reinforce your knowledge. Remember that sometimes these words function as other parts of speech, a fact you will understand as you travel on the road toward competence and confidence.

Prepositions and Prepositional Phrases

about (about time)	into (into my heart)
above (above Matt's head)	like (like his father)
across (across the street)	near (near Annie's home)
after (after the party)	of (of my life)
against (against the wall)	off (off the porch)
along (along the path)	on (on time)
among (among the three men)	onto (onto the roof)

around (around the house)

at (at John and me)

before (before then)

behind (behind the tree)

below (below average)

beneath (beneath the surface)

beside (beside the lake)

between (between you and me)

beyond (beyond time and space)

by (by then)

despite (despite her appearance)

down (down the street)

during (during the trial)

except (except you and me)

for (for him and her)

from (from Matt and her)

inside (inside my brain)

without (without Annie and him)

within (within the house)

out (out there)

outside (outside the office)

over (over the nest)

past (past Matt's house)

since (since that time)

through (through the tunnel)

throughout (throughout the day)

to (to Annie and me)

toward (toward the sheltered side)

under (under the truck)

underneath (underneath the bed)

unlike (unlike her sister)

until (until nine o'clock)

up (up the hill)

upon (upon the roof)

with (with Matt and me)

Multiword Prepositions

according to	contrary to	on account of
along with	except for	on top of
apart from	in addition to	out of
as for	in back of	owing to
because of	in spite of	with regard to
by means of	instead of	with respect to

Prepositional Phrases

The preposition, any modifiers of the object of the preposition, and the object of the preposition itself are called a **prepositional phrase.** The prepositional phrase begins with the preposition (*pre-position*). The preposition is usually followed by modifiers (if there are any) and the object of the preposition, which is generally the last word in the phrase. If you scan the prepositional phrases in the preceding lists, the order of the elements that make up the prepositional phrase will become clear.

Notice that the prepositional phrase contains neither a subject (actor) nor a verb (action). Verbs are covered in Chapter 6, and you will soon understand how the subject and verb must agree in number (see Chapter 9). Prepositional phrases usually function as adjectives or adverbs. Remember that adjectives modify nouns or pronouns; adverbs modify verbs, adjectives, or other adverbs (see Chapter 7). Prepositional phrases also sometimes function as nouns, although not as often. Look at the following sentence in which the parts of the prepositional phrase are identified:

She walked **into the dark room.**

> *into* (preposition)
>
> *the* (modifier of *room*)
>
> *dark* (modifier of *room*)
>
> *room* (object of the preposition, *into*)

Look at the following sentences and notice how the boldfaced prepositions usually imply direction, time, or place. The word group that makes up each prepositional phrase is underlined. See if you can identify the word or words each prepositional phrase modifies.

1. Annie stared **at** Matt as he drove **toward** her home located **in** an exclusive neighborhood.
2. **During** the lightning storm, Matt parked his car **under** a maple tree.
3. Matt looked **at** Annie and said, "I just ended a sentence **with** a proposition."
4. Annie smiled **at** Matt and asked, "Did you say preposition or proposition?"
5. "Oh, I know you can't end a sentence **with** a preposition," replied Matt.
6. Annie look **at** him **in** astonishment and said, "Of course, you can as long as you're not redundant."
7. As thunder shook the car and lightning flashed **around** them, Matt moved closer **to** Annie and whispered, "Can you give me an example?"
8. Smiling **in** the semidarkness **of** the storm, she said, "All right. Listen **to** the following sentence: *That's where it is at.*"
9. "I see what you mean," said Matt. "You simply don't need the *at* **at** the end **of** the sentence."
10. "That's right," said Annie as lightning shot **through** the windows **of** the car.
11. "Then **by** redundant, you mean using words you don't need, **like** *dead corpse,*" said Matt as a symbolic lightbulb flashed **above** his head.
12. "Yes, exactly," said Annie as she looked **at** the rain **through** the headlights **of** oncoming cars. (Notice the stacking of three prepositional phrases.)

8

13. "Annie, when you finish **with** all my language lessons, I'll become one successful man **about** town."

14. "I hope so," replied Annie. "Then we'll discuss ending sentences **with** prepositions and propositions.

15. **After** the storm, he turned the ignition key and shifted the gear **into** drive.

16. A few minutes later, his sleek red car glided **down** the tree-lined street **toward** Annie's home.

By this time, you are beginning to recognize prepositions and their phrases in sentences. Remember that you must be able to do so to ensure subject–verb agreement (that is, if you have a plural subject, you must have a plural verb). You must be able to recognize prepositions to ensure correct capitalization in titles and correct pronoun choices. All these problems are discussed in detail in other chapters. For now, just remember that knowing how to recognize prepositions and prepositional phrases and knowing how to use them correctly are essential to being able to write well.

TIP: When the preposition *to* is followed by a verb, such as *to move* or *to work,* it is not a prepositional phrase. It is called an infinitive. This will become clear later in this chapter. Also, we have two-word verbs in our language. Look at the two examples:

1. He walked **in his father's shoes.**

The phrase *in his father's shoes* is a prepositional phrase.

2. He **kicked in** the door.

Here, *kicked in* is a two-word verb and *door* is the object of the verb. Most of the time you can test to see whether a phrase is a prepositional phrase or a two-word verb by seeing whether you can separate the verb and the preposition that follows it. For example, in the second sentence, you could write: He **kicked** the door **in.** When you can do this, you have a two-word verb.

Pitfalls with Prepositions

Have you, like Matt, ever heard that you should not end a sentence with a preposition? That rule was stressed in the early 1900s, and it has cast its long shadow across the decades of this century. Certainly, we do not want to go out of our way to end a sentence with a preposition, but sometimes we can unwittingly make mistakes by trying too hard to avoid a preposition at the end of a sentence.

Look at the following statement:

X Annie works hard to make the world a better place to live.

The statement makes no sense, but writers who write like this are striving to avoid ending sentences with prepositions. Look at the following sentences:

1. Annie works hard to make the world a better place to live in.

2. Annie works hard to make the world a better place in which to live.

Both versions of this sentence are acceptable. Both statements make sense. In formal writing, most writers would opt for the second one, but in informal conversation or informal writing, the first one is also correct.

Now, look at the following sentence:

Where is he at?

The *at* is unnecessary. People often answer this question by saying, "He's behind the *at.*" They, of course, are sarcastically implying that the speaker should not end a sentence with a preposition. The sentence is incorrect, however, *only* because the last word is not needed. The sentence is as redundant as the phrase *past history* or *advanced planning.* The error is not caused by ending the sentence with a preposition. The fault is in the redundancy.

A second pitfall to be aware of when using prepositions occurs when you use the word *all.* Many people use the preposition *of* in the following constructions: *all of the pages* or *all of my children.* The *of* is not needed. Think about the title of the television soap *All My Children.* The title is correctly written, and remembering it will help you to avoid using the unnecessary *of.*

You should include *of,* however, when you use a pronoun instead of a noun at the end of a phrase. An old song title will help you: "All of Me." You would, then, write *all of them,* but *all the pages.*

Here is a third pitfall. Try to avoid stacking or clustering prepositional phrases in a way that seems monotonous. An example of what not to do follows:

While at home during the evening (around six o'clock) in my office, I write for two hours.

The preceding sentence is composed almost entirely of prepositional phrases. Variety improves writing style. Good writers know that effective writing means lots of rewriting. Don't be afraid to tear a sentence apart and put it back together again and again. In the following rewritten version, the sentence contains only two prepositional phrases as opposed to five in the original sentence.

Around 6:00 P.M., I spend two hours writing in my home office.

You now understand the importance of being able to recognize and use prepositional phrases effectively. As you learn additional rules for writers, you will develop your own style, but it will nonetheless be a style that remains within the boundaries of those rules.

 8.1 EXERCISE FOR RECOGNITION OF PREPOSITIONAL PHRASES

Instructions: Underline the prepositional phrases in each of the following sentences. Write P above the preposition and O above the object of the preposition in each phrase. Do not underline infinitives or two-word verbs.

1. Although grammar has gone out of style, effective writing still demands knowledge and application of the grammar rules.

2. Employers look for good writers.

3. Matt has learned that to move up the ladder at the bank, he must learn to apply the rules of grammar and punctuation to his writing.

4. He has asked Annie, the local writer, to work with him.

5. After much consideration, she agreed.

6. Now, she enjoys their evenings at the Whistle Top Buffet in Goldpage.

7. Matt sometimes writes with a pencil, sometimes with a pen, and sometimes on a computer.

8. Although sitting for long hours at a computer is tiring, Matt prefers the computer.

9. It allows him to make corrections with just a few taps on certain keys.

10. Although Annie gives up precious time for Matt when she could be writing, she is not sorry that she accepted his proposition.

11. Annie is a best-selling writer, but Matt thinks she is a bit of a snob about usage.

12. At home, Matt walked from his kitchen into the living room and anticipated a discussion about pronouns in future meetings with Annie.

13. Annie had promised to bring an autographed copy of her latest book on language.

14. Matt was proud of his own dialect, but he was determined to learn how to write grammatical sentences.

15. He knew that most successful employees at the bank could speak two dialects: the one they spoke during childhood and the one they learned as adults.

8

8.2 EXERCISE FOR IDENTIFYING FUNCTIONS OF PREPOSITIONAL PHRASES

Instructions: For each underlined prepositional phrase, indicate in the space provided whether the phrase is functioning as a noun, adjective, or adverb. Then underline all other prepositional phrases.

1. <u>During the lunch hour</u> is the best time for our meeting. _____

2. The executive committee of the student government association met <u>during the lunch hour</u>. _____

3. The committee debated <u>for one hour</u>. _____

4. They voted to sponsor a writing workshop <u>on May 3</u>. _____

5. This is <u>between you and me</u>. _____

6. The student government has gone <u>from one project</u> to another. _____

7. The writing workshop will be held <u>in the Administration Building</u>. _____

8. It will last <u>for two hours</u>. _____

9. The participants will be reminded to choose all objects <u>of prepositions</u> from the objective case if those objects are pronouns. _____

10. Descriptive writing involves the use of sensory language, which appeals <u>to the five senses</u>. _____

11. Engaging prose is brought <u>to life</u> by the use of sensory language. _____

12. As Matt sat <u>in the warm classroom,</u> he smelled the tantalizing aroma of hotdogs wafting through the open window. _____

13. He tried to concentrate <u>on Annie's comments</u>, but he was captivated by her dazzling smile aimed directly at Amelio and him. _____

14. Plans <u>for next year's workshop</u> are already being discussed. _____

15. It will be held <u>in the same place</u>. _____

Sneaky Verbals

Verbals *are derived from verbs, but they function as other parts of speech.* The term *verbal* is an umbrella term for participles, gerunds, and infinitives. Verbals, although functioning as other parts of speech, masquerade as verbs. They try to travel incognito; they try to trick us. The first verbal to be aware of is the participle. We often let participles dangle, which we cannot do. You will soon understand.

Participles

A **participle** is *a verbal that functions as an adjective, that is, a word that describes a noun or pronoun* (see Chapter 7). The participle may end in *-ing* (the progressive form of the verb), or it may be a past participle. For example, it may end in *-ed* if it is a regular verb. It may end in *-en* or in some other way if it is an irregular verb (see the list of irregular verbs in Chapter 6). Look at the following sentence, in which the participle is boldfaced:

The **running** pig squealed happily.

The verb in the preceding sentence is *squealed; running* is not functioning as a verb in this sentence. It tells something about the pig (*running pig*); it describes the pig. *Running*, then, is functioning as a descriptive word (adjective) because it describes the pig (a noun). *Running* is, therefore, a participle.

Gerunds

Gerunds *are verbals that end in -ing and function only as nouns* (see Chapter 4). Look at the gerund, *running*, in the following sentence:

A. **Running** is good exercise.

Can you find the subject in the sentence? The verb is *is*, a linking verb. The word that precedes the verb is the subject, which is *running*. The word *running* in Sentence A is functioning as a noun, the name of an activity. In the following sentences, *exercising* is a gerund.

B. **Exercising** is healthful.

Exercising is the subject.

C. I like **exercising**.

Exercising in this sentence is the object of the transitive verb, *like*.

D. I sometimes tire of **exercising**.

Exercising here is the object of the preposition, *of*.

E. A healthful habit is **exercising**.

Exercising here is a predicate noun.

In all the sample sentences, *exercising* is functioning as a noun because nouns can serve as subjects (Sentences A and B). Nouns can serve as objects of verbs (Sentence C) and as objects of prepositions (Sentence D). They can also serve as predicate nouns or complements (Sentence E). Gerunds give us fewer problems than participles.

Infinitives

An **infinitive** *is formed by using the present tense or base form of the verb without an -s on the end. It is preceded by the preposition* to. Infinitives can function as nouns, adjectives (words that describe nouns or pronouns), or adverbs (words that describe verbs, adjectives, or other adverbs). The following are examples of infinitives:

to be	to play	to sleep	to write
to grow	to progress	to plan	to initiate
to jump	to learn	to succeed	to rise

Look at the following sentences in which the infinitives are boldfaced:

To work was difficult.

Noun. *To work* is the subject of the sentence.

She worked **to succeed.**

Adverb. The infinitive, *to succeed*, modifies the verb, *worked*.

To work is **to succeed.**

Subject and predicate noun. The first infinitive is the subject; the second follows a linking verb and is a predicate noun or complement.

TIP: An oft-repeated myth that we should not split an infinitive continues to influence writers. The implication is that we should not insert words between *to* and the verb, but look at the examples. You will see that the split infinitive is the best choice.

Annie prepares handouts **to** better **teach** students.

Annie prepares handouts better **to teach** students.

Annie prepares handouts **to teach** better students.

If, then, you must split an infinitive to make your meaning clear—that is, if you must insert words between *to* and the verb—do so. Otherwise, try to avoid such splits.

Verbal Phrases

Remember that a phrase is a group of closely related words without both a subject and a verb, and the phrase functions as a single part of speech.

A **verbal phrase** *is a general term for one of the following: a participial phrase, a gerund phrase, or an infinitive phrase.*

Participial Phrases

A **participial phrase** *consists of a participle (often the introductory word), its object, and any modifiers.* Like the participle, this phrase modifies a noun or pronoun. To make mistakes when using participles or participial phrases is easy, easy, easy. Finding them is difficult. See if you can find any errors in the following sentences, in which the participial phrases are boldfaced:

1. **After working for hours,** the problem was solved.
2. **Staying busy,** the day passes quickly.
3. **Listening to the speaker for hours,** Annie's nerves were on edge.
4. **Reading the essay a third time,** more errors were found.

If you cannot find errors in the preceding sentences, look at each bold-faced word and ask yourself if there is anyone named in the sentence that can do the **working,** the **staying,** the **listening,** or the **reading.** If not, the sentence has a dangling modifier. In other words, the participle has nothing in the sentence to modify or describe, at least nothing that makes sense.

The following sentences have been rewritten to correct the errors.

After working for hours, Matt solved the problem.

In the original sentence, *the problem* had worked for hours to solve the problem. In this sentence, *Matt* worked for hours to solve the problem. Here, to correct the error, we have put someone in the second part of the sentence.

When we stay busy, the day passes quickly.

In the original version, *the day* stays busy to make the day pass quickly. See how silly dangling modifiers can be. Now, we have corrected the error by putting someone in the first part of the sentence. The participle has been deleted.

After Annie listened to the speaker for hours, her nerves were on edge.

Notice again that we have put *Annie* in the first part of the sentence. Annie's nerves, after all, cannot listen to a speaker.

Reading the report a third time, Matt found more errors.

Errors cannot read a report, which is what the original version of this sentences says.

8

Notice that these errors can be corrected only by making sure our participles are describing the right words. Trying to turn the original sample sentences around to correct them would not have worked. We must be sure to put someone or something in the sentence that is being described.

TIP: When a sentence has a participial phrase (a phrase functioning as an adjective), be sure the phrase is modifying the appropriate noun or pronoun. If, for example, you have an -*ing* action word, be sure you have someone in the sentence that can do the action.

Gerund Phrases

Just as gerunds function as nouns, so do gerund phrases. *A* **gerund** *phrase consists of the gerund, its object, and any modifiers.* Following are examples of sentences with gerund phrases, which are boldfaced:

Running around the track is good exercise.

Noun. In this sentence, the phrase is the subject.

She enjoys **running around the track.**

Noun. Here, the phrase is the object of the verb.

Annie's succeeding pleased her family.

Noun. The phrase here is the subject of the sentence, but the gerund itself is preceded by a governing noun (Annie's), which is known as the subject of the gerund. Notice that the possessive form is used before the gerund.

TIP: Generally, use the possessive form of a noun or pronoun when it precedes a gerund. Compare the following:

Annie's success	Annie's succeeding
your enjoyment	your enjoying
their exercise	their exercising

There is an exception to the tip. If the subject of the gerund and the gerund are separated by words, do not use the possessive form for the subject. An example will clarify this.

The students enjoyed **Annie,** an excellent speaker, **discussing** persuasive writing.

Remember that gerund phrases function only as nouns. The most frequently made error is not making the subject of the gerund possessive.

Infinitive Phrases

An **infinitive phrase** *is made up of an infinitive (to followed by a verb), modifiers, if any, and the object of the infinitive.* Infinitive phrases can function as nouns, adjectives, and adverbs. The infinitive phrases are boldfaced in the sample sentences.

To work all day at the computer was difficult.

Noun. The phrase is the subject of the verb, *was.*

He asked **to borrow Annie's book.**

Noun. The phrase is the direct object of the verb, **asked.**

Annie had one book **to lend him.**

Adjective. The phrase modifies the noun, *book.*

Books are written **to entertain and enlighten readers.**

Adverb. The phrase modifies the verb, *written.*

Position the infinitive phrase carefully so that it modifies the words you intend it to modify.

8.3 EXERCISE FOR PHRASE IDENTIFICATION

Instructions: Underline each verbal phrase. In the space on the left, indicate whether the phrase is participial, gerund, *or* infinitive. *In the space on the right, indicate the phrase's function by writing* noun, adjective, *or* adverb.

1. To write effectively is important.

_____   _____

2. Annie likes to write every day.

_____   _____

3. Annie enjoys writing every day.

_____   _____

4. Teaching at the college, Annie has little time.

_____   _____

5. Annie researched to prepare for her lecture on Greek culture.

_____   _____

6. To prepare carefully was important to Annie.

_____   _____

7. Her first lecture focused on the Greeks' dividing and classifying their language.

_____   _____

8. Comedians use humor to soften otherwise painful truths.

_____   _____

8

9. Aristophanes, the Greek playwright, was famous for reflecting human foibles in his comedies.

_____   _____

10. His reflecting the flaws of human behavior was sugar-coated with humor.

_____   _____

11. Maintaining a sense of humor is essential for both individuals and nations.

_____   _____

12. Aristophanes wanted to improve the human condition.

_____   _____

13. Using humor, the playwright enlightened his audience.

_____   _____

14. He wrote to mirror society's flaws.

_____   _____

15. He excelled in writing comedy.

_____   _____

8.4 EXERCISE FOR IDENTIFYING SUBJECTS, OBJECTS, ADJECTIVES, AND ADVERBS

Instructions: The verbal phrase is italicized in each sentence. Give its function by writing in the space one of the following: object of the verb, object of the preposition, subject, adjective, or adverb. If the phrase is functioning as an adjective or adverb, write the word it is modifying.

1. _To write effectively_ is important.

_____

2. Annie likes _to write every day._

_____

3. Annie enjoys _writing every day._

_____

4. _Teaching at the college_, Annie has little time.

_____

5. Annie researched _to prepare for her lecture on Greek culture._

_____

6. *To prepare carefully* was important to Annie.

_____

7. Her first lecture focused on *the Greeks' dividing and classifying their language.*

_____

8. Comedians use humor *to soften otherwise painful truths.*

_____

9. Aristophanes, the famous Greek playwright, was famous for *reflecting human foibles in his comedies.*

_____

10. *His reflecting the flaws of human behavior* was sugar-coated with humor.

_____

11. *Maintaining a sense of humor* is essential for both individuals and nations.

_____

12. Aristophanes wanted *to improve the human condition.*

_____

13. *Using humor,* the playwright enlightened his audience.

_____

14. He wrote *to mirror society's flaws.*

_____

15. He excelled in *writing comedy.*

_____

8

Absolute Phrases

An **absolute phrase** *consists of a noun or pronoun followed by a verbal; however, instead of modifying one part of a sentence, the absolute phrase modifies the entire sentence. Absolute* is derived from the Latin word *absolutus,* meaning free from restriction. This phrase is infrequently used. In any event, it seldom gives us problems as long as we are careful not to confuse it with a participial or infinitive phrase that modifies a specific element in a sentence. An absolute phrase—unlike a participial phrase—has its own "subject." If you were to change the verbal in an absolute phrase to a verb, you would create a sentence. This would not be so with a participial phrase because there is no word to function as a subject. Look at the sample sentences in which the absolute phrases are boldfaced:

- **Her smile demonstrating her enthusiasm,** Annie began to discuss the importance of prewriting activities. (In this sentence, the absolute phrase could be rewritten as a sentence: *Her smile demonstrated her enthusiasm.* We know, then, that the phrase is absolute and not participial.)
- **The bell having rung,** Annie ended her discussion.
- **His mind weary from the test,** Matt went straight home.

Appositive Phrases

An **appositive phrase** *renames a noun or pronoun, and the phrase is in apposition to (placed beside) the word it renames.* Examples of this phrase will clarify the concept.

- Annie, **a writer and instructor of writing,** is passionate about writing and teaching.
- Jim Patrinski, **my caring neighbor,** is a sharp attorney.

Like the absolute phrase, this phrase gives us few problems other than requiring us to decide whether to use commas around it. If the appositive is restrictive, meaning the appositive is necessary for identification of whatever is being renamed, do not surround the appositive with commas. If, however, the appositive is simply adding information, use commas to set off the appositive. For example, if you have two brothers, Jim and Bob, and you mention one of them, you must name him so the reader will know which brother: *My brother Bob is a chemist.* If you have only one brother, Jim, renaming him is not necessary for meaning; you are just adding information, *My brother, Jim, is a writer.*

Accurate Placement of Modifying Phrases

You are already aware of the need for careful placement of one-word modifiers. Modifying phrases must also be placed carefully in a sentence so they modify the word you mean them to modify. Look at the examples of misplaced descriptive phrases. The phrases are boldfaced, and the words they modify are italicized.

X **To prepare for the lecture,** the *research* had to be thorough.

The infinitive phrase is modifying *research*, but *research* cannot prepare for the lecture.

To prepare for the lecture, *Annie* had to research thoroughly.

We have now placed someone in the sentence who can prepare for a lecture.

X **Preparing for the lecture,** the *research* had to be thorough.

The participial phrase here, like the infinitive phrase in the previous example, has nothing to describe—at least, nothing that makes sense.

Preparing for the lecture, *Annie* had to research thoroughly.

You can see the need for placing a pronoun or the name of a person in the sentence. Only people can conduct research.

X The man killed the copperhead *snake* **with a shovel.**

Have you ever seen a copperhead with a shovel?

The *man* used a shovel **to kill the copperhead snake.**

Regardless of the type of modifying phrase you use, be sure it is modifying the appropriate word. If you need to add, delete, or rearrange words to make your meaning clear, by all means, do so.

SUMMARY

You can now define and recognize various types of phrases. You can use and recognize prepositional phrases; you know how to avoid their pitfalls. You can distinguish between prepositional phrases and two-word verbs. You now can avoid errors when writing participial, infinitive, and gerund phrases. You have learned to use the absolute and appositive phrases, although the absolute phrase is rare. You have learned how to avoid inaccurate and confusing placement of modifying phrases. Knowing how to locate and correct dangling participles is in itself quite an accomplishment. ■

8

8.5 END-OF-CHAPTER EXERCISES

Instructions: Identify each italicized phrase by writing in the space on the left one of the following: absolute, appositive, infinitive, participial, gerund, or prepositional. In the middle column, indicate the part of speech (except for the absolute and appositive phrases). If the phrase is a modifier, write the word or words it is modifying in the third column.

1. *Having been stolen during the night,* Annie's Jaguar was seen the following morning wrapped around an old oak tree.

   _____   _____   _____

2. Annie, *an avid writer,* was working at her computer when the state trooper called her.

   _____   _____   _____

3. Shutting down her computer, she left hurriedly *to meet her insurance agent.*

   _____   _____   _____

4. She had been shocked *to receive such a call.*

   _____   _____   _____

5. The Jaguar had been the car *of her dreams.*

   _____   _____   _____

6. Her Jaguar could ascend easily *up the steepest hill.*

   _____   _____   _____

7. *To lose it* seemed unbearable.

   _____   _____   _____

8. *Having been completely destroyed,* Annie's car would have to be replaced.

   _____   _____   _____

9. *Sitting in the insurance office,* she became increasingly frustrated.

   _____   _____   _____

10. A tall man *in a dark blue pin-striped suit* walked across the office toward Annie.

    _____   _____   _____

11. *All things considered,* the man's smile was surprising.

    _____   _____   _____

12. He strode confidently *across the room.*

    _____   _____   _____

8

13. *Smiling at Annie,* he introduced himself as Tom Bisano.

_____ _____ _____

14. Annie almost ran *to keep pace* with the tall man as she followed him to his office.

_____ _____ _____

15. *After examining Annie's car,* Tom (they were now on a first-name basis) shook his head in disbelief.

_____ _____ _____

16. *Sitting at the desk,* the assistant called a cab for Annie.

_____ _____ _____

17. Annie had lesson plans *to finish.*

_____ _____ _____

18. Disgusted by the turn of events, Annie called Matt *to get sympathy.*

_____ _____ _____

19. She later went to bed *to let sleep bury her troubling thoughts.*

_____ _____ _____

20. Her plans *for the next day* included the purchase of a new car.

_____ _____ _____

Instructions: Rewrite sentences to correct dangling or misplaced modifiers. If a sentence is correct, just smile.

8

21. Lying in the grass, the snake startled Matt.

_____

_____

22. Covered with mud, Matt could not see through the windshield.

_____

_____

23. To clean the windshield, it was necessary to drive to the first service station.

_____

_____

24. After parking the car, the windshield received a thorough washing.

_____

_____

25. While leaving the service station, it occurred to Matt that he needed to purchase gasoline.

   _____

   _____

26. Parking his car once again by the gas pump, the attendant smiled and welcomed him back.

   _____

   _____

27. With a clean windshield and tank full of gas, Matt was ready to drive to class.

   _____

   _____

28. After rushing to class, the idea of writing did not appeal to Matt.

   _____

   _____

29. Warming to his topic, however, his essay began to take on a life of its own.

   _____

   _____

30. To write an essay someone else would want to read, the topic had to interest Matt.

   _____

   _____

31. To produce an engaging essay, each sentence had to focus on the topic.

   _____

   _____

32. After formulating a workable thesis statement, the rest should be easy.

   _____

   _____

33. Writing the first draft, the essay could contain surface errors.

   _____

   _____

8

34. Writing the second draft, revisions could be made.

_____

_____

35. When proofreading and editing the final version, all errors would be corrected.

_____

_____

Instructions: Incorporate the following phrases into sentences that you create. Do not add helping verbs to the verb in the phrase. Use such phrases as participial, infinitive, or gerund phrases. Have fun writing sentences that are as creative as possible.

36. to be ready

_____

_____

_____

37. having wandered into the dark forest

_____

_____

_____

38. passing the graveyard

_____

_____

_____

39. sitting in her car

_____

_____

_____

40. walking softly past the church at midnight

_____

_____

_____

41. during the summer

_____

_____

_____

42. to write an essay

_____

_____

_____

43. to prepare for the test

_____

_____

_____

44. despite her having written all night

_____

_____

_____

45. leaving the scene of the crime

_____

_____

_____

46. to sit alone in a dark classroom

_____

_____

_____

47. waiting for copies of the test to be distributed

_____

_____

_____

48. after killing the wasp

_____

_____

_____

49. to listen carefully

_____

_____

_____

50. driving under the influence

_____

_____

_____

51. while listening to my favorite song

_____

_____

_____

52. dancing the night away

_____

_____

_____

53. during a violent lightning storm

_____

_____

_____

54. hearing a loud knocking on the door

_____

_____

_____

55. to hear the crunch of footsteps in the frozen snow

_____

_____

_____

56. frustrated and angry

_____

_____

_____

57. to write with confidence

_____

_____

_____

58. dissatisfied with his essay

_____

_____

_____

59. after leaving the classroom

_____

_____

_____

60. since taking the writing class from Annie

_____

_____

_____

61. having listened to the long speech

_____

_____

_____

62. walking faster and faster

_____

_____

_____

63. no moon shining on that dark October night

_____

_____

_____

64. to succeed in life

_____

_____

_____

65. satisfied with my efforts to learn how to write with power

_____

_____

_____

Instructions: Identify each italicized phrase by writing one of the following above it:

prep. (for prepositional)
inf. (for infinitive)
part. (for participial)
ger. (for gerund)
app. (for appositive)
abs. (for absolute)

66. *In the morning* is a good time *to write.*

67. *All things considered,* the morning is best for me.

68. Some writers like *to write* in the evening.

69. *While lying in bed,* one famous author wrote an entire book.

70. *Using an old typewriter,* another famous writer stood *in front* of a file cabinet.

71. *Resting on top of the file cabinet* was the old typewriter.

72. Ernest Hemingway had cats *to keep him company.*

73. The cats' descendants still live *in the late Hemingway's house,* which is located *in Key West, Florida.*

74. *To read Thomas Wolfe's books* requires a great deal *of time.*

75. *Being biographical in nature,* many of his works focus *on his hometown.*

76. *Having died in his thirties,* Thomas Wolfe, *during his adulthood,* was haunted *by a premonition* that he would die young.

77. *After writing Look Homeward Angel,* he wrote a letter *to his editor.*

78. *In the letter,* he said he would soon be going *to a better home* than any he had ever known.

79. *Within a short time after that,* he died.

80. *Throughout his adult life,* Wolfe was compelled *to write.*

81. *During Wolfe's writing career,* many people from his hometown became angry with him.

82. *Fictionalizing events and people he knew* was, indeed, risky.

83. Today, you can visit the house where he lived *during his childhood.*

84. Located *in Statesville, North Carolina,* his home is open *to the public.*

85. *Sharing tourists with the elegant Biltmore Estate,* the sponsors *of Wolfe's home* know it is humble *by comparison.*

86. *Having the spirit of the author,* Wolfe's childhood home is well worth your time and effort.

87. *To have the opportunity to purchase his books and copies of his letters* is exciting *for visitors.*

88. *Having carved tombstones,* Wolfe's father probably gave the author the idea of an angel looking homeward.

89. *Touring Statesville,* you just might find the actual angel Wolfe's father carved.

90. *Having visited Europe many times,* Wolfe was a sophisticated world traveler.

91. *Drawn to Europe and back to the States again and again,* Wolfe never felt he had a permanent home.

92. *Leaving Wolfe's mother a young widow,* the author's father died.

93. *To feed her family,* she took in boarders.

94. *To keep up with her expanding business,* she had to have more and more rooms built onto the house.

95. Each time young Wolfe thought he had a permanent room *of his own,* his mother would move him *into another room;* it is no wonder he said, "You can't go home again."

C h a p t e r 9

Subject–Verb Agreement

9

Complete Subjects and Predicates

Sentences can be divided into two main parts: the subject and all the words belonging to it (the complete subject), and the verb and all the words belonging to it (the complete predicate). In the following sentence, you can draw a vertical line between *bills* and *can drink* to separate the complete subject from the complete predicate. The word *bills* and everything to its left make up the complete subject. The words *can drink* and everything to their right make up the complete predicate.

Complete Subject	Predicate
Hummingbirds with their long bills	can drink nectar from flowers.

189

As you know, *the* **subject** *is the "actor" or doer in most sentences.* Sometimes, when the verb is "weak," referring to the subject as an actor or doer is stretching things a bit. Nonetheless, *actor* or *doer* best defines the word *subject* to the aspiring careful writer. The subject may be a noun, pronoun, or a phrase. It may even be a clause, a word group with both a subject and a verb within it (see Chapter 10). The following sentences illustrate each type of subject:

Annie is knowledgeable.

Annie, a noun, is the subject.

She is knowledgeable.

She, a pronoun, is the subject.

Learning the rules is important.

Learning the rules, a phrase, is the subject.

What Annie knew surprised the students.

What Annie knew, a clause, is the subject.

The complete subject of a sentence may have modifiers as in the following example, in which the simple subject is boldfaced and its modifiers are italicized:

The tall **man** *in the purple tights* attended the party yesterday.

The subject may also be a **compound subject,** *which means the sentence has two or more subjects connected by the word* **and.**

Knowing how to identify the subject of a sentence will help you to choose the correct verb form.

The **verb** *is the action the subject is doing.* Again, some verbs indicate mere state of being (forms of the verb *be,* for example) or action so slight as to be almost unrecognizable (*has, have, do, does, did, has done*). *The* **simple predicate** *consists of the main verb and any helping verbs. The* **complete predicate** *consists of the verb and all words belonging to it.* These words may include modifiers, objects, and appositives. The sample sentences will help you to identify complete predicates, which are italicized.

The instructor *talked loudly.*

Talked is the verb, and *loudly* is the adverb; together they make up the complete predicate.

The instructor *talked in a monotone.*

Talked is the verb, and *in a monotone* is a prepositional phrase functioning as an adverb. The verb and prepositional phrase make up the complete predicate.

The instructor *wrote the book.*

Wrote is the verb and *book* is the object. *The* is the article modifying *book.* The verb, the article, and the object make up the predicate.

The instructor *wrote Dangling Participles, a bestseller.*

Again, *wrote* is the verb, *Dangling Participles,* the object, and *a bestseller,* the appositive.

To make the subject and verb agree in number, you must be able to identify the subject precisely and to recognize the verb that represents the action the subject is doing or the verb that represents the subject's state of being. When words, such as adjectives and prepositional phrases functioning as adjectives, come between the subject and the verb, you must be able to discard those interrupting words long enough to get the subject and verb to agree in number.

Definition of Subject-Verb Agreement

Authors of English handbooks and English teachers frequently use the term *subject-verb agreement.* Indeed, it is an important term and one that every writer needs to understand. *All we mean by* **subject-verb agreement** *is that a singular subject requires a singular verb and a plural subject requires a plural verb.* We must, then, match singular with singular and plural with plural. In the following examples, notice that a singular verb ends with an *-s,* but a plural verb does not.

Singular subject with singular verb   *The cat* **meows.**
Plural subject with plural verb   *The cats* **meow.**

In the first sample sentence, no *-s* is on *cat,* the subject, but *meows,* the verb, ends in *-s.* In the second sentence, however, just the opposite is true.

Verb Choice When Words Separate Subject and Verb

When the subject and verb are not side by side—that is, when words separate them—it is easy to choose the wrong verb form. For example, if a prepositional phrase separates the subject and verb and the phrase has a plural object, you might erroneously think the object is the subject. Of course, you know that the object of a prepositional phrase is never the subject of the sentence; still, many writers make this mistake. Look at the following sentence:

Mary, along with the other nine students, wants to learn the rules.

In the preceding example, *Mary* is the subject, not *students.* To be able to remove the interrupting words, then, is important in selecting either a singular or plural verb to agree with the subject.

Singular Verb with Third-Person Subject

Remember that when the subject is third person and singular and the verb is in the present tense without helping verbs, the verb will always end with an *-s*, that is, it will always be singular.

In the following sample sentences, the subjects are underlined, and the verbs are boldfaced. Also, notice that the verbals (infinitives, gerunds, and participles) do not affect the tense of the main verb.

<u>Annie</u> **is planning** to write a second book about grammar.

The infinitive *to write* does not affect the tense of the verb *is planning*. Infinitives are tenseless.

<u>She</u> already **has** a list of potential buyers for her book.

Already is an adverb, not part of the verb.

<u>Matt</u> **wants** to buy her book as soon as it is on the market.

The sentence's main clause or statement is *Matt wants to buy her book*. It contains the main verb, *wants*. *As soon as it is on the market* is a dependent clause, in which the verb should also agree with the subject.

Using its expertise, the <u>publisher</u> **plans** to market Annie's book.

As you can see, you already know several facts about subject–verb agreement, which will make this chapter easier for you to understand and remember.

Now, write two sentences in which you use a subject that is third-person singular, and a verb in the present tense with no helping verbs.

1. _____

_____

2. _____

_____

Note: Your verbs should end in *-s*.

Plural Verb with Compound Subject

A **compound subject** *occurs when two or more subjects are connected with the coordinate conjunction* **and.** A plural verb (one not ending in *s*) is usually required with compound subjects. Once again, in the following examples, subjects are underlined and verbs boldfaced.

<u>Matt</u> and <u>Annie</u> **work** together to improve Matt's writing skills.

Notice that in this sentence each subject is singular, but when two or more singular subjects are connected with *and,* you usually use a plural verb. The personal pronoun *they* would replace the two subjects, *Matt* and *Annie.* You know that *they* would certainly require a plural verb. *They work together.*

A <u>desk</u> and <u>chair</u> **complete** the decor of understated elegance in Annie's home office.

Notice that in the preceding sentence, the subject is compound, which means there are two subjects. Remember that two or more subjects connected by **and** demand a plural verb. Therefore, *complete* is correct.

TIP: There is an exception. When two or more subjects are joined by *and* but refer to the same person, place, thing, idea, or animal, use a singular verb, as in the following examples:

- My companion and faithful friend is Fido.

- My colleague and childhood friend encourages me.

- Surprisingly, my critic and companion is the same person.

- Peanut butter and jelly is my favorite combination.

Most of the time, however, you will use a plural verb when two subjects (singular or plural) are connected with *and.*

If the subjects are not connected with *and,* do not be tricked into using a plural verb. Look at the following example:

A <u>desk</u> with a matching chair **completes** the decor of understated elegance in Annie's home office.

With is a preposition, and *chair* is its object. Remember that an object of a preposition can never be the subject of a sentence. This sentence, then, has only one subject, and the verb, *completes,* is correct.)

Now, write two sentences in which you use compound subjects with present-tense verbs without helping verbs. Do not write sentences that demonstrate the exception to the rule.

9

1. _____

   _____

2. _____

   _____

Note: Your verbs should be plural, that is, they should not end in *-s.*

9.1   EXERCISE FOR CORRECT VERB CHOICES

Instructions: Underline the subject of each sentence and write the correct verb in the space provided.

1. Many birds (fly/flies) _____ south in the winter.

2. The female phoebe and its mate (build/builds) _____ a nest in the spring.

3. The female, along with the male phoebe, (search/searches) _____ for twigs and grass for the nest.

4. Our cat and dog often (chase/chases) _____ the birds.

5. One chickadee, as well as several cardinals, (has become/have become) _____ quite tame.

6. Because of an abundant food supply, many kinds of wildlife (visit/visits) _____ our yard.

7. Corn and thistle (attract/attracts) _____ deer, squirrels, and birds.

8. Squirrel-proof feeders (amuse/amuses) _____ the squirrels.

9. A clever animal and a voracious eater (is/are) _____ the squirrel.

10. The many creatures of the forest (has learned/have learned _____ to share in the bounty.

Verb Choice with Either . . . Or and Neither . . . Nor

As you will learn in the next chapter, *either . . . or* and *neither . . . nor* are called correlative conjunctions. When you use *either . . . or* or *neither . . . nor* to connect two or more subjects, the compound-subject rule no longer applies.

Rule 1. If both subjects are singular, use a singular verb as follows:

Either <u>Emily</u> or <u>Paul</u> **is** going to be permitted to attend the workshop.

Do not let the underlining of *Emily* and *Paul* as subjects trick you into believing this sentence has two subjects. Notice that *and* does not connect the two; rather, the correlative conjunctions, *either . . . or,* connect them. This means that one or the other will attend the workshop, not both.

Neither <u>Annie</u> nor <u>Matt</u> **is going** to the next picnic.

Rule 2. If both subjects are plural, use a plural verb as follows:

Neither the board <u>members</u> nor the college's <u>administrators</u> **resent** Annie's fees.

Rule 3. If one subject is plural and one is singular, the verb choice is determined by the subject closer to the verb. Look at this example.

Neither <u>Annie</u> nor the <u>participants</u> **like** interruptions.

The subject closer to the verb, *participants,* is plural; therefore, the verb must be plural. *Like* is a plural verb.

Now, look what happens when the subjects are switched.

Neither the <u>participants</u> nor <u>Annie</u> **likes** interruptions.

Annie, a singular subject, has been moved and is closer to the verb. *Likes,* a singular verb, must now be used.

TIP: If you use *both . . . and* to connect two subjects, you must use a plural verb as in the following: Both Maria and Alonzo make *A*'s on every test.

If *either* or *neither* is the subject of the sentence, use a singular verb, as in the following sentences:

<u>Either</u> **pleases** me.

<u>Neither</u> **pleases** me.

Verb Choice with Indefinite Pronouns

Singular Indefinite Pronouns

Some indefinite pronouns are singular, others are plural, and still others can be either singular or plural depending on meaning. The following pronouns are usually singular and require singular verbs: *another, anybody, anyone, anything, each, either, every, everybody, everyone, everything, much, neither, nobody, no one, none* (meaning not one), *nothing, other, one, somebody, someone,* and *something.* A few sample sentences will illustrate these pronouns. The subject (indefinite pronoun) is underlined, and the verb is boldfaced.

- <u>Everybody</u> **likes** to learn.
- <u>None</u> **fails** the writing tests.
- <u>Something</u> **is** amiss.

Plural Indefinite Pronouns

The following indefinite pronouns are plural and require a plural verb: *both, ones,* and *others.* See the examples in which the subjects are underlined and the verbs boldfaced.

- <u>Both</u> **are** ready for the exam.
- The <u>ones</u> in that stack **are** mine.
- The <u>others</u> **are** yours.

Singular or Plural Indefinite Pronouns

The following pronouns can be either singular or plural, depending on the meaning in the sentence: *all, any, enough, more, most,* and *some.* In each of the following sentences, the indefinite pronoun is underlined and the verb boldfaced. The meaning is conveyed by the word in brackets.

- <u>All</u> [everything] **is** not lost.
- <u>All</u> [students] **have** attended.
- <u>Any</u> [effort] **is** better than none.
- <u>Any</u> [flowers] **are** my favorite.
- <u>Enough</u> [effort] **has been wasted** on that project.
- <u>Enough</u> [trees] **have been planted** in the yard.
- <u>Some</u> of the participants **have** left the restaurant.
- By each day's end, <u>some</u> of the enthusiasm **remains.**

   TIP: Write *everyone* and *anyone* as two words when they are followed by modifying prepositional phrases as in the following sentences:

   Every <u>one</u> of the students **likes** to learn.
   Any <u>one</u> of the restaurants **is** good.

Verb Choice with Relative Pronouns

9

The antecedent of a pronoun, as you may remember, is the word to which the pronoun refers. Whether the verb of a relative pronoun is singular or plural depends on its antecedent. The relative pronouns that function as subjects of the dependent clause (see Chapter 10) are *who, which,* and *that.* In the following sentences, both the antecedent and the relative pronoun are underlined, and the verb of the relative pronoun is boldfaced.

- The <u>man who</u> **lives** in our neighborhood is Count Drack.
- The <u>men who</u> **live** in our neighborhood like Count Drack.
- The <u>desk that</u> **was** in my office has been painted.
- The <u>desks that</u> **were** in my office have been painted.
- My <u>desk, which</u> **was** in my office, has been removed.
- My <u>desks, which</u> **were** in my office, have been removed.
- My desk was one of the <u>desks that</u> **were painted.**

Do not let the last sample sentence trick you. You might rewrite the sentence as follows to help you determine the subject of the relative pronoun: Of all the <u>desks</u> that **were painted,** mine was one.

Inverted Word Order and *There* as a Subject Delayer

When verbs precede subjects, especially compound subjects, you must be careful to look beyond the verb to find the subject or subjects. Once you know whether the subject is singular or plural, you are ready to match it with a singular or plural verb. In this way, the two will get along or agree.

Look at the following examples. See the problems you can encounter if you neglect looking *past* the verb to find the subject or subjects. The subjects are underlined and verbs boldfaced.

In Annie's spacious office **are** a solid cherry Queen Anne <u>desk</u>, a matching <u>chair</u>, and a traditional <u>sofa</u>.

This sentence has three subjects that require the plural verb, *are*. As you can see, subjects are still underlined, and verbs boldfaced.

On her desk **are** a <u>fax machine</u>, a <u>computer</u>, and a <u>telephone</u> with a built-in answering machine.

This sentence has three subjects and, therefore, requires the plural verb, *are*. Notice that *answering machine* (a compound noun) is the object of the preposition, *with.*

Watch for the subject delayer *there.* It introduces an inverted word order. The word *there* itself will not be a subject; it is an adverb of place.

There **are** your <u>manuscript</u> and <u>folder</u>.

On Annie's deck, there are a bird <u>feeder</u>, a hanging <u>planter</u> with red geraniums, an umbrella <u>table</u>, and several <u>chairs</u>.

The last two sentences, could be rewritten as follows:

Your <u>manuscript</u> and <u>folder</u> **are** there.

A bird <u>feeder</u>, a hanging <u>planter</u> with red geraniums, an umbrella <u>table</u>, and several <u>chairs</u> **are** on Annie's deck.

9.2 EXERCISE FOR YOUR AGREEABLE CHOICES

Instructions: Underline the subject. Choose the preferred verb in parentheses and write it in the space provided.

1. Neither the players nor the coach (want/wants) _____ to lose a game.

2. Both the staff members and the faculty members (plan/plans) _____ to speak to the college's vice president about increasing the number of writing workshops.

3. Neither the faculty members nor the vice president (object/objects) _____ to increased training.

4. Neither (want/wants) _____ interruptions during the meeting.

5. None of the students (is/are) _____ apathetic.

6. Each of the ten students now (write/writes) _____ with increased confidence.

7. Either (is/are) _____ capable of making *A*'s.

8. Many of the essays (reflect/reflects) _____ the writers' personal experiences.

9. Some of the participants (has/have) _____ already begun to write.

10. Some of the fear of writing essays (has/have) _____ abated.

11. The student who (create/creates) _____ a good thesis statement builds a good base for an essay.

12. Students who (create/creates) _____ good thesis statements have an advantage.

13. In Amelio's classroom (is/are) _____ a chalkboard, a tattered wall map, and many desks.

14. Either Ameilo or one of the other officers (plan/plans) _____ to speak for the student government,

15. Neither John nor Matt (want/wants) _____ to speak.

16. Either the instructor or the assistants (grade/grades) _____ the objective tests.

17. Either the assistants or the instructor (grade/grades) _____ the objective tests.

18. In Annie's book (is/are) _____ a chapter on descriptive writing with many examples.

19. On her desk (is/are) _____ a combination of paper, paper clips, books, and pencils.

20. There (is/are) _____ too many weak verbs in these sentences, but they provide good lessons.

Verb Choice with Collective Nouns

You have already learned about collective nouns and verb choices. The discussion here is reinforcement. Remember that, like people, collective nouns like to form into groups or cliques. Some examples of collective nouns are *mob, class, committee, task force* (a compound collective noun), *audience, choir, platoon, crowd, army, chorus, family, herd,* and *club.*

If you use a collective noun **as a single unit,** the noun requires a **singular verb.** If, however, you use the collective noun **as individual members** within the group, use a **plural verb.** See the examples.

The family **have** been arriving all morning for the reunion.

The meaning is family members. If you feel uncomfortable using a plural verb with a collective noun, and most Americans do, you can insert the word members after the noun.

The family **enjoys** a reunion every August.

In this sentence, *family* is used as a single unit and, therefore, requires a singular verb.

The committee **is** in the room on the left.

Committee is used here as a single unit.

The committee **have debated** the issue for several hours.

If you look at the meaning of the sentence, at the verb, you can see that more than one person is needed for a debate. The meaning of committee members is clear, but again, you might want to insert the word *members.*

If you use a collective noun as a plural noun, you must be sure that any pronouns referring to the collective noun are also plural. Remember that the word to which a pronoun refers is its antecedent (see Chapter 5). Antecedents must agree in number with their pronouns. Be sure, then, to match plural with plural and singular with singular throughout your sentences. Here are some examples:

The team **have** debated for hours, but they **have** finally reached an agreement.

Notice the first subject, *team,* is plural because a plural verb, *have,* has been used. We must, therefore, use *they,* a plural second subject.

The choir **is** now meeting, but it **plans** to adjourn soon.

Again, notice that the antecedent, *choir,* agrees in number with the pronoun, *it.* Both are singular, and both verbs are singular.

Measurements as Subjects

Measurements of **money, time, length, weight, height,** and **distance** usually require a singular verb. In the following sentences, each subject is underlined, and each verb is boldfaced.

1. <u>Fifty dollars</u> **is** not much money anymore.
2. <u>Two weeks</u> **is** not enough time to relax during a vacation.
3. <u>Three feet</u> **equals** one yard.
4. <u>Twenty pounds</u> **is** too much for me to carry.
5. <u>Five feet</u> **means** she is vertically constrained.
6. <u>Three miles</u> **was** too far for Annie to run.

Sometimes, writers and speakers do use plural verbs with such measurements. They justify their plural verbs by explaining that they are using the measurements as items within the unit. In other words, they use the same explanation that is used with collective nouns.

The Number Versus *a Number*

The number requires a singular verb, but *a number* requires a plural verb.

<u>The number</u> of persons in Annie's workshops **increases** each year.

Here, "The number" acts as the subject and takes a singular verb.

<u>A</u> large <u>number</u> of employees **have registered** for her next workshop.

"A number" is the subject in the preceding sentence and requires a plural verb.

Nouns with Plural Forms but Singular Meanings

Several nouns in our language end in *-s*, that is, have plural forms or spellings but are nonetheless singular in meaning. A few examples are *measles, series, mumps, politics, physics,* and *news*. Such nouns require singular verbs. Here are some examples:

1. <u>Measles</u> **is** a serious disease.
2. Annie's <u>series</u> of workshops **has helped** the students.
3. Bad <u>news</u> **increases** program ratings and newspapers sales.

Plural Words Within Titles

When titles have plural words within them, the titles nonetheless require singular verbs. See the following examples.

1. Annie's *Business Writing Strategies* **has** become the careful writer's bible.

2. *Writing Rules* has dropped on the best-selling list because of Annie's book.

3. Annie's speech to the local Rotary Club, *Connections Between Writing Skills and Succeeding*, **was published** and **has become** a bestseller.

4. *All My Children* is a popular television soap opera.

9.3 | EXERCISE FOR SUBJECT-VERB AGREEMENT

Instructions: Underline the correct verb in parentheses.

1. The football team (has/have) new uniforms.

2. Twelve inches (equal/equals) one foot.

3. The number of investors (have/has) recently increased.

4. The amount of $1 million (is/are) not as much as it was in the past.

5. The baseball series (has/have) ended.

6. The choir (sing/sings) each song beautifully.

7. *Greece and Rome* (is/are) a wonderful book.

8. A large number of students (has/have) begun to enjoy poetry.

9. At least two months (is/are) required for planning a formal wedding.

10. The class (receives/receive) a writing assignment each week.

11. Linguistics (focuses/focus) primarily on oral language.

12. Some people feel that the news (is/are) slanted.

13. Measles (is/are) a serious disease.

14. Mathematics (is/are) capitalized when it is referred to as the title of a course.

15. The family (lives/live) in a brick house.

SUMMARY

After reading this chapter, you should not have further problems getting your subjects and verbs to agree in number. You have learned the definition of the phrase *subject-verb agreement,* along with rules to help you achieve it. You know that when a subject is third-person singular and the verb is in the present tense with no helping verbs, you must always use a singular verb, that is, a verb ending in -*s*. You know what is meant by a compound subject and that it usually requires a plural verb. You now know how to choose the correct verb with *either . . . or* and *neither . . . nor*. You can distinguish between plural and singular indefinite pronouns. You have been alerted to the pitfalls of inverted word order with respect to choosing a singular or plural verb. Collective nouns and verb choices as to number should no longer be a problem if you consider whether the noun is a single unit or members within the unit. You have learned the rule governing subject-verb agreement with measurements. You now know that the phrase *a number* requires a plural verb, but *the number* requires a singular verb. You have been alerted to those nouns, like *news*, that are plural in form but still require singular verbs. Finally, you know that even when a title contains a plural noun and seems for all the world to be plural, you nonetheless match it with a singular verb. After all, one title, regardless of its content, is still just one title.

When you construct a sentence, be sure that all verbs agree with all subjects in number. Be sure that all pronouns agree in number with their antecedents. When you proofread, check to be sure you have matched plural with plural and singular with singular. ■

9

9.4 END-OF-CHAPTER EXERCISE

Instructions: Correct each mistake in verb choice in the following essay by drawing a line through the incorrect verb and writing the correct verb above it.

Gwendolyn Brooks: A Living Poem

Gwendolyn Brooks, one of the most talented of American poets, like to be referred to as black rather than African-American. The first black writer to receive the Pulitzer Prize, she is now Poet Laureate Gwendolyn Brooks of Illinois. Carl Sandburg was the first to serve in this position. Brooks have followed him. A series of awards have come her way, including the Shelley Memorial Award and two Guggenheim Fellowships. There was also the American Academy of Arts and Letters Award and the Anisfield-Wolf Award, to mention only a few. Named in her honor is the Gwendolyn Brooks Junior High School and the Gwendolyn Brooks Cultural Center. Indeed, the number of awards she have received are too numerous to list. She and her husband lives in Chicago. The poet, as well as her daughter, are talented. Among Brooks' many publications is an autobiography, one novel, several books of poetry, and writing manuals. Although linguistics are not her specialization, her poetry and prose lets the reader know she is nonetheless a sculptor of language. A large number of people who loves poetry is among her fans. What is more, the number of her fans continue to increase as they become acquainted with her works. One of her latest books have a cover resembling a notebook that an elementary student might use. Enclosed in a marbleized black and white cover, *Children Coming Home* are about the size of a school notebook.

Brooks, like other fine poets, skillfully use sensory language. "Kitchenette Building," one of her many poems, penetrate to the core of naked reality. An appeal to our five senses and this naked reality is sharply delineated. When the battle between the dream world and real

9

life begin, the necessity of day-to-day survival "gray" away any chance for dreams to emerge as victors. The first lines of this poem sets a universal theme in motion. "We" convey an image of all people, through no fault or plan of their own, who is forced to live in a substandard environment. Imagery, which is etched in desolation and hopelessness, pervade the poem. In the last stanza, the dream, along with any hopes of a dream, have vanished. Brooks, like the best of other poets, succeed in making us sense, see, smell, hear, and taste quiet desperation. The reality of being left without dreams have been made concrete in this poem.

Gwendolyn Brooks has, indeed, earned the continuing series of awards that have come her way. It is no wonder that her life itself has been referred to as a living poem.

9

Chapter 10

The Conjunction–
Punctuation Connection:
Connecting Words and Clauses

10

▶ OBJECTIVES

In this chapter, you will learn to

••• recognize the coordinate conjunctions (FANBOYS) and subordinate conjunctions

••• understand the roles of independent (main) clauses and dependent (subordinate) clauses in sentences

••• punctuate correctly when using conjunctions

••• recognize conjunctive adverbs and use them correctly

••• understand the need for parallel structure with correlative and coordinate conjunctions

••• identify the structure of a sentence and appreciate the need to vary sentence structures

••• avoid comma splices, run-on sentences, and sentence fragments

Smart Connections

You already understand that excellent writing skills are acquired by learning and applying the rules of grammar. Rules of punctuation and grammar are inextricably intertwined. You will see in this chapter that learning to identify and use correctly the coordinate and subordinate conjunctions, as well as conjunctive adverbs, will enable you to write effective sentences, vary the structure of sentences, and punctuate them correctly.

A **conjunction** *is a word that connects <u>or</u> links words <u>and</u> groups of words in a sentence.* In the preceding sentence, look at the underlined words, *or* and *and*. Both words are conjunctions because each connects the word preceding it and the word following it. Conjunctions serve as valuable tools for writers. They can be used to avoid writing short, choppy sentences. If you use conjunctions wisely, you can smoothly connect words, phrases, and clauses—the important sentence components you will learn about in this chapter.

10

Also, when you choose a particular conjunction, you are telling your reader that the parts of the sentence you are connecting are of either equal or unequal status. It is important that you know the subclasses of conjunctions and how they work.

Each will be discussed in detail. The four subclasses of conjunctions follow:

- coordinate conjunctions
- subordinate conjunctions
- conjunctive adverbs (or adverbial conjunctions)
- correlative conjunctions

Coordinate Conjunctions (FANBOYS) and Independent Clauses

A **coordinate conjunction** *is a linking word that connects two or more words, phrases, or clauses that are similar in grammatical structure; that is, coordinate conjunctions link such items as -ing verbs with -ing verbs, nouns with nouns, phrases with phrases, and clauses with clauses.* When you connect two persons' names with the word *and,* you are using the coordinate conjunction *and* (Mary *and* James). The two words or groups of words that are connected by the conjunction are of equal status.

There are only seven coordinate conjunctions in our language, and you can form an acronym, a word made up of initials from the first letter of each coordinate conjunction. This acronym—FANBOYS—will help you to memorize the seven coordinate conjunctions. Here are the FANBOYS, those conjunctions that connect elements of similar grammatical structure in a sentence:

for, and, nor, but, or, yet, so

Be sure to memorize them before you read further. You must be able to recognize the FANBOYS so that you know which specific words within a title you cannot capitalize (see Chapter 14 on capitalization). You must know the FANBOYS so you will correctly punctuate compound sentences. You must know the FANBOYS so you can correctly punctuate items in a series, and you must know the FANBOYS so you will use parallel structure. All these requirements will become clear as you continue through this chapter.

But right now, if you have not memorized the seven words, *do it.*

Now, we are ready to proceed. The comma (**,**) is the most frequently used and *misused* punctuation mark. If you review the following information on comma usage and the FANBOYS, you will understand more about using this troublesome mark.

The Phrase Defined

Let us begin by reviewing the definition of a phrase, given in Chapter 8. A **phrase** *is a group of words that does not have both a subject and a verb.* You

10

already know how to recognize prepositional phrases, such as *under the bed* and *during the lecture.* You also know how to recognize verb phrases, such as *has been running, will have run, has already gone,* and *had been.* You also remember those verbal phrases, such as *running across campus* and *to look at the speaker* (see Chapter 8). Remember that the modifying/participial phrases can dangle. There are also adverbial phrases, such as *because of you* and *while there.* Now that you have refreshed your memory on phrases, let us move to clauses.

The Clause Defined

A **clause** *is a group of words that has both a subject and a verb.* Recall that a subject is the "actor" in the sentence, and the verb expresses the action the subject is doing or expresses the subject's state of being. There are two subclasses of clauses: independent and dependent. *An* **independent clause (or main clause)** *can stand alone as a sentence; it delivers a complete thought.* An independent clause may be part of a sentence. The first part of this sentence is an independent clause, although it is not standing alone as a sentence. See what I mean? Almost every word group in this book that begins with a capital letter and ends with a period or question mark is made up of at least one independent clause, and many have more than one independent clause.

Commas and Coordinate Conjunctions

Look at the following sentences:

Matt works at the bank.

Annie writes books.

The two sentences if placed side by side in a paragraph might be choppy. The FANBOYS help us to combine short, choppy sentences. When we use coordinate conjunctions, each sentence becomes an independent clause in a longer (compound) sentence. Look at the following combination:

Matt works at the bank**, and** Annie writes books.

Do you see one of the FANBOYS in the preceding sentence? Where is the comma? It is placed according to the rule for punctuating with one of the FANBOYS. Read and memorize the following rule, and you will always know how to use the comma when you have this structure:

Rule (FANBOYS)

When two independent clauses are joined by one of the FANBOYS, you place a **comma before the FANBOY.** Remember that the word groups preceding and following the FANBOY must be independent clauses; that is, each must have a subject–verb combination and express a complete thought.

10

TIP: Do not use a comma before the FANBOY if the word group following the FANBOY is not an independent clause:

Annie writes books and presents writing workshops.

Notice that we cannot place a comma before *and* because the words following *and* cannot stand alone as a sentence. It is, therefore, not an independent clause.

Now read the following sample sentences that demonstrate the use of the comma in compound sentences (sentences with two or more independent clauses). All seven coordinate conjunctions (FANBOYS) are illustrated.

1. **F** (**for**) Annie wanted to go to the picnic, for she knew Matt would be there.

2. **A** (**and**) Matt arrived early, and Annie arrived five minutes later.

3. **N** (**nor**) Annie did not like the hot weather, nor did she like the ants at the picnic.

4. **B** (**but**) Annie remained until after the fireworks, but she had grown weary of the activities.

5. **O** (**or**) Matt would go home after the picnic, or he would return to the bank to catch up on his paper work.

6. **Y** (**yet**) Annie thought Matt was intelligent, yet she wished he knew more about punctuation.

7. **S** (**so**) She knew he was an eager learner, so she continued to work with him.

TIP: When *or* and *nor* are used as coordinate conjunctions, a choice is implied. Also, the word order following *nor* is reversed. See Sentence 3 in the preceding examples.

10.1 EXERCISE FOR YOUR COMMA PLACEMENT WITH INDEPENDENT CLAUSES

Instructions: Insert commas where needed in the following sentences. If the sentence is correctly punctuated, celebrate.

1. The Milky Way is a galaxy and it contains approximately 100,000 million stars.

2. Traveling a light-year is beyond our comprehension and technology.

3. A light-year represents the distance required for light to travel in one year but such a distance is still beyond our comprehension.

4. A light-year is beyond our comprehension for it is a distance of almost 6 trillion miles.

5. The Sun is a star and it is located 30,000 light-years from the center of the galaxy.

6. No human has ever traveled 6 trillion miles nor is anyone expected to travel such a distance in the near future.

7. Some galaxies are much farther from Earth than the Milky Way so their light requires 10 billion years to reach Earth.

8. Congress may increase funding for space exploration or it may decrease funding.

9. Our Solar System contains the Sun and also boasts nine planets.

10. Our Solar System includes many comets and meteorites.

10.2 EXERCISE FOR YOUR SENTENCE COMBINING

Instructions: Combine the short sentences. For each pair of sentences, use one of the coordinating conjunctions to combine them. Be sure to use commas correctly.

1. Mercury is located closer to the Sun than any other planet in our Solar System. Pluto is located farthest from the Sun.

2. Earth's journey around the Sun lasts one year. Mercury's journey requires only 88 days.

3. Pluto is farther from the Sun than any of the other planets. It travels almost 248 years to complete its journey around the Sun.

4. The Sun is 93 million miles from Earth. It appears much closer because of its dazzling radiance.

5. The Hubble Space Telescope was named after Edwin Hubble. It is the largest telescope ever launched into space.

6. The giant telescope was launched in 1990. Its orbit is 404 miles from Earth.

7. This distance allows the telescope to clear Earth's atmosphere. The Hubble provides a clearer picture of the universe than is provided by Earth-bound telescopes.

8. Venus has valleys and mountains. Much of its surface is similar to that of Earth.

9. Nothing can live on Venus. Its surface temperature is about 900°F.

10. People used to think that Earth was at the center of the universe. Nicolaus Copernicus, a Polish astronomer, demonstrated that the Sun was at its center.

11. Planets in science fiction often have more than one moon. Some planets in our Solar System also have more than one moon.

12. Neptune has 8 moons. Uranus has 15.

10

13. Writers of excellent science fiction research carefully. Many planets in their works have more than one moon.

14. The zodiac comprises 12 constellations. They are the 12 signs used in astrological forecasts.

15. These forecasts are viewed by many people as mere superstition. Others read their astrological forecasts every day.

Dependent Clauses and Subordinate Conjunctions

A **dependent clause** *connected to the rest of the sentence by a subordinate conjunction can never hope to stand alone as a sentence, although it has both a subject and a verb.* If it does stand alone, it can be nothing more than a fragment, a piece of a sentence, alas, an incomplete thought. Just as dependents must rely on someone to support them, so are dependent clauses forced to rely on independent clauses. Without help, a dependent clause can never offer a complete thought. Shortly, when you read about the subordinate conjunction in this chapter, the relationship between the dependent and independent clauses will become clear.

You need to know that scholars sometimes refer to a dependent clause as a subordinate clause. They are the same. Do not let the terminology upset you. Remember that *sub-* as a prefix implies that something is secondary or beneath. Look at the words *subcommittee, subcontractor,* and *subsoil.* A subordinate conjunction, then, connects the secondary or unstressed part of a sentence (the dependent or subordinate clause) to the independent clause.

A **subordinate conjunction** *introduces a clause that cannot stand alone as a sentence.* The subordinate conjunction is the word that renders the clause dependent or subordinate. This is an important fact for writers to know. As you are aware, there is a punctuation rule you follow when you use coordinate conjunctions to connect clauses. There are also punctuation rules to follow when you use subordinate conjunctions, but you must first become familiar with the subordinate conjunctions themselves.

Unfortunately, the first letters of the subordinate conjunctions, regardless of their order, do not provide us with a memorable acronym. Read the following lists of subordinate conjunctions several times until you have them memorized or at least until you are sure you would recognize them.

The following words introduce dependent or subordinate clauses:

after	as soon as	even if
although	as though	even though
as	because	if
as if	before	in order that
as long as		once

10

provided that	though	where
rather than	unless	wherever
since	until	while
so that	when	why
that	whenever	

The relative pronouns *who, whose, which,* and *that* also introduce subordinate clauses. These clauses function as adjectives, modifying the antecedent of the pronoun.

TIP: Be aware that some of the subordinate conjunctions also function as prepositions. You must, therefore, be able to distinguish between a prepositional phrase and a subordinate clause. Following is a prepositional phrase: *After the game.* Here is a dependent or subordinate clause: *After I went to the game.* Look for a subject and a verb following the subordinate conjunction.

Following is a sample sentence that begins with a dependent or subordinate clause. The subordinate conjunction is boldfaced, and the subordinate (dependent) clause is underlined.

When Annie prepares handouts for her workshops, she realizes how difficult writing can be.

Remember that the subordinate conjunction means the dependent clause cannot express a complete thought without the help of the independent clause. If you read separately the two clauses of the sample sentence, you will realize that the last clause can stand by itself, but the first cannot. Also, notice where the comma is placed. You must learn two punctuation rules regarding subordinate conjunctions and dependent clauses.

Rule 1. (Subordinate Conjunctions)

When the subordinate or dependent clause introduces a sentence, a comma is placed after the dependent clause (not after the subordinate conjunction).

A number of sample sentences follow to help you understand and apply this rule. The subordinate conjunction is boldfaced, and the entire dependent clause is underlined. Each time you read a sentence, notice where the comma is placed.

1. The fact **that** Annie enjoys the students is obvious.

2. **As** she sat at her desk, she completed an exam.

3. **After** she finished the handouts for her workshops, she relaxed.

4. **Before** she began to write the first draft, she brainstormed and researched.

5. Goldpage, the small town **where** Annie was born, is sparsely populated.

10

6. **Since** <u>each of Annie's sample sentences begins with a subordinate clause</u>, she must use a comma immediately following the clause.

7. **So that** <u>her participants will understand the concept</u>, she is creating several sample sentences.

8. **Because** <u>specific rules guide Annie</u>, she uses commas correctly.

9. **After** <u>she endured the agony of writing</u>, she enjoyed the ecstacy of having written.

10. **While** <u>she drove to her writing workshop</u>, she saw two deer.

Except for Entries 1 and 5 in the preceding examples, all other sentences begin with subordinate clauses. If you understand the rule governing comma usage when the subordinate clause begins a sentence, you are ready for the second rule with respect to subordinate conjunctions and dependent clauses.

Rule 2. (Subordinate Conjunctions)

You usually omit the comma **when** <u>the subordinate clause follows the independent clause.</u>

In the preceding sentence, note that the subordinate conjunction is boldfaced, and the subordinate (dependent) clause is underlined. Notice also that there is no comma before the dependent clause (before *when*).

After you have memorized this rule, memorize the following exception: Use a comma when the clause begins with the subordinate conjunction *although* regardless of the placement of the dependent clause. In other words, even if the dependent clause follows the independent clause, you still use a comma when *although* introduces the clause. Sometimes, writers use a comma with a *because* clause regardless of its placement. They do this to show the clause is an afterthought and is not necessary to the meaning of the sentence.

Sample sentences will make this rule and its exception clear. Again, the subordinate conjunctions are boldfaced, and the subordinate clauses are underlined.

1. Annie enjoys teaching **because** <u>she enjoys the participants</u>.

2. She wrote in her journal **as** <u>she sat in front of her computer</u>.

3. She relaxed **after** <u>she had finished the handouts for her workshops</u>.

4. Annie brainstormed and researched **before** <u>she began to write the first draft</u>.

5. You would know the rules of comma usage with subordinate conjunctions **if** <u>you were Annie</u>.

6. Annie cannot use a comma before the subordinate clause **since** <u>her sentence ends with the dependent or subordinate clause</u>.

7. Annie is creating several sample sentences **so that** her participants will understand the concept.

8. Writing can be both agony and ecstasy, **although** she feels compelled to write.

9. She experiences the agony **before** she begins writing and during the process.

10. The ecstasy begins **after** she has completed a book.

11. Annie uses commas correctly **because** specific rules guide her.

12. Her participants can use commas correctly **once** she presents her series of grammar workshops.

TIP: Be careful not to place periods or semicolons after a dependent clause when the clause begins the sentence.

Conjunctive Adverbs

Conjunctive adverbs *describe the relation between two main clauses.* Some authors refer to conjunctive adverbs as sentence adverbs or as adverbial conjunctions. Whichever term is used, these words are unlike coordinate conjunctions. They cannot link two independent clauses unless a semicolon is used. Here is a list of the most commonly used conjunctive adverbs.

Adverbial Conjunctions

accordingly	meanwhile
also	moreover
anyway	namely
besides	nevertheless
certainly	next
consequently	nonetheless
finally	now
further	otherwise
furthermore	similarly
however	still
incidentally	then
indeed	thereafter
instead	thus
likewise	undoubtedly

There is a handy way to distinguish conjunctive adverbs from coordinate conjunctions. The coordinate conjunction cannot be moved around in a sentence, but an adverbial conjunction can.

Examples will make this clear.

Annie likes to write; she has little time, however.

Annie likes to write; she, however, has little time.

Notice that the adverbial conjunction *however* has been moved from the end of the sentence.

Annie likes to write; however, she has little time.

Notice that *however* has been moved yet again.

Had we used *but* instead of *however,* we could not have moved it to another place in the sentence. The conjunctive adverbs give us a bit more flexibility if we want to switch emphasis from one place to another.

Now here is a rule for punctuating conjunctive adverbs.

Rule. (Conjunctive Adverbs)

When two independent clauses are joined by a conjunctive adverb, a semicolon (;) is usually placed before the conjunctive adverb, and a comma is placed after it. Look at the following formula. **CA** stands for conjunctive adverb. The formula is followed by a sample sentence that applies the formula.

independent clause + ; + CA + , + independent clause + .

Annie likes to write; however, she has little time.

[independent clause] ; [CA] , [independent clause] .

The conjunctive adverb *however* can be replaced with the coordinate conjunction *but.* The meaning is not changed, but the punctuation is different. Look at the two sentences that follow:

Annie likes to write; however, she has little time.

Annie like to write, but she has little time.

If the conjunctive adverb is not located between two independent clauses, the formula changes. If a conjunctive adverb is the first word in a sentence, put a comma after it. See the example in which <u>however</u> is underlined.

Annie likes to write. <u>However,</u> she has little time.

If a conjunctive adverb is surrounded by fragments (pieces of sentences or incomplete thoughts), surround the conjunctive adverb with commas. Here is an example.

Matt likes to write. He, <u>however,</u> still has much to learn.

If a conjunctive adverb comes at the end of a sentence, place a comma in front of it.

Matt like to write. He still has much to learn, <u>however</u>.

Notice that clauses with conjunctive adverbs in the preceding sample sentences can stand alone as sentences, unlike dependent clauses.

Conjunctive adverbs provide us with still another tool for expressing our ideas and feelings. The more you know, the more confidence you gain as a writer.

Parallel Structure with Coordinate and Correlative Conjunctions

The **correlative conjunctions** *come in pairs, and most consist of one of the coordinate conjunctions combined with other words.* The following **correlative conjunctions** give us few problems:

as . . . as

both . . . and

either . . . or

neither . . . nor

not only . . . but also

whether . . . or

However, when you use correlative conjunctions, you must be careful to use parallel construction if possible. You must also use parallel structure when using coordinate conjunctions. **Parallel structure** *means that you use the same grammatical structure before and after the conjunction.* If, for example, you connect verbs with *and*, you must be sure that all three verbs are the same form. You could not use an *-ing* ending on one verb and a simple infinitive for the others. Sample sentences will clarify this concept.

Annie enjoys garden**ing**, walk**ing,** and writ**ing.**

Notice that each verb ends in *-ing*, which means the structure is parallel. Look at the nonparallel structure in the following sentence:

X Annie enjoys garden**ing**, walk**ing,** and **to write.**

Neither the participants nor the trainer liked interruptions.

The correlative conjunctions, *neither* and *nor,* connect the subjects, *participants* and *trainer.* Since *participants* and *trainer* are both nouns, the sentence is structured correctly.

Annie's latest book, *Easy Writer,* is a symphony that soars, a world that entices, a story that captivates.

Notice that the *and* has been omitted for the sake of rhythm, but the parallel structure is still intact. The *and* is understood and, therefore, dictates parallel structure.

As you can see, parallel structure can make writing memorable. Sometimes, however, parallel structure is not possible. Look at the following sentence:

10

Matt likes reading, painting, and mathematics.

In the preceding sentence, it is impossible to end mathematics in *-ing*. Whenever the language permits, however, use parallel structure with coordinate and correlative conjunctions. You will learn about parallel structure for phrases and sentences in Chapter 12.

10.3 EXERCISE FOR PUNCTUATING SENTENCES WITH DEPENDENT CLAUSES

Instructions: Insert commas if they are needed to set off dependent clauses. If the sentence is correctly punctuated, do nothing.

1. Because reading is a prerequisite to effective writing writers of engaging prose are also readers.
2. If you introduce me to a reader you introduce me to a fascinating person.
3. You cannot become an effective writer unless you learn the rules of writing.
4. Until Matt memorized all the rules for comma usage he was unsure about comma placements.
5. So that he would understand comma usage Matt practiced applying the rules to actual writing.
6. As his knowledge increased his prose improved.
7. While he edited his essays Matt sometimes had to look up a rule for comma placement.
8. He has now learned most of the rules although writing is still hard work for him.
9. After Matt polishes an essay he has a real sense of accomplishment.
10. He has a real sense of accomplishment after he polishes an essay.

10.4 EXERCISE FOR IDENTIFICATION OF INDEPENDENT AND DEPENDENT CLAUSES

Instructions: Underline each independent clause; place brackets around each dependent clause. In this exercise, look also for dependent clauses that begin with relative pronouns.

1. I know the town where Annie was born.
2. Annie, who is a famous writer, was born in Goldpage.
3. We cannot apply the rules of writing until we have learned them.

4. After we learn the rules of punctuation, our self-confidence soars.

5. I can write with increased self-confidence when I use commas correctly.

6. Whenever I submit an *A* paper, I know that self-esteem is rooted in knowledge.

7. My self-esteem really soared when I received my first check for a published essay.

8. Although I did not want to become a professional writer, receiving money motivated me.

9. I can now write at home in the evenings and receive money for my efforts because I have both knowledge and a computer.

10. Annie Penwright, who led our workshop at the college, has had a tremendous influence on Matt and me.

10.5 EXERCISE FOR COMBINING INDEPENDENT AND DEPENDENT CLAUSES

Instructions: Combine each pair of sentences to create a sentence with a dependent clause and an independent clause. Introduce some of your sentences with dependent clauses and others with independent clauses. Be sure to insert commas where needed.

1. I want to impress my instructor. I attend every class.

2. I attend each class. I at least let the instructor know about my dependability.

3. The instructor knows I am a serious student. I complete every assignment.

4. I work at a part-time job. I still find time to study.

5. I often study late at night. I work and go to college during the day.

6. Life is not always easy. I sometimes become discouraged.

7. I receive an *A* on a writing assignment. I become encouraged again.

8. I spend time and money to attend college classes. I must do my best to learn.

9. I graduate. My chance to receive excellent instruction will be gone.

10. College instructors work hard to help me learn. I must do my part.

11. I understand the importance of this time in college. My time could be wasted.

12. I receive a writing assignment. I think about it a great deal.

10

13. I have learned that logical thinking is a requirement for clear writing. I think now before writing.

14. I first approach a writing assignment. I often brainstorm.

15. It is easier to write a rough draft. I follow steps in the writing process.

16. I brainstorm, freewrite, and research. I write a rough draft.

17. I learned the recursive nature of writing. Writing was difficult for me.

18. I do not begin a rough draft now. I have brainstormed.

19. I formulate a preliminary thesis statement. I am ready to write the rough draft.

20. My reader will want to read my prose. I work hard to make it engaging.

10.6   EXERCISE FOR ACHIEVING PARALLEL STRUCTURE

Instructions: Rewrite sentences to correct any errors in parallel structure. If the sentence is correctly written, rejoice.

1. Students can either learn the rules or suffering the consequences.

   _____

   _____

2. Reading, writing, and arithmetic are considered to be the basics of education.

   _____

   _____

3. Both writing in a vacuum and to write without knowledge lead to failure.

   _____

   _____

4. Annie's favorite activity was not only writing, but also she enjoyed teaching.

   _____

   _____

5. She made her students understand that effective writing required both the knowledge of rules for writing and applying those rules to writing.

   _____

   _____

10

6. Neither a part-time job nor a schedule that was heavy would discourage Matt.

_____

_____

7. Whether you submit your essay or are rewriting it matters not to me.

_____

_____

8. Annie was speaking about parallelism and looked at Maria.

_____

_____

9. Not only was Annie attractive, but also she was being intelligent.

_____

_____

10. Annie likes to write in the early morning, gardening in the afternoon, and to teach in the evening.

_____

_____

Types of Sentences

Since you are now familiar with parts of speech, phrases, and clauses, you can easily understand the various types of sentences.

As you know, clauses have both subjects and verbs but can be dependent or independent. Every sentence has at least one independent clause.

You have probably been told many times by English teachers to vary your sentences, both in length and in structure. Learning the structural types of sentences will help you to choose the length and structure that best suit your purpose. The four types of sentences are simple, compound, complex, and compound–complex.

A **simple sentence** _is a sentence with only one independent clause, that is, one subject-predicate combination._ It is important that you understand, however, that a simple sentence may have more than one verb (a compound verb). A simple sentence may also have more than one subject (a compound subject). A simple sentence may even have a compound subject and a compound verb, but it will not have more than one independent clause. All the following examples are simple sentences. In each, the complete subject is underlined, and the complete predicate is boldfaced.

10

Simple Sentences

1. <u>This sentence</u> **has only one independent clause.**

2. <u>This sentence</u> **has one independent clause and no dependent clauses.**

Notice that sentence 2 has two direct objects of the verb, but it still has only one subject-verb combination.

3. <u>Annie and Matt</u> **work together on language skills.**

The preceding sentence has a compound subject, but it still has only one independent clause.

4. <u>Matt and Annie</u> **work during the day and dine in the evening.**

In the fourth sentence, we have two subjects and two verbs but still only one independent clause. It is, therefore, a simple sentence.

A **compound sentence** *has two or more independent clauses.* Each clause can stand alone as a sentence.

Compound Sentences

1. Matt worked late at the bank, but Annie went to the party.

The word *but* joins two independent clauses. Notice that each of these independent clauses could stand alone as a sentence.

2. Matt met Count Drack at the Whistle Top; Annie worked late and joined them for dessert.

The semicolon replaces a comma followed by one of the coordinate conjunctions.

A **complex sentence** *has only one independent clause and one or more dependent clauses.* In the following examples, the dependent clauses are underlined, and the independent clauses are boldfaced.

1. <u>While Annie worked at the computer</u>, **Matt dined with Count Drack.**

Remember that a comma must follow the dependent or subordiante clause when it introduces the sentence.

2. **Annie,** <u>who was the town's best writer</u>, **worked at the computer** <u>while Matt dined at the Whistle Top Buffet</u>.

Notice that the first dependent clause is embedded between the main subject, *Annie*, and the main verb, *worked*.

Now, you can practice writing complex sentences by adding words to the words already provided. Insert commas as needed.

1. <u>While I</u> _____

_____

2. _____

_____ as we _____

10

3. <u>Although Annie</u> _____

_____

_____

Here are some tips to help you check your complex sentences.

1. In the first sentence, you must have a comma after the introductory dependent clause—not after _while_. Then you should have a word group after the comma that could stand alone as a sentence.

2. In the second sentence, you will probably not have a comma before _as we_. You will have an independent clause before _as_.

3. You should have a comma after the _although clause,_ not after _although._

   A **compound–complex** sentence _contains at least two independent clauses and at least one dependent clause (possibly more)._ In other words, a compound-complex sentence combines a compound sentence with one or more dependent clauses. Again, the dependent clauses are underlined and the independent clauses boldfaced.

Compound–Complex Sentences

1. <u>While Annie was working at her computer,</u> **Matt was dining with Count Drack,** and **the bank president was playing golf.**

This sentence has two independent clauses connected with _and,_ which makes part of the sentence compound. It has an introductory dependent or subordinate clause combined with the two independent clauses. The combination makes this sentence a compound–complex sentence.

2. <u>The trainer taught,</u> and <u>the participants took notes</u> **as their participles dangled.**

In this sentence, the dependent clause follows the two independent clauses.
   Again, you can apply what you have learned by writing compound–complex sentences in the spaces provided.

10

1. _____

_____

2. _____

_____

3. _____

_____

Check your compound–complex sentences to be sure you have two clauses that could stand alone as sentences. Each of your sentences must also have at least one subordinate or dependent clause.

10.7 EXERCISE FOR IDENTIFYING TYPES OF SENTENCES

Instructions: Identify the type of each sentence by writing one of the following in the spaces provided: simple, compound, complex, or compound–complex.

1. She arranges all her canceled checks in numerical order, and then she matches the amount of each check with the amount in her records. _____

2. Each month, Annie reconciles the ending balance on her bank statement with the ending balance in her checkbook. _____

3. She writes "out" beside each amount in her checkbook that represents an outstanding check. _____

4. She totals the amounts of all outstanding checks, and she is careful to check the amount on the check with the amount that she has recorded in her records. _____

5. On the back of her bank statement, she records the ending balance that is shown on the statement, and then she totals all deposits and credits not shown on her statement. _____

6. She adds the total of all deposits not shown on the statement to the ending balance that she has recorded on the back of her statement. _____

7. From this balance, Annie subtracts the total amount of outstanding checks. _____

8. She is careful to subtract from this amount any charges for checks or any other debits shown on the statement that are not shown in her records. _____

9. After she follows all these steps, the balance she gets should agree with the balance in her checkbook. _____

10. If she is lucky, the two figures are alike. _____

10

Common Errors: Comma Splices, Run-On Sentences, and Sentence Fragments

To avoid certain kinds of errors in punctuation, you must fully understand the terms *comma splice, run-on sentence,* and *sentence fragment.* Memorize or at least understand the following definitions.

Definition of a Comma Splice

A **comma splice** *occurs when two or more sentences are connected with commas only, that is, without any conjunction.* This means that the writer has ended a sentence with a comma and has written the next sentence without capitalizing the first word. Of the following sentences, the first contains a comma splice. The others illustrate the methods you can use to correct comma splices.

X 1. Matt wants to improve his writing skills, then, he may receive a promotion.

2. Matt want to improve his writing skills; then, he may receive a promotion.

3. Matt wants to improve his writing skills. Then, he may receive a promotion.

4. Matt wants to improve his writing skills because he may receive a promotion.

Notice that in Sentence 4 I deleted the word *then* because it was no longer necessary. The subordinate conjunction *because* was sufficient. Also, notice that I corrected the comma splice by using three methods. First, I replaced the comma with a semicolon (do this rarely). Second, I replaced the comma with a period. This method is the most common and most preferred. Third, I inserted a subordinate conjunction. Sometimes, a coordinate conjunction (FANBOYS) can be used. Following is another example of a comma splice and its corrected version with the use of *and.*

X Annie attended the concert with Albert, Maria went with John.

Annie attended the concert with Albert, and Maria went with John.

If necessary, review the rules that govern punctuation when you use conjunctions.

Definition of a Run-On Sentence

Contrary to what many people believe, a run-on sentence is not a sentence that runs on and on and on. For example, in William Faulkner's *The Sound and the Fury,* one sentence "runs on" for several pages, but it is not a run-on sentence. It includes appropriate conjunctions and is correctly (some think miraculously) punctuated.

10

Actually, the term *run-on sentence* is a misnomer because it implies that only one sentence is involved. A comma splice becomes a run-on if the comma is deleted and nothing is inserted to replace it. *A* **run-on sentence,** *then, occurs when two or more sentences are "run together" without any punctuation or connecting words.* A run-on (or *fused*) sentence can be corrected by using the same methods used for correcting comma splices. Here is an example:

X Matt wrote an engaging essay he was later recognized for for his efforts.

A semicolon, a period, or a comma followed by a coordinate conjunction should be placed between *essay* and *he.*

Be sure to end every sentence with an end mark—a period, a question mark, or an exclamation point (use this one rarely).

Definition of a Sentence Fragment

If you accidentally drop a glass and break it, you will find pieces or fragments of glass on the floor. These fragments, caused by an accident, are similar in many ways to sentence fragments. *A* **sentence fragment** *is only a piece or part of a sentence because it fails to express a complete thought, although it begins with a capital letter and ends with an end mark.* To write sentence fragments accidentally or unintentionally is to make errors in your writing. Sometimes, writers create sentence fragments deliberately, and they work. Novelists, when writing dialogue, must write fragments. We routinely speak in fragments. An accidental written grammatical fragment, however, never works. It is an error.

A sentence, unlike a fragment, gives the listener or reader a complete thought. It has a subject (although sometimes an understood subject) and a verb. A sentence fragment may lack a verb or a subject or both. It can, however, have both a subject and a verb, but because of a subordinate conjunction, it may fail to express a complete thought. It may leave the reader hanging. Look at the following fragment: *When I finished my last essay.* The reader of this fragment naturally wants to know what happened after the writer fininshed the essay. Even if the next sentence explains the fragment, the fragment is still written as a sentence and is, therefore, an error. The fragment must be attached to a main or independent clause: *When I finished my last essay, I celebrated.* A sentence fragment can also be revised into sentence form: *Finally, I finished my last essay.*

Look at the following sentences that demonstrate sentence fragments. The accidental fragments are underlined.

X   1. Annie loves desserts. <u>For example, chocolate mousse</u>.

This is an added-detail fragment. It can be corrected by either attaching it to the preceding sentence or by transforming the fragment into a sentence that contains both a subject and a verb.

Corrected Versions

> **a.** Annie loves desserts, for example, chocolate mousse.
>
> **b.** Annie loves desserts. For example, she loves chocolate mousse.

X 2. <u>Because Annie wanted to complete the book</u>. She worked every day.

This is a fragment caused by the subordinate conjunction *because*. Beware of the subordinate conjunctions. Be sure to place commas (not semi-colons or periods) at the end of every dependent introductory clause. To correct this sentence, you can either remove *because* or replace the period with a comma and attach the dependent clause to the following independent clause. You can also insert a comma followed by a coordinate conjunction. See the corrected versions.

Corrected Versions

> **a.** Annie wanted to complete the book. She worked every day. (This is correct but a bit choppy.)
>
> **b.** Because Annie wanted to complete the book, she worked every day. (This is a good method of correction, but remember the next option, too.)
>
> **c.** Annie wanted to complete the book, so she worked every day. (By replacing a subordinate conjunction with a coordinate conjunction, you create a different structure. Awareness of all the options will help you to vary your sentences.)

X 3. Annie greeted Matt. <u>Sitting at a table in the Whistle Top Buffet</u>.

Corrected Versions

> **a.** Annie greeted Matt, who was sitting at a table in the Whistle Top Buffet.
>
> **b.** Sitting at a table in the Whistle Top Buffet, Matt greeted Annie.

To make sure you have not written a fragment, follow these steps:

1. Look for the subject (the actor) in a sentence.

2. Look for the verb (the action). Be sure that an *-ing* verb (if it is not a participle or gerund) has a helping verb.

3. Look for introductory subordinate clauses to be sure they do not end with periods or semicolons.

TIP: Here is a reliable method for detecting and correcting comma splices, run-ons, and fragments. During one of the several times you proofread your writing (always proofread your prose), begin by reading the last sentence first. Then, read backwards through the first sentence. In this way, your proofreading will not become just reading. Also, by isolating each "sentence," you can check to see if you really have a sentence. This technique will help you to find and correct comma splices, run-ons, and fragments.

10.8 EXERCISE FOR EDITING FOR COMMA SPLICES, RUN-ONS, AND FRAGMENTS

Instructions: Proofread the following paragraph and correct all comma splices, run-on sentences, and sentence fragments.

Proofreading Tips

As soon as we have written our last draft. We should proofread carefully. There are so many kinds of errors to look for. For example, misspelled words, comma splices, run-ons, fragments, and errors in grammar. Reading the last sentence first and continuing to read backwards. We can more easily find word groups that are not really sentences. Also, if we begin reading the last word, then the second to last, and so on. We can isolate words, then, we can more readily catch misspelled words. After all, computer spell-checks do not catch every misspelling, they will, for example accept *their* when we meant to write *there*. We should also ask someone else to read our writing, another proofreader will not have fallen in love with our prose. We do tend to love our own writing it is, after all, our baby. Regardless of its deformities and ugliness. We think it is beautiful. Because we want to find all our errors. Before our reader sees them. We must learn to proofread carefully, this means we must proofread small amounts of writing at one time. So that we do not become too tired to catch our mistakes. Also, it is a good idea to put our work in "cold storage" for as long as possible, retrieve it, and proofread it again. Proofreading and correcting all errors. We can be assured of receiving a high grade. At least, if the content is compelling. Knowing the steps in the writing process is important. Especially knowing those steps involving proofreading and editing.

10.9 EXERCISE FOR CORRECTING COMMA SPLICES, RUN-ONS, AND FRAGMENTS

Instructions: Rewrite each of the following items to correct the comma splices, run-on sentences, and sentence fragments. You may need to combine or separate the word groups. Be sure to insert punctuation marks correctly. If you find no mistakes in the item, be happy.

1. Because Matt learned a great deal about science fiction from his discussions with Annie. His interest in the genre increased, and he continued to learn.

   _____

   _____

   _____

2. The main genre to deal with technology. Good science fiction is usually a combination of scientific facts and the writer's imagination.

   _____

   _____

   _____

3. Frank Herbert wrote excellent science fiction. *Dune,* for example.

   _____

   _____

   _____

4. The characters in his famous *Dune* must conserve water, for example, they wear body suits that recycle their bodies' water.

   _____

   _____

   _____

5. However, *Dune* is much more than a story about the physical world, it is a story about the human mind, including its strengths and its weaknesses.

   _____

   _____

   _____

10

6. Offering one theme of power and its corruption. Herbert personifies evil in one of his characters.

_____

_____

_____

7. The obese character leans over a globe of his world. Placing one hand over the entire globe.

_____

_____

_____

8. Wearing expensive rings on his chubby fingers. The character is the personification of unlimited power and the evil it often generates.

_____

_____

_____

9. "I Have No Mouth, and I Must Scream" is a chilling science fiction story by Harlan Ellison, its main character is a computer that overpowers humankind.

_____

_____

_____

10. The last character living in the world is trapped inside the giant computer. Which plays cat and mouse with the character.

_____

_____

_____

11. Wanting at least to scream, the character has no mouth. He is doomed to silent and eternal entrapment.

_____

_____

_____

12. Many works of science fiction focus on our preoccupation with technology, perhaps to the subordination of human feelings, one example is Robert A. Heinlein's short story "The Roads Must Roll."

_____

_____

_____

13. Never a genre that highlights only technology. Science fiction explores the human condition.

_____

_____

_____

14. Annie discusses many science fiction works with Matt. Especially those works focusing on environmental and feminist issues.

_____

_____

_____

15. Containing all the themes of mainstream fiction; science fiction has much to teach us.

_____

_____

_____

16. From distant galaxies to the inside of a water drop. Science fiction offers a potpourri of worlds for our enjoyment and exploration.

10

_____

_____

_____

17. An organization of fine science fiction authors. The Science Fiction Writers of America was founded in 1965.

_____

_____

_____

18. After the association was founded. Writers of science fiction had an organization that would look out for their professional interests.

_____

_____

_____

19. Many science fiction writers of this century have distinguished themselves, included in a long list of such writers are Isaac Asimov, Ray Bradbury, Edgar Rice Burroughs, Ursula LeGuin, Theodore Sturgeon, A. E. van Vogt, Roger Zelazny, and, of course, Frank Herbert.

_____

_____

_____

20. Since both works weave technology and machinery into timeless fiction, Mary Shelley's _Frankenstein_ and H. G. Wells' _Time Machine_ have continued to influence science fiction writers.

_____

_____

_____

10.10 EXERCISE FOR USING COMMAS WITH COORDINATE AND SUBORDINATE CONJUNCTIONS

Instructions: Follow the instructions for each numbered entry. Answers will vary, and will not be given in the Answers to Exercises at the end of this book.

Examples

A. Use _and_ in a compound sentence.
   I am enjoying this class, and I am learning a great deal.

B. Use _and_ in a simple sentence.
   I am enjoying this class and learning a great deal.

1. Use _and_ in a compound sentence that you create.

_____

_____

2. Use *and* in a simple sentence that you create.

_____

_____

3. Write a compound sentence in which you use the coordinate conjunction *for*.

_____

_____

4. Write a complex sentence that begins with a "because clause."

_____

_____

5. Write a complex sentence that ends with a "when clause."

_____

_____

6. Write a compound–complex sentence. Choose your own conjunctions.

_____

_____

7. Write a complex sentence that begins with an "although clause."

_____

_____

8. Use the coordinate conjunction *so* to write a compound sentence.

_____

_____

9. Use the coordinate conjunction *or* to write a compound sentence.

_____

_____

10

10. Use the subordinate conjunction *whenever* to write a complex sentence. Begin your sentence with *whenever*.

_____

_____

11. Use the subordinate conjunction *as* to write a complex sentence that ends with an "as clause."

_____

_____

12. Write a sentence in which you have three items in a series.

_____

_____

13. Write a sentence with two subjects.

_____

_____

14. Write a sentence in which you include a "who clause."

_____

_____

15. Write a sentence in which you include a "whose clause."

_____

_____

SUMMARY

In this chapter, you have learned the subclasses of conjunctions and how to use them correctly. Remember that there are fours types of conjunctions:

1. coordinate conjunctions (FANBOYS) that connect words, phrases, and independent clauses of equal value and require parallel structure

2. subordinate conjunctions that connect dependent and independent clauses (unequal value)

3. conjunctive adverbs (words like _however_, _nevertheless_, and _moreover_) that show a relationship between two independent clauses

4. correlative conjunctions that connect words requiring parallel structure

You now understand the roles of independent and dependent clauses, and you know how to use and punctuate them correctly. You understand parallel structure and when to use it. You know the different types of sentences and their different structures. You have learned how to avoid the following errors when combining phrases and clauses: comma splices, run-on sentences, and sentence fragments. You are on your way to becoming a competent and confident writer. ■

10

10.11 END-OF-CHAPTER EXERCISE

Instructions: Annie's "letter" to a friend has been altered to include comma splices, run-ons, and fragments. Your assignment is to correct all such errors. Use correct punctuation.

Dear Jill,

Your request that I offer advice on advertising for your new gourmet restaurant was a welcome one. Because you and Jack have been helpful to me in the past.

You should choose a color for the paper of your brochure that is beautiful yet elegantly understated. For instance, a tint that might resemble the color of a gallon of white paint with only four drops of rich brown added. Ah, yes, that would do it. The color of the paper would dictate the color of the printer's ink, it, of course, would have to be chocolate brown.

The cover of your brochure might feature an artist's sketch of the famous old home. That will house your restaurant. The name of your restaurant, Top of the Hill, could complete the cover.

The language must appeal to a certain group, for example, it should have some snob appeal. After all, a connoisseur has acquired a taste that is discriminating, then, you should include the words *discriminating taste* in your brochure. Also, you can banty about a few choice words. For example, *bon appetit, elegant,* and *dining pleasure.* Scratch the last one, it has become a cliché. *Palate* is still good. If, that is, it is combined with the right words.

Jill, short of writing your brochure for you. I'll just mention a few tips with respect to the magical world of advertising. The language can provide a powerful tool, it can seduce, titillate, excite, and thereby bring customers—nay, clients—through your doors. Like the subtle color of your brochure that the customer never notices. The language itself will not be noticed consciously for what it is really doing, for instance, the diction suggested in the beginning of this letter appeals to

10

the reader's desire to be in a class apart. You can also appeal to your clients' other desires, they want to be happy and healthy. They want to belong, so choose words that appeal to those desires. *Highest standards, exclusive clientele, superb service,* and *ambiance,* for example.

Sculpted like a work of art. Language can serve your marketing purpose. You must, however, include some basic information. Amid the fluff of seductive advertising. Containing the name, address, and phone number of your restaurant, the time and days your establishment is open, meals served, and a mention that reservations are required. Your brochure will launch your new business. Do not mention prices, if clients need to ask, they cannot afford you.

If you couch the above information in persuasive language that is enfolded between the covers of a tasteful brochure. Your new restaurant will soon become the famous Top of the Hill. If I can be of further help, Jill. Just let me know.

Best wishes,

Annie

10

Chapter 11

Punctuation:
Additional Rules

11

▶ OBJECTIVES

In this chapter, you will learn to

- ••• apply rules for comma usage
- ••• use quotations marks with other punctuation
- ••• insert ellipses, brackets, and *sic* in quoted material
- ••• use end marks, colons, and semicolons
- ••• master hyphens, dashes, and parentheses

Punctuation marks are used to guide readers through your writing. If a mark is misplaced, the reader can become easily confused. Look at the following sentence:

X While Matt ate his dog slept.

Only when you read the last word do you begin to understand that the sentence is not saying at all what you first thought it was saying. You know a comma is needed because you know the sample sentence is introduced by a dependent clause. Once you see the word *slept,* you know where the introductory clause ends. The comma, then, should be placed after the word *ate,* that is, after the introductory clause.

While Matt ate, his dog slept.

The sample sentence with the inserted comma clarifies the meaning. The confusion is gone.

This chapter will help you to decide when and where to use punctuation marks correctly. Know, however, that even professional writers sometimes agonize over punctuation, especially commas. You will soon understand that rules for comma usage are sometimes contradictory. At other times, it is difficult to decide whether a part of the sentence is necessary for sentence sense (whether it is restrictive) or whether it can be deleted (nonrestrictive). We need to know such facts if we are to know whether to insert or omit a comma. Read the rules for comma use several times.

11

235

Comma Usage

Several of the following rules are already familiar to you but have been repeated for reinforcement.

Commas for Clarity

Rule 1. Use a Comma Before a Coordinate Conjunction That Connects Two Independent Clauses

The coordinate conjunctions are **f**or, **a**nd, **n**or, **b**ut, **o**r, **y**et, **s**o (FANBOYS).

Matt went home**, but** Annie lingered at the party.

If there are three or more independent clauses (a series), use a comma between the clauses and one before the coordinate conjunction.

Matt went home, Annie lingered at the party, and José went to a friend's house.

Rule 2. Use a Comma to Separate Items in a Series (three or more items)

However, be aware of disagreement among scholars and writers about one aspect of this rule. Here are examples.

Annie enjoyed the food, the music, and the sunset.
Annie enjoyed the food, the music and the sunset.

As you can see, the first sentence has a comma before the *and,* but the second does not. If journalism is your major, you will probably omit the comma. Most handbooks of English, however, recommend use of the comma before one of the FANBOYS in a series. Certainly, the comma prevents confusion that might occur if the items themselves are compound. Look at the following example.

X Annie enjoyed the delicious food and lively music, the beautiful sunset and warm breezes and the friendly people and relaxing atmosphere.

or

X Annie's dogs are brown, white and black and tan.

In each of the preceding sentences, the absence of a comma before the *and* that divides the items causes confusion. In the second sentence, we do not know if one of Annie's dogs is brown and black or if one is black and tan. How many dogs does she have? If we place a comma before either the first *and* or the second *and,* the confusion disappears.

Now try applying what you have learned. Write three sentences by placing words before and after each of the following conjunctions. Be sure to insert commas if you have an independent clause both before and after the coordinate conjunction.

1. _____ and I _____

_____

2. _____ so he _____

_____

3. _____ but _____

_____

Now, write three sentences in which you have at least three items in a series.

1. _____

_____

2. _____

_____

3. _____

_____

Rule 3. Use a Comma After an Adverb That Introduces a Sentence

First, we should begin with comma usage.

Suddenly, she saw the light of knowledge.

Again, know that some writers feel the omission of the comma after the adverb is also correct. To avoid confusion and to be consistent, use it.

Rule 4. Use a Comma Following a Long Introductory Phrase and an Introductory Clause

To write with confidence, the participants worked hard to learn the rules. (Introductory phrase.)

If you learn these rules, you will punctuate sentences with confidence. (Introductory clause.)

Learning the rules, the participants began to write with confidence. (Introductory participial phrase.)

Do you remember the dangling participle (see Chapter 8)? You already know that you must follow an introductory participial phrase with a comma. You also remember that you must be sure the _-ing_ verbal (participle) is describing the right word in the sentence, that someone or something is in the sentence doing the action. Look at the two examples.

11

X **Proofreading the essay,** a misspelled word was found.

In this sentence, there is no one who can proofread an essay. A misspelled word cannot read; therefore, the sentence contains a dangling participle.

> **Proofreading the essay,** the student found a misspelled word.

Proofreading modifies student; there is now someone in the sentence who can proofread an essay.

Rule 5. You Should Usually Use a Comma Following a Short Introductory Phrase

> **Because of you,** my heart is on fire.
> **During the winter,** Annie writes.

Writing is far more flexible than, say, math. The same flexibility, however, that makes creativity possible also presents gray areas that often make comma usage difficult. A few—very few—experienced writers omit the comma after a short introductory phrase if they think the sentence is clear without the comma. Part of the problem with omitting the comma after a short phrase is that when a longer phrase is written with a comma following it, inconsistency results. Throughout this book, I have strived for consistency by using commas after short introductory phrases. See my comma after *book* in the preceding sentence. I used such commas consistently for two reasons: I want my writing to be as clear as possible, and I want my punctuation to be consistent. You must ultimately make such decisions on your own.

Reinforce the preceding rules by applying what you have learned. Insert commas where needed in the following sentences. If you are not sure where to put a comma, check the rule noted in parentheses.

1. Feeling giddy Matt decided to leave the picnic. (Check Rule 5.)
2. Next he decided to stop at the Whistle Top Buffet. (Check Rule 3.)
3. He remembered Annie's saying that he should avoid words like *things stuff* and *interesting* in his writing. (Check Rule 2.)
4. While he was driving to the Whistle Top he remembered the difference between *farther* and *further.* (Check Rule 4.)
5. Driving farther up the hill Matt saw Goldpage's original character taking his evening walk. (Check Rule 5.)

See how well you did by checking the corrected sentences.

1. Feeling giddy, Matt decided to leave the picnic.
2. Next, he decided to stop at the Whistle Top Buffet.
3. He remembered Annie's saying that he should avoid words like *things, stuff,* and *interesting* in his writing.

11

4. While he was driving to the Whistle Top, he remembered the difference between *farther* and *further*.

5. Driving farther up the hill, Matt saw Goldpage's original character taking his evening walk.

Rule 6. If Part of a Sentence Is Essential to the Meaning of Another Part of the Sentence, It Is Said to Be Restrictive, and It Should Not Be Set Off with Commas; if Part of a Sentence Is Not Essential to the Meaning (Nonrestrictive), Set it Off with Commas.

Notice that the following "who clause" is not set off with commas because it is essential to the meaning of the sentence:

Supervisors **who work hard** will get more work.

If the "who clause" were deleted, we would not know which supervisors would get more work. We must not, therefore, set off the "who clause" with commas because we cannot throw out the "who clause." It restricts the meaning of supervisors (it is restrictive).

If part of a sentence is not essential to the meaning of another part of the sentence to which it refers, it is called **nonrestrictive** and should be set off with commas. In other words, you could take the commas by their tails and throw the material surrounded by those commas out of the sentence. The mention of commas' tails is simply a mnemonic device to help you remember that nonrestrictive material should be set off with commas.

Annie, **who is Goldpage's renowned writer,** is a trainer and lecturer.

In the preceding sentence, *Annie* has been named and identified. The "who clause" is simply additional information about her. It must, therefore, be set off with commas.

When you are using modifying phrases, clauses, or appositives, your inclusion or omission of commas will depend on their restrictive or nonrestrictive nature.

Rule 7. Use Commas to Set Off an Absolute Phrase, which is a Phrase that Does Not Modify or Connect Grammatically to Any Single Part of the Sentence but Rather Modifies the Entire Sentence

Unlike the dangling modifier, the absolute phrase has an implied subject. You could insert or delete a verb or change its form in an absolute phrase and, thereby, create a sentence.

The report completed, Matt left the bank for a stroll through the park. (The report was completed.)

The traffic having snarled, the driver began to lose patience. (The traffic snarled.)

11

The nervous chatter subsiding, the students began to take the test. (The nervous chatter was subsiding.)

The evening gossip exhausted, the writers went home. (The evening gossip had been exhausted.)

Rule 8. Use Commas to Set Off Parenthetical or Interrupting Expressions. A Parenthetical Expression Is One That Explains or Supplements

Examples will clarify this.

Writing on an electric typewriter, **for example,** is like traveling on the interstate in a horse-drawn buggy.

Even some authors, **many critics say,** need to learn the rules for writers.

Some fiction writers, **according to Annie,** could use lessons in comma usage.

Annie, **having finished the manuscript,** sighed with relief.

Apply what you have learned by inserting any necessary commas in the following sentences.

1. Count Drack called that because of his flowing cape was actually a riverboat gambler. (See Rule 8.)

2. Count Drack who was the town's most eccentric character liked to eat at the Whistle Top Buffet. (See Rule 6.)

3. Diners who eat at the town's most famous restaurant see both friends and foes there. (See Rule 6.)

4. No parking spaces available at the Whistle Top's parking lot Matt decided to go home and have a frozen dinner. (See Rule 7.)

5. The person who has patience can usually find a parking space. (See Rule 6.)

Check your comma placements with the following answers.

11

1. Count Drack, called that because of his flowing cape, was actually a riverboat gambler.

2. Count Drack, who was the town's most eccentric character, liked to eat at the Whistle Top Buffet.

3. Diners who eat at the town's most famous restaurant see both friends and foes there.

4. No parking spaces available at the Whistle Top's parking lot, Matt decided to go home and have a frozen dinner.

5. The person who has patience can usually find a parking space.

Rule 9: Use Commas to Set Off Phrases Using Words Like *Not* and *Hardly* to Show Opposition

The beginning writer needs more help, **not more criticism.**

Annie's brains, **not her looks,** made her a success.

The rocking of the boat, **hardly gentle,** kept the passengers off balance.

Rule 10. Use Commas to Set Off Tag Questions

It has been said that more women than men end their sentences with tag questions, **hasn't it?**

Supposedly, women's insecurity causes their sentences to end with tag questions, **doesn't it?**

Annie has never ended a sentence with a tag question, **has she?**

Rule 11. Use Commas to Set Off *Yes* and *No*

Yes, Annie is a confident person.

No, I don't believe I have ever heard her use a tag question.

Now, write two sentences. In one sentence, use *yes* and in the next, use *no*.

1. _____

   _____

2. _____

   _____

(Check Rule 11 if you need help.)

To reinforce the rules you have learned, at the end of each of the following word groups, write a tag question. Be sure to insert a comma if one is needed. Also, remember to place a question mark at the end of each sentence. (See Rule 10 if you need help.)

1. I do not end sentences with tag questions _____

2. Most people love grammar _____

3. Ending a sentence with a tag question does not mean we are insecure _____

Check your answers.

1. I do not end sentences with tag questions, do I?

2. Most people love grammar, don't they?

11

3. Ending a sentence with a tag question does not mean we are insecure, does it?

Continue connecting rules to actual writing by inserting commas where needed in the following sentences:

1. Annie not Matt teaches the writing classes at the bank. (Rule 9.)

2. Matt attends every session not every other session. (Rule 9.)

3. Writing is not easy is it? (Rule 10.)

Again, check your answers.

1. Annie, not Matt, teaches the writing classes at the bank.

2. Matt attends every session, not every other session.

3. Writing is not easy, is it?

Rule 12. Use a Comma to Set Off the Name of a Person You Are Addressing Directly (direct address)

Your shoulder pad has slipped and formed a strange hump on your back, **Annie.**

Annie, don't lose your confidence because of the shoulder pad.

TIP: Do not confuse names of people to whom you are writing or speaking (direct address) with people about whom you are writing or speaking.

- I like you, Eddie. (Second person/direct address.)
- I like Eddie. (Third person.)

Practice what you have learned by inserting commas where needed.

1. Jack you are applying the rules of comma usage.

2. I like your essay Teresa because of your vivid descriptions.

3. When writing an essay Tiffany you should brainstorm and list ideas before writing.

4. I told José to use a colon after the salutation in a letter of application.

5. Are you still with me Robert?

(See Rule 12 for help with comma usage in these sentences.)

Check your commas by noting the following corrections:

1. Jack, you are applying the rules of comma usage.

2. I like your essay, Teresa, because of your vivid descriptions.

3. When writing an essay, Tiffany, you should brainstorm and list ideas before writing.

4. I told José to use a colon after the salutation in a letter of application.

5. Are you still with me, Robert?

Rule 13. Use a Comma to Set Off a Mild Interjection (words like *oh*, *well*, *hey*, or *shucks*)

Oh, I thought a comma could be used after a salutation in a business letter.

Gee, what made you think that?

Rule 14. Use a Comma to Separate Coordinate Adjectives

Remember that coordinate means of equal value. In other words, each coordinate adjective modifies the word referred to in its own way, that is, without help from the other adjectives. Examples will clarify this.

The broccoli was fresh, tender, and tasty.

The Whistle Top Buffet's decor is quaint, cozy, and friendly.

The famous, controversial, and intelligent woman caught the diners' attention as she entered the Whistle Top.

TIP: When adjectives are coordinate, they can be rearranged in sentences. Also, you can place *and* between the adjectives. These two tests will help you to decide whether the adjectives are coordinate (and need commas) or whether they are cumulative (and do not need commas). Look at the example of coordinate adjectives:

The interior of Annie's home is large, cheerful, and sunny.

Notice that we could rearrange the adjectives or replace the comma between *large* and *cheerful* with *and*, which means commas must be used. Now look at an example of a sentence with cumulative adjectives:

The two small cats belong to Annie.

In this sentence, we cannot rearrange the adjectives, nor can we separate them with *and*. We, then, cannot use commas between the adjectives.

Rule 15. Use a Comma Within and Following Addresses, Place Names, Dates, and Long Numbers

My address is 68 Willowby Boulevard, East.

Goldpage, West Virginia, is Annie's hometown.

11

Notice that a comma is also used to separate the name of the state from the rest of the sentence.

Since September 14, 1985, she has been the town's famous writer.

More than 3,675,000 readers have enjoyed her books. ·

Rule 16. Use Commas to Set Off Words Identifying the Speaker or Writer of a Quotation

Matt said, "I feel giddy."

"I know," said Annie.

TIP: Note that the comma and the period are placed **inside** the **second** quotation mark. "Believe me," said Barney, "I want to write well."

Rule 17. Use Commas to Separate People's Names from Their Titles

Annie Penwright, Ph.D.

Rule 18. Use Commas for Appositives Only if the Appositive Is Adding Information, That Is, Could Be Deleted Without Leaving an Unclear Sentence

Remember that an appositive renames:

My husband, John, is also my classmate.

John renames *husband*; *John* is surrounded by commas because a woman can have only one husband, so *John* is adding information and could be deleted. The sentence would still make sense.

Look at the additional examples:

Annie's book *Easy Writer* was a bestseller.

In this sentence, *Easy Writer* is necessary because Annie has written several books, and we need to know which book the writer is calling a bestseller. For that reason, no commas are needed.

Nancy's dissertation, *The Way of the Wasp*, was not a bestseller.

In this sentence, Nancy has written only one book, so we know that the book mentioned has to be *The Way of the Wasp*. We, therefore, must enclose the title in commas.

One of Nancy's books *The Cricket on the Hearth* hit the bestseller list.

Again, Nancy has written more than one book, so the title cannot be deleted without loss of meaning. We do not separate such words with commas.

Rule 19. Use a Comma After a Salutation in a Friendly Letter and After the Complimentary Close

Dear John,

It's all over. We cannot see each other again.
With deepest regrets,

Missy

Review these rules often and use them for easy reference when you are writing. A general rule of thumb for comma usage is to determine if the material is restrictive or nonrestrictive. Can it be deleted without loss of meaning? If so, use commas to separate it from the rest of the sentence. If the material is necessary (restrictive), do not use commas.

11.1 EXERCISE FOR COMMA USAGE

Instructions: Correct any errors in comma usage by either deleting or inserting commas as necessary. If the sentence is correctly punctuated, be happy and move on to the next sentence.

1. Annie was invited to participate in a panel discussion for a local organization and she wrote a letter in which she accepted the invitation.

2. Her topic would center on her organizational skills so she prepared a few notes.

3. On the day of the dinner meeting she arrived early.

4. She was ready to serve on a three-member discussion panel but she learned she would have to speak instead.

5. She of course had no speech prepared.

6. She could not write a speech in such a short time nor could she speak without some kind of outline.

7. Self-assured, and knowledgeable she would move to Plan B.

8. She decided to read humorous excerpts from her letter, involve her audience, and end with a reinforcing statement of her main point.

9. Armed with hurriedly scribbled notes her letter and lots of speaking experience she approached the lectern.

10. Although, she was dressed appropriately, the communication breakdown had upset her.

11. Yes she had reason to be concerned for she had been prepared for a panel discussion.

12. She began with a deep breath, and a brief pause.

11

13. Next, she aimed a confident smile at her audience.

14. Dressed in a dark blue suit, a white blouse, and medium-heeled blue shoes she began her speech.

15. After thanking the program chairperson for inviting her she shared parts of her letter.

16. You asked me to tell you how I organized my time when I was a college student pet owner part-time employee community volunteer and writer.

17. Not knowing what this will do to your nervous system I must confess that I am not an organized person.

18. Margaret, whose opinions I respect, thinks of me as organized.

19. I may be organized but I regard perseverance and commitment to be as important as organizational skills.

20 With respect to my college days, I remember spending each evening with a different writer.

21. I might have spent Monday evening with Amy Tan Tuesday evening with Richard Rodriguez Wednesday with Mary E. Mebane Thursday with Russell Baker, Friday with Cherokee Paul McDonald and Saturday with Annie Dillard.

22. Actually I spent my evenings with their works not with them.

23. On Sundays I did countless chores for I no longer had the luxury of procrastinating.

24. Attending college is in itself a full-time job don't you agree?

25. Setting priorities, and learning to juggle became an everyday part of my life.

26. Yes I had to adjust to dust on my furniture.

27. I adjusted to frozen dinners, stacks of laundry, and dustbunnies on the floor.

28. I had after all more important things to do for I had dates with exciting writers.

29. During those long sessions of reading I encountered the prose of Annie Dillard.

30. Her descriptive prose is excellent but her imagination is divine.

11.2 EXERCISE FOR EDITING PRACTICE

Instructions: In the following paragraph, insert necessary commas that have been omitted.

Commas for Clarity

When we write commas must be used to set off mild interjections such as *oh* or *well.* Of course we should use such interjections sparingly. Writing that is clear concise complete and concrete is easy to read and understand. Commas may not do much to make writing concise complete and concrete but they certainly do help to make writing clear. We know for example that commas should be used in long numbers like 6324940. Also they should be used between city and state. Examples are New York New York and Charleston West Virginia. (Yes there is another Charleston.) A comma should also be used between the date of the month and the year. An example follows: July 4 1997. If you write a personal letter you must use a comma after the salutation. A business letter of course requires a colon after the salutation. All in all commas are handy little squiggles and each one guides the reader along the road to understanding meaning in any piece of writing. You do agree don't you? Since they help us writers to make our meaning clear we should use them with care.

Quoted Material and Quotation Marks

Quotation marks are used in pairs (" "). The first of the pair is used to open a direct quotation; the second is used to close it. By quotation, I mean the exact words that have been said or written by someone the writer is quoting. Anything that is quoted word for word should be enclosed with quotation marks. Quotation marks are not used, however, for indirect quotations. See the following examples:

Matt said, "I am working on my M.B.A." (Direct quotation.)

Matt said that he was working on his M.B.A. (Indirect quotation.)

If quoted material extends beyond four lines, you can indent an additional five spaces to set the quoted material off. Then, you can omit the quotation marks. Be sure your introduction to the long quotation makes clear that the words are quoted from a specific source.

If the quotation extends beyond one paragraph, begin each paragraph with quotation marks, but end only the last quoted paragraph with quotation marks. See the example. In her *How to Say Something in 500 Words,* Dr. Annie Penwright makes the following comments about writing clearly:

11

"It is certainly possible to write beautiful prose without saying anything at all. Have you ever read an article and wondered what the author was saying? Most of us have had this experience. The writer has not impressed us.

"The more educated we are, the more likely we are to stretch the language to its farthest banks. We, perhaps unwittingly, become linguistic peacocks, totally disregarding our reader's ability to understand what we are saying. We need, therefore, to ask ourselves continually why we are writing.

"If we are writing to communicate our ideas, that is, if we are writing to an audience, then we need to keep that audience in mind. We have a moral obligation to use language that is clear and to the point; otherwise, we have failed to communicate our ideas. We have failed to be considerate writers."

When you have a quotation within a quotation, use single quotation marks for the internal quotation.

The bank president said to Annie, "Matt told me he was going to 'work all evening' until he finished your assignment."

Quotation Marks with Other Punctuation

A period is used to end a statement. **When the statement ends with quoted material, the period (.) is placed inside the closing quotation mark.** See the following example:

Annie said, "Matt, I successfully defended my dissertation."

TIP: If you are using in-text citations, that is, placing your source at the end of quoted material, the period is placed after the citation. This is an exception to the period-quotation rule. See the following example:

According to a recent study, "M.B.A. graduates from prestigious colleges frequently cannot write grammatical sentences" (Hunk and Bright 1996).

Unlike periods and commas, which are placed inside the closing quotation marks, **the placement of question marks and exclamation points is determined by what is actually the question or exclamation.**

If the quoted material itself is a question, the question mark is placed inside the closing quotation mark. If, however, the entire sentence is a question, the question mark is placed on the outside. The same is true of an exclamation. If the quoted material is exclamatory, the exclamation point is placed inside the closing quotation mark. If the entire sentence is exclamatory, the exclamation point is placed outside the closing quotation mark.

Matt asked, "Has Annie gone to lunch yet?"

> or

"Has Annie gone to lunch yet?" asked Matt.

Did Matt say, "I want to take Annie to lunch"?

The manager said to the assistant, "Your computer is on fire!"

The assistant, according to one observer, ran out of the room "like a gazelle"!

When both the entire sentence and the quoted sentence are questions, the question mark is placed inside the closing quotation.

Did Matt say, "Has Annie gone to lunch yet?"

Colons are placed outside the closing quotation marks.

It has several ambiguous meanings, that word "relationship": it can mean going steady, playing the field, being engaged, or being friends, enemies, or friendly enemies.

Semicolons should be placed outside the closing quotation mark.

Annie says that her success is due to her "doing instead of dreaming"; she has shared that statement with her participants.

Quoted Material with Ellipses, Brackets, and *Sic*

When you use quoted words in your writing and you want to omit one or more of those words, there are specific—almost picky—rules you must follow.

If you omit words at the beginning of a sentence, you do not need to use ellipses, which are a series of dots. The following sentence will be used several times to show different situations for using ellipses: *Matt began talking about grammar and its connection to writing.*

"talking about grammar and its connection to writing."

No ellipses are needed because words have been deleted from the beginning of the sentence.

If you wish to delete words *within* a sentence, you must use three ellipses. To use them correctly, look closely at the following example. Pay *close* attention to the number of dots and the spacing. Notice that there is a space before and after each of the **three** dots.

"Matt began talking about grammar . . . its connection to writing."

The ellipses indicate that the word *and* has been omitted.

The rule changes if you are going to delete words at the end of a quoted sentence. This time, you will notice that four dots have been used. The last dot is the period for the sentence. Also, notice that there is no space between *connection* and the first dot.

11

"Matt began talking about grammar and its connection. . . ."

The dots at the end of the sentence indicate that the words *to writing* have been omitted. In an actual document, you would not know which words had been omitted; you would know only that words had been omitted.

If you want to add words to quoted material, you use brackets [ ].

The article said, "To understand nature [it was referring to nature's dark side], you must be an objective observer."

Sometimes, when you are quoting another writer, you may find an error. You do not have the authority to change the writer's wording, but you do not want your reader to think you have made the error, whether it is a grammatical mistake, a misspelled word, or simply inaccurate content. In this situation, you can write in brackets the word *sic,* which is Latin for *thus.* This insertion tells the reader that you are simply quoting, that the archaic spelling or misspelling or whatever is not yours. Here is an example.

"Matt began talking about grammer [sic] and its connection to writing."

Notice that *sic* immediately follows the error.

11.3   EXERCISE FOR PERFECT QUOTATIONS

Instructions: Insert necessary quotation marks in the following sentences. Where necessary, add commas or end marks with the inserted quotation marks.

1. Annie said Matt, remember that you must use commas to set off names of persons you are addressing directly

2. Annie said that she wanted the house specialty.

3. How does it feel to have your latest essay published asked Matt.

4. It was a thrill to see The Apostrophe's Catastrophe published replied Annie.

5. Matt asked, Was that really the title of your essay

6. When Annie replied in the affirmative, Matt said Wow

7. Annie said, Not to change the subject, Matt, but have I told you about the time I was asked to participate in a panel discussion

8. No, Annie, but I want to hear about it replied Matt

9. She said It could have been a disaster

10. The server approached the table hurriedly and said The restaurant is on fire

11. Standing in the parking lot, Matt asked Is that fire shooting from the roof

11

12. It certainly is said Annie.

13. He said This reminds me of the maxim about the best-laid plans of mice and men, Annie

14. Anyway, I do want to hear about your panel discussion added Matt

15. Oh, it wasn't a panel discussion; I learned when I arrived at the club that I had to make a speech, not serve on a panel said Annie as she laughed.

Question and Exclamation Marks

Always use a question mark (**?**) when the sentence asks a question. Use an exclamation point (**!**) when the statement indicates strong emotion. Remember that interjections, such as *ouch*, *zowie*, and *wow*, also indicate strong emotion and are followed by exclamation points when the interjections are used in isolation.

TIP: Always use exclamation points sparingly. Certainly, never use more than one at the end of a sentence. Overuse of exclamation marks will dull their effect. It is better to use words to express emotions effectively.

Colon Usage

Colons (**:**) are nice marks because they tell the reader that something else is coming. They are used for several other purposes.

Use colons to introduce a series if the introductory statement can stand alone.

We need the following items: pencils, pens, and staples.

Note, however, if the introduction to the series ends with a verb, such as *is* or *are*, a colon should not be used.

The items we need are pencils, pens, and staples.

Use a colon to connect two independent clauses when the second clause offers an explanation, amplification, or illustration of the first.

The bank has offered an incentive to its employees: It has agreed to pay for each employee's college tuition.

Use a colon in bibliographical items.

Penwright, Annie. *Easy Writer*. Boston: Mirror Press, 1996.

Use a colon between the hour and minutes, between volume and page numbers in bibliographical listings, and between bible chapter and verse.

6:30 P.M.

III:293–300

Matthew 12:1

11

Use a colon after a salutation in a business letter:

Dear John:

Semicolon Usage

Use a semicolon (;) between two independent clauses when no connecting word is used. Notice that a period could replace the semicolon in the following example:

Annie asks participants not to abuse the use of the semicolon; she stresses that too many people overuse it.

Use a semicolon between two independent clauses even when an adverbial conjunction (*however, nevertheless, therefore*) **is used.**

Annie enjoys writing; however, she has little time for it.

Use a semicolon to divide items in a series if the items have commas within them.

The participants included Don Bott, a doctor from Goldpage, West Virginia; Jonathan Smyth, a law student from Chicago, Illinois; and Jan Worthington, an engineering major from New York, New York.

Use a semicolon between two independent clauses joined by a coordinate conjunction if one or both clauses contain commas.

Working hard to motivate the participants, Annie felt she had succeeded; and, by day's end, she knew she had achieved her goal.

Hyphens

Acupunctuation
by
Lois-McBride-Terry

Hyphens gave me headaches—
I was half-insane, in-sane;
I suffered more from hyphen wounds
than semi-colon pains!
No remedy could bring relief,
till, out of desperation,
I found a perfect antidote
for splitting-word sensation:
I changed my writing style to one
called Hyphen-Ventilation.
Now no-more-pain upon my page,

11

from border unto border—
I'm hyphenating-every-thing-
in-one-big-new-Word-Order!

Use a hyphen to separate syllables in a word when the word comes at the end of a line. However, you should never divide a one-syllable word, and never divide a word at the bottom of a page. You cannot place part of a word on one page and the other part on another page.

The hyphen is used between adjectives that *precede* a noun and act as one unit. Look at the following examples:

gray-haired professor

20-page report

20- to 30-page report

Notice that the word *page* has been omitted after the figure *20,* but the hyphen is still used.

A hyphen is also used between an adverb and adjective that precede a noun and function as a single unit *if* the adverb does not end in *-ly*.

well-written report

but

clearly written report

Hyphens are used to form some compound words.

five-year-old

son-in-law

editor-in-chief

Hyphens are used in fractions and compound numbers.

two-thirds	forty-one
one-fourth	thirty-three
one-half	twenty-nine

Hyphens are also used to attach some prefixes. When a prefix is attached to a capitalized word, a hyphen is used.

un-American activity

pre-Civil War days

The prefixes *self-, all-,* and *ex-* usually require hyphens regardless of the words to which they are attached.

self-made woman	ex-convict	all-knowing
self-esteem	ex-employee	

11

Hyphens must also be used if the attachment of the prefix without a hyphen could cause confusion.

recreation or re-creation

recover or re-cover

TIP: Remember that the hyphen is only half as long as the dash, which is explained in the following section. Be careful not to type or write a dash when you mean to use a hyphen.

Dashes and Parentheses

Commas are neutral punctuation marks. Dashes are twice as long as hyphens. **Dashes (—) are used to emphasize, and parentheses ( ) are used to de-emphasize.** These important bits of information will help you to use these three punctuation marks to coincide with your emphasis or lack thereof. Look at the following sentences. Each should be read in a different way. Sentence 1 should be read in a neutral tone. Sentence 2 should be read with stress on the part between the two dashes. Sentence 3 should be read with a de-emphasis on the words within the parentheses.

1. Dashes, twice as long as hyphens, are used to emphasize words.
2. Dashes—twice as long as hyphens—are used to emphasize words.
3. Dashes (twice as long as hyphens) are used to emphasize words.

As you can see, dashes or parentheses can replace commas to set off a nonrestrictive part of a sentence.

Dashes are also used to set off a series within a sentence.

The essay—redundant, vague, and poorly organized—must be rewritten.

A dash can be used to signal a contrast or shift in direction in a sentence or to set off an inserted clause that is emphasized.

She wanted to write—not teach.

He deceived us—I don't think he meant to—when he asked us to believe him.

Use the dash sparingly; otherwise, it loses its value as an emphasizer. *Never use the dash to replace a period.*

Parentheses are used to enclose words that add information or interrupt. Commas can be used to separate such material from the rest of the sentence; therefore, parentheses can replace commas to de-emphasize parenthetical material.

The Civil War (1861-1865) divided our nation and sometimes even family members.

Mrs. Penwright (she is Annie's mother) will be here shortly.

Parentheses are used for initialisms, acronyms, and numbers that are repeated.

The Internal Revenue Service (IRS) has a great deal of power.

forty-five (45)

TIP: When you use dashes or parentheses to set off a sentence within a sentence, do not use a period.

Annie (she is a good writer) won an award.

If, however, the sentence within a sentence (set off with either dashes or parentheses) is an exclamatory statement or a question, use the appropriate end mark.

My 85-year-old mother—can you believe this?—just wrote a book.

My 85-year-old mother (can you believe this?) just wrote a book.

In any case, do not capitalize the first word of any sentence enclosed with dashes or parentheses.

11.4 EXERCISE FOR YOUR PUNCTUATION PERFECTION

Instructions: Insert necessary punctuation marks in the following sentences. If you find an error in quoted material, show that the error is not yours. If the sentence is punctuated correctly, just smile.

1. "Commas and periods should be placed inside the closing quotation marks" said the trainer.

2. Annie said that she especially enjoyed teaching at the bank.

3. Matt said, "Annie I especially enjoy your teaching at the bank"

4. Annie said, "Matt, the essay The Verbal and the Gerbil is my favorite."

5. "Can you tell me why the exclamation point and question mark are placed sometimes inside and sometimes outside the closing quotation marks" asked Annie.

6. Pounding her fists on the podium, Annie yelled with emotion, "You can use only one exclamation point in a lifetime"

7. Did she say, "You get only one in a lifetime"

8. Annie was joking when she said only one in a lifetime she makes learning fun.

9. The author's quotation is worth mentioning: "Grammer is an easy word to misspell."

10. Your computer is on fire

11.5 EXERCISE FOR CORRECT USE OF COLONS AND SEMICOLONS

Instructions: Replace incorrectly used commas with either colons or semicolons. If the sentence is correctly punctuated, be happy.

1. Annie's mother, Mrs. Penwright, wrote an essay on high school reunions, it was written in first person.

2. Just as she pulled the final page from her computer, she heard a loud explosion.

3. She had no electricity, the house was dark.

4. She wondered which of the following to do, drive to Annie's apartment, call 911, or stay calm and wait.

5. Suddenly, the lights came on, she could hear the hum of the refrigerator.

6. She turned on the radio, and the announcer gave the following information, a large gas line had exploded, and the forest was on fire.

7. Mrs. Penwright smelled smoke and saw fire, it was time to take action.

8. She went to the garage and retrieved her water hose, then she pulled it to the back of the house and connected it to the outdoor faucet.

9. Aiming the hose at the roof of her brick house, she turned the water on full force.

10. She heard her phone ringing, therefore, she turned off the water and rushed inside.

11. It was Annie she said that she and her friends were coming to help fight the fire.

12. Thirty minutes later, the following helpers arrived, Annie, Mrs. Penwright's devoted daughter, Matt, Annie's good friend, and José, a friend to both Matt and Annie.

13. All of them went to the garage and collected the following, rakes, hoes, shovels, and weedeaters.

14. The fire was out of control, indeed, flames shot high into the night air.

15. Firefighters could not get close enough to do anything, nevertheless, they were ready to work as soon as they could.

16. Wildlife scurried about as their habitat was swallowed by flames.

17. Annie saw many frightened animals that night, deer, rabbits, squirrels, raccoons, skunks, opossums, and groundhogs.

18. Eventually, the fire subsided, and Annie's mother prepared sandwiches for the hard-working crew.

19. Looking out the windows, they saw miles of smoldering embers and blackened and leafless trees silhouetted against a full autumn moon, miraculously, no one had been seriously injured.

20. Tired, hungry, and sad, the weary firefighters ate in silence.

11.6 EXERCISE FOR CORRECT USE OF HYPHENS, DASHES, AND PARENTHESES

Instructions: Insert hyphens, dashes, and parentheses as needed. In a few of the sentences, you may wish to use commas rather than punctuation to emphasize or de-emphasize. If the sentence is punctuated correctly, sigh.

1. A knock at the door it interrupted the silence startled the diners.

2. The knock came from a redheaded firefighter.

3. The firefighter a 20 year old woman was invited to eat.

4. She talked about the time she had worked a 24 hour shift.

5. The woman tired, hungry, and sleepy was obviously courageous.

6. The whole crew wanted to sleep not talk.

7. José his face was smudged with black smoke looked tired.

8. The food hearty sandwiches, potato salad, and raw vegetables soon disappeared.

9. José despite his smudged face was handsome.

10. José tall, dark, and intelligent had fought hard to save the forest and Mrs. Penwright's house.

11. Nonetheless, at least two thirds of the forest had been destroyed.

12. The redheaded firefighter it was later learned, by the way had earned countless awards for her bravery.

13. Her name this was learned during the introductions was Thelma Martinique.

14. Thelma a petite 5 foot woman enjoyed both the food and the camaraderie.

15. The conversation eventually turned to Mrs. Penwright's well written essay, and José asked if he could share a copy with his sister in law.

SUMMARY

In this chapter, you have learned the rules governing comma usage. You have learned that a nonrestrictive part of the sentence means a part that could be thrown out, that it interrupts or adds information. You have learned that such parts of a sentence should be enclosed with commas. You have learned how to use both double and single quotation marks correctly. You have learned how to combine them with other punctuation marks. Also, you now know the correct techniques for deleting words from quoted material or inserting your own words into quoted material. You can now distinguish between the dash and the hyphen, as well as use them correctly. You understand that punctuation marks can themselves change meaning or shift stress in a sentence. You have come a long way. Congratulations! ■

11.7 END-OF-CHAPTER EXERCISES

Instructions: Correct all errors in punctuation by either deleting, adding, or replacing punctuation marks.

High School Reunions   My high school reunion will be held in a few weeks, it will be my fortieth. Although, I have never attended before, I have decided to attend this highly-touted celebration. Each time that I received a well written notice in the past I tossed it in the trash because I thought I should wait. I thought my looks would improve if I waited, I would be beautiful thin and young looking. Alas Father Time continues to scratch a deep lined surface on my face. My lips and eyes continue to shrink but everything else gets bigger. I really should have attended earlier when I looked like Liz Taylor in National Velvet. Now, I just look like National Velvet, the horse. Of course I'm sure everyone else will have aged more than I, that's the real advantage of attending reunions.

My husband thinks that I don't know where he got such an idea I was an outstanding student beautiful, brilliant, and popular. I'll be hard pressed to explain to him why no one at the reunion will even remember my name.

You must wonder why I have chosen to attend this time; given my Delta Dawn looks and unpopular status. The years do; indeed, leave a philosophic mind. At last, I know my classmates will look beyond such superficial characteristics right as beauty and popular status. I have a successful marriage of thirty four years, I have a career that is often gratifying sometimes not, but that's another story and a business that grows steadily.

Father Time isn't winning all the battles, I may not be svelte and beautiful, but I still love life. For a 57 year old, I'm doing all right. I'll see you at the reunion, please remember my name, for Tom Penwright my husband will be with me.

Instructions: Correct all errors in punctuation. If the sentence is correctly punctuated, do not try to correct it.

1. One of Mrs. Penwright's recent essays "A Pocketful of Love" was published in a prestigious periodical.

2. While it is an essay about her grandmother; it is still timely.

3. Describing her grandmother, the author says My grandmother was remarkable in many ways.

4. Of Elmira Frame, her grandmother, she wrote the following, "She moved about her old house with regal dignity".

5. She wore her gray hair wound into a circle at the top of her head, it looked like a silver crown that belied her small income and simple homespun life.

6. A profile of my grandmother's character, industry, frugality, and charity, was the epitome of the Puritan ethic.

7. Work was her life, even when she sat down to rest, she was snapping beans or making the long magic curl of an apple peeling fall into a shallow pan.

8. Cataracts had damaged her eyesight; but her vision enabled her to see things most people never noticed.

9. As time passed we both grew older.

10. Despite her failing eyesight she made all her clothes.

11. Tiny stitches these were hand sewn stitches secured a large pocket to the front of each of her several aprons.

12. Filled with a variety of treasures, a change purse with money, gum, mints, and a handkerchief, that pocket came to be a symbol of her love.

13. Actually I never saw everything in her pocket, however, I can still see her hand reaching into it to give me a surprise.

14. Sometimes, she retrieved a small black change purse which she opened to fulfill my request for a dime or a quarter.

15. Whenever my childish heart was broken or my knee was skinned; she would again reach into that bulging pocket and pull out a bit of happiness in the form of gum or candy.

16. One day, she said to me, "Rebecca you must write about your childhood in Goldpage West Virginia".

17. My grandmother was always able to distinguish between my need and my greed; when I asked for a second piece of candy.

18. She said, "You must learn to use a little and save a little."

19. As I gained some of her insight. I began to understand just how little she had to use or to save.

20. In retrospect, I marvel at her ability to have managed her income so that something was always there for a rainy day.

21. She lived in a time when a woman's place was in the home, she accepted that most of the time.

22. Occasionally, I saw a dreamy far away look in her faded brown eyes.

23. Nevertheless her feet remained on practical ground.

24. She was a product of her time oh what she might have been in another day.

25. She had something special something that would transcend death, live beyond the grave, and endure through the ages, she had a pocketful of love.

Chapter 12

Transitions and Effective Writing Structures

▶ OBJECTIVES

In this chapter, you will learn to

- • • recognize the importance of transitions
- • • use pronouns as transitions
- • • choose appropriate transitional expressions
- • • master the art of repetition and parallel structure
- • • avoid illogical constructions

The Importance of Transitions

Without transitions, writers would be unable to write prose that smoothly leads the reader from one idea to the next. Without transitions, writers would be forced to use unnecessary repetition. Without transitions, writers would be unable to use repetition for special emphasis. Indeed, transitions provide the oil that helps readers glide easily through a well-written piece of prose.

Read aloud the next paragraph about transitions in writing. As you read, you will notice that the sentences sound choppy, that the repetition serves no purpose. No connecting devices link each sentence to other sentences. There are a few transitions within sentences, and they help. The paragraph could have had far more needless repetition. Several sentences have been "saved" by transitions.

Transitions in Writing

12

Transitions are important devices for writers. Transitions serve as guides to the writer and the reader. Transitions offer logical connections between words, phrases, clauses, and sentences. Transitions can transform short, choppy sentences into smooth-flowing prose. Transitions provide logical connections between sentences. Transitions can move the reader from one paragraph to the next by connecting paragraphs. The reader glides from one idea to the next. Transitions signal similarities, contrasts, and additions. Transitions announce sequence of time and place. Transitions indicate examples, intensification, and cause and effect. Transitions signal conclusions. Transitions provide choppy prose with rhythm, logic, and smoothness.

Almost any sentence in the preceding paragraph could be pulled from the paragraph and not be missed. Most effective writing is not like that. Everything must be bound to something else. The preceding paragraph is like a brick wall that has been laid with no cement to bind one brick to another. The paragraph is little more, then, than a stack of sentences that could easily fall apart.

Pronouns as Transitions

In the sample paragraph, using pronouns to replace the much-repeated word *transitions* at the beginning of several sentences would help. Pronouns prevent such needless echoing. The personal pronouns, as you remember from Chapter 5, refer to nouns and can, therefore, connect sentences logically and smoothly. If you reread the paragraph, using *they* sometimes, instead of endlessly repeating *transitions*, you will see an immediate improvement in the style.

Transitional Expressions

Transitions help you to direct readers through your prose in much the same way that road markers direct travelers to their destinations. Readers know what to expect because of transitions. They help you to show similarities, to make comparisons. With transitions, you can add information or put a series of items in proper sequence. You can also indicate differences and contrasts. Giving examples, emphasizing information, and showing cause and effect are all easier because of that wonderful writing device, the transition. Listed are some of the most commonly used transitions.

Transitions to Indicate Similarities

also	in comparison
in the same way/manner	likewise
similarly	

Transitions move readers smoothly from one idea to the next. **Likewise,** they offer certain expectations **in the same way** road signs offer clues to destinations.

12

Transitions to Indicate Additions or Sequence

in addition	also
moreover	and
and then	next
then	finally
last	furthermore
in the first place	meanwhile
first, second, third . . .	

In the first place, sentences strung together without transitions are often choppy. **Furthermore,** such omissions can cause confusion.

Transitions to Show Contrast

although (even though)	but
however	despite
nevertheless	on the contrary
otherwise	yet
regardless	still

on the other hand (Be sure you have used *on the one hand,* first.)

Regardless of the writer's correctly constructed sentences, a lack of transitions is a flaw. **Despite** a writer's excellent choice of words, sentences strung together without transitional expressions are unsatisfactory.

Transitions to Indicate Examples or Intensification

for example	for instance
indeed	in fact
specifically	truly
to illustrate	of course
after all	

Learning to use transitions effectively can, **indeed,** improve the flow of our writing. **After all,** we want our reader to have a sense of direction.

Transitions to Indicate Cause/Effect

as a result	consequently
because	therefore
then	thus
accordingly	since

Beginning writers frequently omit transitions. **As a result,** their sentences seem disjointed. **Because** these writing devices provide an excellent device for achieving smooth prose, we should use them.

12

12.1 EXERCISE FOR SMOOTH TRANSITIONS

Instructions: Rewrite the paragraph in this chapter, which is titled "Transitions in Writing." This time, insert transitions. Also, you may wish to combine sentences, delete words, or otherwise improve the style.

Transitions in Writing

Repetition and Parallel Structure

Repetition and parallel structure are powerful writing devices. Although pointless or accidental repetition can create monotony, deliberate repetition, properly used, can strengthen writing and reinforce the message or main point. If you reread the first paragraph in this chapter, you will find an effective use of repetition. The words *without transitions, writers would be* are repeated at the beginning of the first three sentences. Such purposeful repetition gives the prose rhythm—a beat—that intensifies the message. Repetition and parallelism give your prose cadence. Look at the following excerpt from one of my speeches, in which I have boldfaced the repetition:

When my young world was green and full of promise, **when my** friends and I could fly high over rooftops and emerald green hills, **when** we could be Captain Marvel, Superman, and movies stars rolled into one, **when** anything was possible, Sattes Cemetery was a focal point in our lives.

In the preceding example, both repetition of words and grammatical patterns (parallel structure) work together.

Parallel structure *is the repetition of the same grammatical structure, and like repetition of words, it can be a powerful force in both writing and speaking.* Parallelism used in successive sentences can be effective.

Some plots **were surrounded by metal fences.** Others **were marked by white picket fences.** Still others **were enclosed by neat borders of grass.** Each plot was different.

Notice the passive construction in each of the first three sentences. The last sentence receives emphasis partly because of its brevity and partly because of its change in structure.

Occasionally, you can replace commas in a series with *and* to suggest an ongoing process or to emphasize the message with the structure itself. When you do this, use parallel structure. Read aloud the excerpt from the same speech.

Many of the names on the tombstones had been obliterated by wind and rain and snow and, of course, the unrelenting passage of time.

Notice that the last item in the series contains the required noun, but the noun *passage* is preceded by an adjective and followed by a prepositional phrase. The addition of words in the last item prevents monotony. Now read aloud the same sentence with commas.

12

Many of the names on the tombstones had been obliterated by wind, rain, snow, and, of course, the unrelenting passage of time.

Which do you think is more effective? These are stylistic choices, but what a difference your choices can make.

Repetition of grammatical patterns works well in the following examples taken from my book review of Curt Leviant's novel *The Man Who Thought He Was Messiah*. (The review was published in the *Charleston Daily Mail*, March 1, 1991.)

"Caught between **darkness and light, order and chaos, flesh and spirit,** Nachman begins a spiritual journey in search of self-identity. . . ."

In each of the three boldfaced phrases, the coordinate conjunction links nouns. The parallel structure provides rhythm.

"Leviant's latest work is **a symphony that soars, a mystical world that entices, a story that captivates.**"

Here, each of the three boldfaced word groups begins with the article, *a.* In the first and third word groups, a noun follows *a,* but in the second, the adjective, *mystical,* precedes the noun, *world.* Such slight deviation is acceptable. All three word groups end with *that* plus a verb. Notice that there is no *and* used to connect the middle and last word groups. This was a stylistic decision. You can read the sentence aloud, first inserting the *and,* then omitting it. This is how I made the decision not to include the conjunction.

To increase your awareness of the beauty and structure of language, you must read, read, read. As you continue to become more aware of language and structure, you will develop an increasingly sensitive "ear" for what works and what does not. Repetition, parallelism, and other kinds of transitions must be used carefully, lest they become wooden, mechanical.

Pitfalls with Parallelism

In Chapter 10, you learned about the need to maintain parallel constructions in elements joined by correlative and coordinate conjunctions. Whenever you need parallel structure, you must make sure that your structures *are* parallel. As you can see by the examples, you can easily makes mistakes if you are unaware of parallelism.

Coordinate conjunctions require parallel structure.

X Her workshops were both informative and appeared to be fun.

Her workshops were both informative and enjoyable.

X Annie likes to write personal essays, teach writing workshops, and working in her garden.

Annie likes to write personal essays, teach writing workshops, and work in her garden.

When comparing two elements, be careful to include parallel structure; otherwise, you might confuse the reader.

X William Faulkner's writing is quite different from Ernest Hemingway.

William Faulkner's writing is quite different from Ernest Hemingway's writing.

X José is not tall as Matt.

José is not as tall as Matt.

When using correlative conjunctions, be sure to complete the second half of your parallel structure.

X Not only did Hemingway create short sentences, but also few adjectives.

Not only did Hemingway create short sentences, but also he used few adjectives.

For parallel structure with two "that clauses" connected by *and,* repeat *that.*

X Matt told Annie that he enjoyed her workshops, and he planned to attend others.

Matt told Annie that he enjoyed her workshops and that he planned to attend others.

If you repeat an adjective or a modifier in a series, repeat it with each item; otherwise, use the modifier with only the first item.

X The firefighters enjoyed their sandwiches, their colas, and salads.

The firefighters enjoyed their sandwiches, their colas, and their salads.

or

The firefighters enjoyed their sandwiches, colas, and salads.

Be sure to include all necessary words in parallel structure.

X Mrs. Penwright was proud and interested in Annie's writing.

Mrs. Penwright was proud of and interested in Annie's writing.

Be sure to use parallelism with *neither . . . nor.*

X Annie was not a mathematician, and neither was her mother.

Neither Annie nor her mother was a mathematician.

12

12.2 EXERCISE FOR IDENTIFYING REPETITION AND PARALLELISM

Instructions: Underline all parallel structures and effective repetition in the following excerpt from one of my speeches. Just above each underlined structure, identify the repetition or parallelism by writing one of the following: coordinate conjunction, correlative conjunction, comparison, effective repetition.

The Devil Made Me Do It

First, I want to ask you a few questions. Are you a leader or a follower? Are you a dreamer or a doer, a whiner or a winner? Are you a protester against authority or a provider of fresh ideas?

Before you answer these questions, travel with me on an armchair journey all the way back to the Great Depression in the early 1930s. Most people in West Virginia, my home state, were poor, had been poor, and would continue to be poor. Poverty during those bleak, gray days was so severe, so widespread that you might think crime was rampant. It was not. Despite the poverty, people seldom locked their doors.

Today, crime is repeatedly blamed on poverty, but the experiences of West Virginians during a time of abject poverty do not support such an oft-repeated assertion—an assertion that has become a myth. People from both poor and wealthy backgrounds commit crimes.

The big myth I am shattering is the myth that people commit dastardly acts because of the system or because of their parents or because of their unfair teachers or because of society as a whole. We have ready excuses for almost any negative behavior, and the excuses make the perpetrator feel purged, exonerated. The rest of us are burdened with guilt for others' actions: those of us who have obeyed the laws, who have worked hard, who have been good students, good parents, and good citizens. We have worked and planned and made wise decisions, but we have nonetheless been targeted as the bad guys.

It is time we put a halt to this devil-made-me-do-it mentality. If I decide to take that first drink, smoke that first cigarette, or experiment with that popular drug of the day, that decision is mine and mine alone. If I blame society for the consequences, I am a whiner, a mimic.

Think about it. When you make decisions to avoid addictive and destructive behavior, you are paving the way to becoming a winner—not a whiner, a leader—not a follower, a thinker—not a mimic.

Despite your supportive teachers and professors, you cannot succeed unless you make a commitment to learning, unless you study, unless you read, unless you complete the assignments. It is, then, not who your parents are, but who you are; it is not who your friends are, but who you are. It is not where you live or where you attend college. Peer pressure cannot make you commit any act you do not wish to commit. You alone must take responsibility for your decisions. You will live with their rewards or their consequences.

Additional Faulty Constructions

Sometimes, we write such a long sentence that the meaning conveyed in the sentence is not what we really intended to say at all.

X The ability of Annie to write effectively teaches others by providing samples of her own works.

Although we do not mean that *ability* can teach and provide examples, that is exactly what this sentence is saying.

Annie, because she writes effectively, can teach others by providing examples of her own work.

When we try to impress instead of communicate, we often construct unclear sentences.

X It is incumbent upon us participants, subsequent to Annie's request, that all assignments be completed with care.
We participants must comply with Annie's request to complete all assignments with care.

When using *not so much,* use *as* instead of *but rather.*

X Mrs. Penwright was not so much shy but rather reserved.
Mrs. Penwright was not so much shy as she was reserved.

12

When using *seemed more like,* be careful not to insert *rather* when you need only *than.*

X Annie seemed more like a leader rather than a follower.

Annie seemed more like a leader than a follower.

TIP: Do not be afraid to break up long confusing sentences into two or more shorter sentences that are clear.

SUMMARY

This chapter has alerted you to the importance of transitions. You have learned that transitions can be used to make comparisons and to add information. They can help you to organize information into proper sequence. They can show contrasts, give examples, emphasize information, and show cause and effect. You now are aware of the difference between needless repetition and repetition used for a specific purpose. You have been cautioned to check for parallel structure. You know the pitfalls to avoid when using parallelism. You have learned to check your sentence structures to be sure they have not become so cumbersome they mislead the reader. You know to look for additional pitfalls in structure. You can use with confidence transitions, repetition, and parallelism to produce effective—even powerful—prose. ∎

12.3 END-OF-CHAPTER EXERCISES

Instructions: Rewrite each sentence, correcting all faulty constructions. If the sentence is correct, smile.

1. The Declaration of Independence says, "Prudence, indeed, will dictate that Governments long established should not be changed for light and transient causes. . . ."

   _____

   _____

   _____

2. Life is both rhythmic and appears to be cyclic.

   _____

   _____

   _____

3. The rhythm created by repetition and parallelism in writing is similar to life.

   _____

   _____

   _____

4. Still, repetition in writing is not consistent as repetition in life.

   _____

   _____

   _____

5. Not only does Annie use parallel structure in her prose but also repetition.

   _____

   _____

   _____

6. Annie tells her participants that life has cadence, and it has repetition; therefore, we are pleased when we find rhythm in writing.

   _____

   _____

   _____

7. Life's rhythm can be found in the cycle of seasons, the cadence of heartbeats, repetition of day and night, and even in routines of all living creatures.

_____

_____

_____

8. To be sensitive and aware of life's cyclic nature is to understand the need for rhythm in our own writing.

_____

_____

_____

9. Matt was not a naturalist, and neither was Annie.

_____

_____

_____

10. Like a person wearing too much makeup, the man's prose was peppered with unfamiliar words, nonparallel structures, and long garbled sentences.

_____

_____

_____

11. He was not so much trying to communicate, but rather was trying to impress.

_____

_____

_____

12. He seemed more like a beginning writer rather than an author.

_____

_____

_____

13. Under Annie's guidance, his prose gradually became clear, rhythmic, and powerful.

_____

_____

_____

14. His writing—like life itself—was pleasant in its cadence, effective in its repetition, and clarity.

_____

_____

_____

15. To promote unity, the writers of the *Declaration of Independence* ended the famous document with these words: "we mutually pledge to each other our lives, our Fortunes, and our sacred Honor"; they understood the power of parallelism.

_____

_____

_____

Instructions: Write a well-developed paragraph (at least ten sentences) on peer pressure. Use the writing techniques covered in this chapter. Be sure to proofread for errors in grammar, punctuation, word choice, and constructions. Answers will vary and will not be given in the Answers to Exercises at the end of the book.

_____

_____

_____

_____

_____

_____

_____

_____

_____

_____

_____

_____

_____

_____

_____

_____

12

PART III

**Spelling, Capitalization,
Mechanics, and Numbers**

Spelling, Pluralization, and Apostrophe Usage

13

OBJECTIVES

In this chapter, you will learn to

••• gain a more positive attitude toward spelling skills

••• learn how computer spell checkers can help and hinder

••• form the habit of using the dictionary

••• discover an approach to mastering your own spelling demons

••• understand the value and shortcomings of spelling and pluralization rules

••• use the apostrophe correctly

Attitude Toward Spelling

Once you feel confident about choosing the precise words for your specific audience and purpose, you must be sure that all your words are spelled correctly.

If you have been a weak speller for many years, you probably need first to change your attitude about yourself. For example, most poor spellers think of themselves as poor spellers. It is as if the label they attach to themselves offers an enduring excuse that will permit them to continue misspelling words. They seem to believe they cannot improve their spelling skills any more than they can change the natural color of their eyes. This is simply not so; poor spellers can and do become better spellers. Believe it, and your attitude will offer promise of improvement.

Here are two facts to let you know you are not alone with your spelling weaknesses: (1) Many of the best professional writers have spelling problems, and (2) many words in our lexicon cause spelling problems for everyone. Be aware that all writers have certain words they will look up again and again as long as they write.

13

279

Aids in Spelling Correctly

Besides gaining a positive attitude toward your ability to become a better speller, you should form habits that will improve your spelling. Learn to use your dictionary and spell checker on your computer. In addition, keep a list of the words you frequently misspell.

Computer Spell Checkers

If you write with the aid of a computer, and I hope you do, your software probably has some kind of spell checker. Use it. Every time you add words to your manuscript, use it.

Computer spell checkers are helpful, but they do have limitations. For example, if you have used the word *their* when you meant to use *there*, most spell checkers will not catch your error. If you have mistakenly added an *-s* to a word or omitted an *-s*, your computer will accept your error gleefully, we often think. If you have software that calls attention to errors in grammar, and the addition or deletion of an *-s* has caused such an error, your computer will catch it. Nonetheless, even after you have used a computer spell checker, you still must proofread carefully.

Use of Dictionaries

As noted in Chapter 2, dictionaries are essential aids in choosing words, and they are also essential in spelling words correctly. You can purchase several kinds of dictionaries, but your most valuable aid is a hardback collegiate dictionary. Since our language is constantly changing, dictionaries become outdated quickly. Try, then, to have a dictionary that is current, certainly not more than about five years old. Remember that new words are added to our lexicon continually.

Some words are listed in the dictionary with more than one spelling. Choose the first listing. For example, most dictionaries list *judgment* as a first choice, followed by *judgement* as a second choice. The first spelling, without the extra *e*, is the American spelling of the word; the second choice is the British spelling. American edited English is the English of business and academia within the United States. Also, be alert to connotations of words, those implied meanings. Use a collegiate dictionary to check all listed definitions; then think about implied meanings.

You can find other kinds of information about words listed in a collegiate dictionary. You can, for example, find a word's part of speech, its source, its pronunciation, and its various definitions. Also, most hardback collegiate dictionaries contain listings of colleges and universities, names and biographical sketches of famous people, geographical information, symbols, tables, and frequently used foreign words and phrases. As you can see, an up-to-date dictionary is a priceless tool for every writer. Keep one handy as you write.

13

A thesaurus is another kind of dictionary. Depending on its type, a thesaurus will give you synonyms or antonyms arranged according to category. You must exercise some caution when you use a thesaurus to find a synonym. The synonym listed beside the boldfaced word you have looked up is the synonym that best replaces the boldfaced word. As the synonyms move farther and farther from the boldfaced word, the less likely they are to be suitable replacements. In other words, the synonyms are arranged in diminishing order insofar as their ability to replace the boldfaced word.

Do not use a thesaurus just to find a longer or more impressive word. The simple, easy-to-understand word is likely to be the most effective word (of course, you should avoid slang except for special effect in fiction or informal writing).

As also noted in Chapter 2, usage dictionaries offer yet another kind of information, and they are valuable for the precise writer. These dictionaries tackle the often controversial usages of words. For instance, some collegiate dictionaries might offer *disinterested* as a synonym for *uninterested*. A usage dictionary will not. Instead, its editors typically poll a panel of language scholars and give the consensus of that panel on the usage of a particular word. A usage dictionary usually keeps the fine-line distinction between similar or frequently misused words. It would, for example, indicate that *disinterested* means impartial or fair and that *uninterested* means not interested.

Lists of Troublesome Words

In Chapter 2, you studied pairs and sets of words whose spellings are often confused. Of course, there are many other words that present spelling problems. Here is a list of commonly misspelled words with tips to help you remember their spellings. Obviously, this list is far from comprehensive. Its point is to show you examples of memorable tips you can create for words that give you trouble.

Demon Words	Memorable Tips
accommodate	**C C** the **M** and **M.** This word has **two c's** and **two m's.**
a lot	**A** whole **lot** is slang for a great deal. **A lot** is *always* two words with a hole (space) between **a** and **lot. A lot** also means a parcel of land.
all right	**All right** is just like **all wrong.** Write both expressions as **two words,** always.
congratulations	Congratulations for crossing both *t*'s in **congratulations.** Never put a *d* in this word.

13

conscience	**Con** plus **science** will help you to spell **conscience.**
dessert	**Dessert** has sugar and spice in the middle (**ss**) when it means sweets at the end of a meal. Otherwise, you must **desert** one of the *s*'s. **Desert** means to abandon something or someone. It can also mean a dry, sandy area.
dilemma	**Emma** can spell **dilemma** because it ends with her name.
familiar	**Familiar** (unlike *similar*) ends with the word **liar.**
hypocrisy	One who practices **hypocrisy** is a **hypocrite.**
mathematics	In **mathematics, ma** is followed by **the matics.** Remember that ma**the**matics has the word **the** in it.
niece	**Niece** is the word *nice* with an *e* dropped right in the middle. She is a **nice niece.**
opossum	Many people pronounce **opossum** as if it were spelled *possum.* Just remember to begin it with one *o,* followed by one *p.*
ptomaine	The **PTO** boat is from **Maine. Ptomaine** poisoning is food poisoning.
pursue	I will pursue **u** and **u.**
separate	**Separate** is often misspelled, but if you look closely, you will see **a rat** in the middle of sep**ara**te.
sincerely	Be **sincere** when you write this word; then just add **ly.**
truly	You cannot put *true* in **truly.** Omit the *e.*

Obviously, you will be able to think of many other hard-to-spell words, especially if you brainstorm with your peers. You will want to keep a list of words that give *you* spelling problems, along with memorable tips you can create to help you learn to spell correctly *your* troublesome words. You might also check for any patterns of spelling problems you have. For example, words ending in either *-able* or *-ible* may cause you confusion.

Like *ptomaine,* many words are difficult to find in a dictionary because of their strange beginnings. A few examples are **opossum, mnemonic, pneumonia, aerobics,** and **psychology.** When you cannot find a word in the dictionary, try searching for a synonym. If that fails, ask someone for help. If that fails, completely reword your sentence to avoid the word you cannot spell. After all, the versatility of our language gives us the leeway to pursue other words and grammatical structures if we so desire.

13

Spelling Rules, Exceptions, and Frustrations

Although a few spelling rules in American English are helpful, most are long, complicated, and burdened with numerous exceptions. One helpful rule is the doubling-of-the-consonant rule.

Doubling the Consonant

Do you write *cancelled* or *canceled, travelled* or *traveled?* A comparatively simple rule exists to help guide you. If the accent is placed on the first part of the word (as is true in both *cancel* and *travel*), then you do not double the consonant. The correctly spelled words are **canceled** and **traveled.** If, however, the accent is placed on the second syllable, then you do double the consonant. Examples are **admitted** and **committed.** Beware of **commitment;** it is another frequently misspelled word.

Now, let us look at the *i*-before-*e* rule as an example of a rule loaded with exceptions. Most writers remember only the first two lines of the rule; a few remember all four. Almost no one remembers all the exceptions to the verse, which follows:

Use *i* before *e*

Except after *c*

Unless the word sounds like *a*

As in *neighbor* and *weigh.*

Here are just a few of the many exceptions to this rule: *ancient, conscience, deficient, sufficient, financier, society, either, neither, seize, leisure, height, sheik, weird,* and *their.* Some writers have divided all the exceptions into categories. It's far easier to look the word up if you are unsure about its spelling.

Rules for Pluralization

Not all rules are as difficult to apply as the *i-e* rule. Look at the plural forms of *city* and *toy: cities* and *toys.* Have you ever wondered why you drop the *y* and add *-ies* to *city* but simply add an *-s* to *toy?* The answer provides a good rule you can follow. If the *y* is preceded by a consonant, you drop the *y* and add *-ies* to make the word plural. Look at the following lists of examples:

lady/ladies	but	boy/boys
baby/babies	but	day/days
body/bodies	but	key/keys
cry/cries	but	bay/bays
try/tries	but	money/moneys

13

The exception to this rule involves proper nouns, that is, words that name specific persons, families, places, and things. Examples are *two Bettys* and *the McHenrys.*

Most nouns, in fact, simply require the addition of an *-s* to make them plural. If, however, you must add an additional syllable to make it possible to pronounce the *-s,* the word will end in *-es.* Examples are *bush, fox, buzz, church,* and *mass.* When you pronounce each of these words in its plural form, you will need to add an additional syllable. When you write these words in their plural forms, then you must add *-es.* The plural spellings follow: bush**es,** fox**es,** buzz**es,** church**es,** and mass**es.** (Notice that no apostrophe has been used to make any of these words plural.) To test this rule, **pronounce the plural form aloud.** If you hear the extra syllable in the plural word, add *-es* when you write the plural form.

Remember, too, that if a word already ends with an *e,* like *judge,* you add only an *-s* despite the additional syllable.

The word *fish* deserves special mention. If you mean more than one species, then you make *fish* plural by adding *-es.* You must write *all the fishes swim in the sea.* However, if you write the plural form of *fish* and you are referring to only one species, you write *fish.* The following sentence will help you to remember these rules:

Forty **goldfish** swim in my pond, but countless **fishes** swim in the ocean.

Another exception requires that you take special care when you make words plural that end with *f* or *fe.* For example, the singular word **roof** becomes **roofs** when pluralized, but **hoof** becomes **hooves. Chief** becomes **chiefs,** but **thief** becomes **thieves** and **leaf, leaves. Knife** and **wife** are pluralized as **knives** and **wives.** If you are unsure about the plural spelling of a word ending in *f* or *fe,* check your dictionary.

You must also beware of words that end in *o.* The best rule is to look them up when you question their spellings. Here is a general rule, however, that might prove helpful: Usually, if the word ends in *o* and the *o* is preceded by a vowel, simply add an *-s:* **barrio/barrios, radio/radios,** and **video/videos.**

If the *o* is preceded by a consonant, add *-es:* **hero/heroes** and **potato/potatoes.**

Here is an exception you are going to love. If you are using a word symbolizing something musical, add only an *-s* for pluralizing, even if the *o* is preceded by a consonant. Is this rule already losing its helpfulness? Examples are **concerto/concertos** and **piano/pianos.** When I am unsure about the *o*-ending words, I look them up.

Now we turn to a whole class of exceptions. A few irregular words form their plurals in unusual ways. It is important that you know how to spell these plural forms not only for correctness in spelling but also for correctness in apostrophe usage. You will, then, see some of these words again near the end of this chapter when we deal with the apostrophe.

13

Look at the following examples of irregular nouns and their plural spellings:

Singular	Plural
child	children
goose	geese
louse	lice
man	men
mouse	mice
ox	oxen
tooth	teeth
woman	women

You may never need to write the word **mongoose,** but in case you do, be sure to form its plural by writing **mongooses.** Frustrating, isn't it?

Sometimes, we do not even change singular words to make them plural. I live in the country and often see many **deer** (**NEVER deers**) in my back yard. **Deer** is one of several words that keep the same spelling in both their singular and plural forms. Examples follow:

Singular	Plural
deer	deer
dozen	dozen (exception: indefinite number as in *dozens of donuts* but *twelve dozen*)
fish	fish (one species)
fish	fishes (more than one species)
sheep	sheep
trout	trout

Foreign words can present special problems. Latin words, for example, do not usually require the addition of *-s* or *-es* for pluralization, although in some cases, this is changing. Remember that our language, a living language, is constantly changing.

Not too long ago, for example, we always wrote *memoranda* as the plural of *memorandum*. Now, most dictionaries list *memorandums* as the preferred spelling. Also, we used to write the plural of *index* as *indices*. Again, this has changed. The preferred plural form now is *indexes*.

Not all foreign words have changed in their plural forms. Many still have the original plural endings. Look at the examples listed:

Singular	Plural
alumna (woman)	alumnae (women)
alumnus (man)	alumni (men or men and women)
analysis	analyses

13

Singular	Plural
basis	bases
crisis	crises
criterion	criteria
datum	data
medium	media
phenomenon	phenomena
syllabus	syllabi (*Syllabuses* is preferred in some dictionaries, a preference that helps the communication process.)

Compound and hyphenated words also need special consideration. When you pluralize compound words, such as *cupful* or *spoonful*, simply add an *-s* at the end: **cupfuls** and **spoonfuls.** However, when you pluralize hyphenated words, such as *editor-in-chief, mother-in-law,* and *passer-by*, you add the *-s* to the word that symbolizes whatever is actually increasing in number. For example, when we say or write the words **mother-in-law,** we actually mean **mother (according to law).** If we are referring to more than one mother (according to law), we logically must place the *-s* on the word *mother*. Look at the following lists:

Singular	Plural
editor-in-chief	editors-in-chief
daughter-in-law	daughters-in-law
father-in-law	fathers-in-law
sister-in-law	sisters-in-law
passer-by	passers-by

Reinforcement of Spelling Tips

1. **Change your attitude** if necessary. You *can* improve your spelling, regardless of your spelling weaknesses.
2. **Keep your dictionary handy.** Consult it as necessary.
3. **Use your computer's spell checker.**
4. **Keep a list of the words you frequently misspell.** Beside each word try to write a tip that will help you remember the correct spelling. For example, for years, I had to look up the word **pursue** every time I wrote it. I couldn't remember whether I should write *per* or *pur*. Then one day, I thought of the following tip: *I will pursue **u** and **u** .* This may seem silly, but I have not had to look up this word again.
5. **Proofread your writing not only forwards but also backwards,** beginning with the last word. This backward reading isolates each word and prevents proofreading from becoming just reading.

13

6. **Pronounce words carefully.** Mispronunciations can cause misspelled words. Look at the following frequently mispronounced and, therefore, often misspelled words: *library, humble, mathematics, height* (height ends with *ht*, not *th*), *February*, and *athlete*.

13.1 EXERCISE FOR CHOOSING CORRECTLY SPELLED WORDS

Instructions: Write in the space provided the preferred word in parentheses.

1. (approachs/approaches) Annie Penwright uses unusual _____ when she presents writing workshops.

2. (Kelly's/Kellys) The _____ live across the hall from Annie.

3. (editor-in-chiefs/editors-in-chief) The publishing company has three _____ .

4. (benefitted/benefited) The employees _____ when they participated in Annie's workshops.

5. (judgment/judgement) Matt's _____ with respect to word choices improved.

6. (committment/commitment) He had made a _____ to improving his writing.

7. (accomodations/accommodations) Annie asked her secretary to reserve _____ for her next workshop at The Greenbrier.

8. (recieved/received) She had _____ excellent evaluations when she last presented a workshop there.

9. (deer/deers) She especially enjoyed watching the many _____ at the famous resort.

10. (its'/it's/its) The grounds reminded her of her mother's country place with all _____ wonderful wildlife.

11. (Memorys/Memories) _____ , like a child's slinky, travel back and forth on the road of experiences.

12. (delimma/dilemma) Annie's memory raced back to that night when an explosion and subsequent fire created a _____ for firefighters.

13. (familar/familiar) News stories of forest fires are _____ during dry seasons, especially in California.

14. (desert/dessert) After the fire that night, the landscape behind her mother's house was as barren as a _____ .

15. (conscious/conscience) No one that night suffered from a guilty _____ because of the fire.

16. (congradulations/congratulations) The fire chief offered _____ to all the courageous firefighters.

13

17. (opossum/oppossum) Annie remembered watching as a frantic _____ scurried to safety.

18. (truely/truly) It had _____ been a tragic event.

19. (seperated/separated) In an effort to keep the fire _____ from Mrs. Penwright's property, the volunteers cleared the land.

20. (arobics/aerobics) The volunteers worked tirelessly because they were all regular participants in _____.

21. (travelling/traveling) After _____ for several miles, the volunteers arrived in time to help Mrs. Penwright.

22. (calender/calendar) A glance at the _____ had confirmed the arrival of the dry season.

23. (There/Their) _____ efforts and hard work touched both Annie and her mother.

24. (its'/it's/its) _____ been a long time since the fire occurred.

25. (cancelled/canceled) After the fire subsided, the safety director _____ the emergency.

13.2 EXERCISE FOR SPELLBOUND EDITING

Instructions: Correct all misspelled words by drawing a line through the misspelled word and writing the correct spelling just above the error. Use your dictionary if you are unsure about a spelling mistake.

The Picnic

It seemed like a lifetime ago sense Matt had become acquainted with Annie at the bank's picnic. Its' picnic had been held in July of that memorible year. The two of them had sat on adjoining benchs. They watched various species of fish swimming in the blue lake. Two large red foxs darted through the woods on the opposite side of the lake. Suddenly, a green snake slithered beneath Annie's bench. Not afraid of nonpoisonous snakes, Annie laughed and told Matt she was glad no mongeese could threaten there native snakes. During the next hour, Matt discovered that Annie was an alumni of his college.

13

Not yet working on his M.B.A., Matt remembered saying, "Your an alumna of my college." This comment led to a discussion of the college cafeteria's food, especially it's mashed potatos. They both agreed that the taste must surely have been similiar to wallpaper paste. So engrossed in their conversation were Matt and Annie, they did not see the many passer-bys, three young deers, or the four sheeps that were grazing on a nearby hill. Only when a women exclaimed that three trouts had swum to the surface of the water did they once again notice there surroundings.

Yes, Matt remembered well there first conversation. That was even before he had recieved his undergraduate degree. That was before Annie had worked with several editor-in-chiefs. That was the begining of a long freindship. That was a lifetime ago. Remembering thier many sessions in which he had learned valuable writting tips, Matt was now ready to call Annie. He was planning to end another sentence with a proposition.

Apostrophe Usage

Many writers mistakenly use the apostrophe to make words plural; they should not. The apostrophe looks like a nervous comma that has jumped above the line. Look at the following example of an apostrophe in a sentence:

Matt took **Annie's** word that apostrophes generally should not be used to make words plural.

Notice that the apostrophe before the *s* does not mean that there is more than one Annie. Instead, it indicates ownership or possession. The word belongs to Annie; it is **her word** that convinced Matt to avoid the apostrophe for pluralization.

Now that you know how to recognize an apostrophe in a sentence, you must know when and where to use this frustrating mark. The **apostrophe** is used primarily for two purposes:

13

1. to show possession (Annie's word)

2. to indicate missing letters in contractions (can't/wouldn't)

Possession

The apostrophe is used with an *s* to show possession. The general rule is to use the apostrophe followed by *s* with a singular noun and to use the apostrophe by itself with a plural noun ending in *s*. When a plural noun does not end in *s*, to make it possessive, you add an apostrophe followed by an *s*. Examples are *media's coverage* and *the alumni's reunion.* When you do not know whether to put the apostrophe before or after the *s*, remember to **first write the word in its singular or plural form.** If you remember to do this, you should not have a problem with this demon mark.

The following examples demonstrate the use of the apostrophe with both singular and plural nouns. Notice that the plural nouns do not contain apostrophes.

Singular	Singular Possessive	Plural	Plural Possessive
woman	woman's	women	women's
Jones	Jones' or Jones's	Joneses	Joneses'
goose	goose's	geese	geese's
mongoose	mongoose's	mongooses	mongooses'
editor-in-chief	editor-in-chief's	editors-in-chief	editors-in-chief's
lady	lady's	ladies	ladies'
bench	bench's	benches	benches'
medium	medium's	media	media's
Smith	(Ms.) Smith's	(the) Smiths	(the) Smiths'
deer	deer's	deer	deer's

Look at the words in the second column. Notice that, in each case, we wrote the word in its singular form **before** we dealt with the apostrophe. Also, notice that with *Jones* (as is true with any **singular word that ends in *s***), you have a choice for making the word possessive. You can add just an apostrophe after the *s* or you can add an apostrophe and another *s*. If you add only the apostrophe, you will have one less syllable when you pronounce the word. The way, then, that you want your reader to pronounce the word should govern whether or not you add an *s* after the apostrophe. Are you still with me on this? If not, just avoid adding the extra *s* every time. (Do not ever pluralize *Jones* by writing it as either *Jones'* or *Jones's.*) Notice that the apostrophe and an *s* are added to the last word to make *editor-in-chief* possessive.

Next, look at the words under the heading **Plural.** You do not see any apostrophes at all. This should reinforce the fact that apostrophes are not

13

used to form plurals of words. Notice, too, that we followed the pronunciation rules for making **Jones** plural. You do need to pronounce an additional syllable and, therefore, must add *-es*. You must write (the) **Joneses** with no apostrophe. Notice that **editors-in-chief** is correct because we pluralize *editor,* not *chief.* Also, we kept the Latin pluralization of **medium,** thus writing **media.**

The word **women's** in the column labeled **Plural Possessive** can never be written with the *s* attached to the word itself. When we changed the *a* within the word to an *e,* we pluralized it. We cannot pluralize it again by adding an *s.* Many people misspell *women.* For some reason, it seems to be a spelling demon. Remember that it is **wo-man** (singular) and **wo-men** (plural), without the hyphens, of course.

The singular possessive of words such as *Moses, Odysseus,* and *Ulysses* requires only an apostrophe at the end of the word.

Moses' tablets

Odysseus' adventures

Ulysses' adventures

You will remember from studying pronouns in Chapter 5 that when you write **its,** meaning that something belongs to it, you do not use an apostrophe.

The book is exciting, but **its** title is boring.

The cat ate all **its** food.

The word *its'* **does not exist**—ever. Do not use it.

Separate Ownership

Let us suppose that Matt Murray and Annie Penwright are attending a picnic. Annie drove her car, and Matt drove his. The two cars are parked under a maple tree. Since each owns a car, you would give each name an apostrophe, as in the following sentence:

Annie's and Matt's cars are parked under a maple tree.

Remember, then, that if you are indicating separate ownership, each owner's name must have an apostrophe.

Joint Ownership

Let us now suppose that two people are attending the same picnic. Marge and Bob McHenry have traveled to the event in their red convertible. Since they own their car jointly, only the second name gets an apostrophe. See the following example:

Marge and Bob's car is a red convertible.

A few final words on using the apostrophe for possession. Notice that the following phrases cannot really be labeled possessive. We nonetheless must use the apostrophe with each.

St. Valentine's Day
New Year's Eve
a stone's throw
in harm's way
Mother's Day
New Year's Day
St. Patrick's Day
April Fools' Day
All Saints' Day

If you are insecure when using the apostrophe to show possession, you should read this section several times until you feel confident that you have mastered its usage.

Contractions

If you want your writing to have an informal tone, perhaps to bring the reader closer, you might use contractions occasionally. Remember to let your audience govern your choice on this. Avoid contractions in formal writing, and most academic writing is formal. Unless, then, you are writing dialogue, quoting directly, or writing informally, avoid contractions. A few samples of contractions follow:

Words	Contractions of Words
it is/it has	it's
cannot	can't
should not	shouldn't
will not	won't
is not	isn't

Letters and Numbers

The apostrophe can be used for a third purpose. If you are writing letters of the alphabet, figures, or plurals of words as words, you can use the apostrophe to avoid confusion. For example, the plural of *a* may look like *as* if you do not use an apostophe (*a*'s). This usage is unusual. You may need to use this only a few times in your entire life. It is correct to pluralize letters, numerals, and words without the apostrophe if the reader is not confused.

Look at the following sentences for examples of **apostrophe usage with letters of the alphabet:**

13

1. Matt learned the *abc*'s of writing.

2. Write your lowercase *a*'s like this.

3. Be sure to dot your *i*'s and cross your *t*'s.

You can see that you will not be using the apostrophe with the alphabet much at all.

Now, look at the following sentence for **examples of apostrophe usage with figures:**

My son has difficulties writing 5's and 8's.

Do not use an apostrophe when indicating a decade:

The 1960s launched many social changes in the United States.

Remember that when you pluralize words used as words (rather than as symbols of reality), use the apostrophe. The following sentence will help you to understand this concept:

James changed the *there*'s to *their*'s to correct his errors.

Notice that letters and words used as words are italicized.

13.3 EXERCISE FOR POSITIVE APOSTROPHE EDITING

Instructions: Correct all errors in apostrophe usage by deleting unnecessary apostrophes and s*'s. Insert apostrophes and* s*'s where needed.*

1. New Years Day is a time for beginnings.

2. Its a time for reviewing accomplishments and setting goals.

3. A decades beginning presents an even greater challenge to set goals.

4. One womans goals were recorded in her journal, which she began on the first day of the year.

5. Mrs. Marsha Jones journal contained many references to her experiences in Annie's writing classes.

6. The Joneses daughter, Carletta, had attended the writing classes with her mother.

7. The two womens essays won high praise from Annie.

8. Marsha and Carlettas essays always focused on different topics.

9. Marsha wrote about her own experience's.

10. Carletta wrote an essay on Odysseus's adventures.

11. The women lived only a stones throw from the college.

12. They certainly learned how to dot all their *i*s and cross all their *t*s in Annies class.

13. The Jones house was near Annies luxurious apartment building.

13

14. The Jones had lived there for many years.

15. Marsha often wrote about todays society with its' many problems and its' many opportunities for solutions.

16. She wrote to her hearts content.

17. She wrote about the spirit of love that could create its' own juncture where all people could meet and live in harmony.

18. Annie sometimes thought that Mrs. Jones writing was a bit much, but she encouraged her anyway.

19. During one session, Annie told the class about the time a woman had wanted to take credit for Annies writing.

20. She said that she could not imagine anyones wanting to claim authorship of someone elses work.

SUMMARY

Remember that to become a better speller, you must first understand that regardless of your spelling weaknesses, you can take specific steps to improve your skills. Also, understand that even professional writers often struggle with spelling; this will give you confidence. Learn the few helpful rules. Make a habit of using your computer spell checker *and* your dictionary. Keep a list of your frequently misspelled words and create your own tips to help you remember how to spell them correctly.

You have learned that you use the apostrophe for only two principal purposes: to show possession and to write contractions. The third use (a rare use) is with figures, letters of the alphabet, and words used as words.

Be sure to proofread everything you write to check for spelling errors and correct apostrophe usage. You have all the information you need, and you can do it. ■

13.4 END-OF-CHAPTER EXERCISES

Instructions: Except for errors within quotation marks, correct all other errors in spelling and apostrophe usage by rewriting each sentence that contains errors.

1. The sentences that follow are excerps from a new book by one of Annies former students; it's title is *The Book of Esther: Mother Tongue.*

_____

_____

_____

2. My mother called recently to say shed met a nurse who knew everything.

_____

_____

_____

3. The nurse, according to my mother, had an additional degree in Sychology.

_____

_____

_____

4. My mother said that the nurse said, "When you have any desease ending in *-itis,* like bronchitis or arthritis, you have some kind of information."

_____

_____

_____

5. Laughing at her comments', I said, "You surely mean *inflammation,* dont you, Mom?"

_____

_____

_____

6. Mother said impatiently, "Whatever, I'll talk to you latter."

_____

_____

_____

7. My mother creates' her own words and, therefore, often needs an interpreter; Im usually it.

_____

_____

_____

8. My mothers doctor was puzzled one time when she told him her "years had been eetching."

_____

_____

_____

9. The doctors repeated question about her symptoms did not surprise me.

_____

_____

_____

10. I explained that my mothers ears had been itching.

_____

_____

_____

11. Despite her creative language, my mother understands peoples behavior and motivations better than anyone I know.

_____

_____

_____

12. When I was young, wise, witty, sharp, and all-knowing, she told me who my real friends' were.

_____

_____

_____

13. Her advise only irritated me because naturally I knew more than she ever could.

_____

_____

_____

14. In retrospect, I realize that her assessments were alright.

_____

_____

_____

15. A daughters hairstyle should never be discussed between mother and daughter.

_____

_____

_____

16. My mother asked me one day, "Your going to get a haircut soon, arent you?"

_____

_____

_____

17. I said that I liked my hairs length but might get a perm.

_____

_____

_____

18. "You get to many perms," said Mother.

_____

_____

_____

19. "Its been four months, Mom," said I with a sigh.

_____

_____

_____

20. "Well," she countered, "you truely get to many, in my opinion"; Id been waiting for her opinion.

_____

_____

_____

13

21. Later, during a writing conference that Mother attended with me, she said, "Lets leave. I'm not one bit 'insterned' in this."

_____

_____

_____

22. After alot of puzzled thoughts about "insterned," I concluded that she had blended *interested* and *concerned* to create *insterned.*

_____

_____

_____

23. This kind of blending takes nothing short of brilliance, all of which proves that people who's dialects are "different" can be brilliant.

_____

_____

_____

24. When the Bushs lived in the White House, my mother called them "the Booshes."

_____

_____

_____

25. Cushions' are "cooshions," according to my mothers pronunciation.

_____

_____

_____

26. Mother Esthers pronounciation of *push* is "poosh."

_____

_____

_____

13

27. Not a linguistic snob, I know that my mother is wise, wonderful, and witty, which is why I like writting about her.

_____

_____

_____

28. With no more than a third-grade education, she taught herself to read and write, although she sometimes writes' on a recipe card, "Sprinkle a little time [sic] on the feesh [sic]."

_____

_____

_____

29. Annie Dillards mother inspired Annie because of her mothers expertise with language.

_____

_____

_____

30. Because of my mothers linguistic inventiveness, spoonerisms, Bunkerisms, and several other linguistic *-ism*s, I, to, have been inspired.

_____

_____

_____

Instructions: Draw a line through each incorrectly spelled word. Also, draw a line through each word with an error in apostrophe usage. Write your corrected versions in the spaces provided. There may be more spaces than you need.

31. José watched the bright autumn sun shinning through the labary windows. _____

32. He had been studing for three hours. _____

33. After three hours study time, he was eager to meet his friends for lunch. _____

34. Proofreading his biology report, José changed all the *hes* to hes or *shes*. _____

35. Josés friends would be waiting for him. _____

36. The two cafeterias food had improved. _____

37. Although the food wasnt the best, its' servers were friendly. _____

38. José chuckled as he thought of the sign on the cafeterias facade accross the street. _____

39. Our fresh lettuce compliments our hamburgers. _____

13

40. To remove the sign would be to loose its' humor.
_____

41. He had choosen the local college for its conveniance.
_____

42. Leaving the libary, José saw Maria and Bill's biology books on the table.
_____

43. To lose them would be disasterous, so he retreived them for his friends.
_____

44. Later, he met them in the cafeteria, where he ordered coffee with alot of caffiene.
_____

45. Through the large glass windows of the cafeteria, José saw his mom's and dad's car.
_____

46. His dads' old car had a bad carberator.
_____

47. The new cars red paint glistened in the October sun.
_____

48. Amoung the four friends at the table, José was the one planing to be a medical doctor.
_____

49. The other's schedules were also demanding.
_____

50. Annie and Matt sat at an adjoining table; thier conversation seemed serious.
_____

14

Chapter 14

Capitalization

▶ OBJECTIVES

In this chapter, you will learn to

••• use capital letters to begin sentences

••• recognize and capitalize proper nouns

••• capitalize names of specific places, institutions, companies, organizations, committees, boards, departments, and events

••• capitalize correctly specific words in titles

••• apply capitalization to names of specific deities, religions, and nationalities

••• capitalize names of months, holidays, days of the week, languages, and course titles

••• apply capitalization correctly to courtesy and professional titles, abbreviations, specific letters of the alphabet, and brand names

••• capitalize correctly in salutations, complimentary closes, and addresses

When writing, you must know which words require capitalization. Although there are some gray areas in capitalization, this chapter will help you capitalize words correctly.

Gray Areas in Capitalization

If you are in doubt about capitalizing a word, you can look up the word in a dictionary. If the word is one used within your discipline or within your company, and there are no guidelines, determine capitalization by considering the importance of the reality for which the word stands. For example, chapter titles in books are capitalized, but page numbers are not. This rule was undoubtedly formulated by consideration of the importance of a chapter in comparison to a page. There are gray areas in capitalization, but with the help of dictionaries, company guidelines, style sheets, or your own logic and the information in this chapter, you should be able to capitalize correctly and confidently most of the time.

First Words in Sentences

The first letter of the first word of a sentence must be capitalized. Even words that begin sentences within quotation marks must be capitalized.

Notice in the following example that the whole sentence begins with a capitalized word, as does the quoted sentence:

The gray-haired man at the nearby table said,

"Did someone end a sentence with a proposition?"

Proper Nouns: An Overview

You will recall from Chapter 4 that **proper nouns** *name specifically*. However, to say that a proper noun names a specific person, place, thing, or animal can be somewhat confusing. For example, if Annie refers in her writing to the university she attended as "my university," she is certainly referring to a specific university, yet she does not capitalize *university*. If, however, she refers to her university as Yale, she is giving the specific name of the university and must therefore capitalize it. Phrased as a rule, this probably sounds confusing, but do not panic. Instead, look at the following lists, which should help clarify the difference between common and proper nouns. (You can also refer to the list in Chapter 4.) Look at the following two lists:

Proper Nouns	Common Nouns
Annie Penwright	woman/writer/trainer
Elsie	the farmer's cow
Snickers	the brand name of a candy bar
Elizabeth Tailless	Annie's cat
Bowser	Matt's dog
Monday	today
Lookout Lane	the street
General Grant	the general

Within each section of this chapter, you will find additional examples of various kinds of proper nouns.

Specific Names of Places, Institutions, Companies, Organizations, and Events

Capitalize the specific names of cities, counties, states, countries, continents, rivers, lakes, seas, oceans, and places otherwise specifically named.

Boston

Dade County

Massachusetts

United States

North America

Potomac River

Lake Superior

Mediterranean Sea

Pacific Ocean

Far East (When compass directions indicate place, they are capitalized. When they indicate direction, they are not.)

Capitalize the specific names of institutions, companies, and organizations, as well as divisions within them. These include divisions such as committees, boards, and departments. Specific names of events are capitalized. The following will clarify these rules:

Marshall University	institution
Arts and Humanities	division within institution
Board of Trustees	governing board of institution
Accounting Department	division within company
Mirror Press	publishing company
Boy Scouts of America	organization
World War II	event

Titles of Published Works, Television Programs, Movies, Compact Discs, and Songs

Titles of published works, such as books, magazines, journals, essays, articles, poems, songs, columns, and plays, as well as television programs, movies, and compact discs, have specific rules for capitalization.

1. Always capitalize the first and last words in a title regardless of the parts of speech.

2. **Do not** capitalize the articles *a*, *an*, and *the* if they fall **within the title.**

3. **Do not** capitalize prepositions with four or fewer letters if they fall **within the title.** Examples include *to, into, with, out, of, for*, and *at*.

4. **Do not** capitalize conjunctions with four or fewer letters if they fall **within the title.** Examples include *for, and, nor, but, or, yet, so* (the FANBOYS of Chapter 10).

You already understand the reasons for knowing the parts of speech, but capitalization of titles offers yet another reason. Notice the capitalization of the following titles.

Dictionary of Word Origins (book)

Newsweek (magazine)

14

A Handbook to Literature (book)

The Taming of the Shrew (published play)

"Singing with the Fundamentalists" (essay)

All My Children (television program)

Kiss of Death (movie)

Ode on a Grecian Urn (poem)

No Time to Kill (compact disc)

"A Good Run of Bad Luck" (song on compact disc *No Time to Kill*)

Deities, Religions, Nationalities, and Ethnic Groups

Names of deities, such as the Holy Ghost, Jehova, Allah, and Christ, are capitalized. Names of religions are capitalized. Examples include Catholicism, Protestantism, Judaism, and Islam. The names of followers of religions are also capitalized: Catholic, Protestant, Jew, and Muslim. Titles of the sacred documents of religions are capitalized. Examples include the following: the Bible, the Koran, the Old Testament, and the New Testament.

Names of nationalities and ethnic groups are capitalized. Examples follow:

African-Americans

Americans

Chinese

French

Native Americans

When referring to Caucasians or African-Americans as whites or blacks in writing, you must make a decision with respect to capitalization. To ensure consistency, you should capitalize both (*Blacks* and *Whites*) or capitalize neither (*blacks* and *whites*). Generally, African-Americans now want to be referred to as African-Americans. However, this is not always so. Gwendolyn Brooks, the poet laureate of Illinois, for example, likes to be referred to as Black and she capitalizes *Black*. Several dictionaries indicate that *Black* is often capitalized. The implication, of course, is that sometimes it is not. My preference is lowercase for both terms.

Days of the Week, Months, and Holidays

Days of the week, months of the year, and holidays are capitalized.

Sunday

December

New Year's Eve

Good Friday

14

Hanukkah
Labor Day
Martin Luther King, Jr. Day
Thanksgiving

Remember, though, that seasons of the year are not capitalized: spring, summer, autumn/fall, and winter.

Names of Languages and Course Titles

Names of languages and specific course titles are capitalized:

English 401
an English class
Biology 201
a biology class

Because *biology* is not the name of a language, you cannot capitalize *biology* unless you are writing the specific title of the course.

John is taking three **biology** classes this semester.
Bob is taking **Accounting 301.**
He will take one **accounting** class next semester.

Courtesy, Professional, and Family Titles

When courtesy and professional titles precede the names of persons, they are capitalized.

Ms. Penwright
Professor John Johnson
Senator Grubb

If the professional title **follows** the person's name, it is not usually capitalized.

John Grubb, senator of our state
John Johnson, professor of English
John Williams, our doctor
John Miles, our division manager, is calling a meeting.

Heads of state are capitalized even when the name of the person is not included.

14

The President of the United States will speak this evening.
The Queen of England owns many precious jewels.

Titles of relatives, such as *aunt* and *uncle,* are usually not capitalized unless they precede the person's name or are used as replacements for names. Here are some examples.

Uncle Matt is Toby's favorite uncle.

My father loves autumn.

Yes, Father enjoys autumn.

Abbreviations and Certain Letters of the Alphabet

Abbreviations as replacements of words that are capitalized are usually themselves capitalized. Examples follow:

FBI (Federal Bureau of Investigation)

NOW (National Organization for Women)

UCLA (University of California at Los Angeles)

Ph.D. (Doctor of Philosophy)

Also, certain letters of the alphabet are capitalized in special situations. When a writer uses the pronoun *I,* the *I* is always capitalized. When the letter *O* is used as a replacement for *oh,* the letter should be capitalized. Finally, when letters indicate shapes or are names, they are capitalized. Examples include the following:

T cell

T-square

X-ray

vitamin C

U-turn

L-dopa

Brand Names

Brand names must be used with caution in writing, and each should be capitalized if the company capitalizes its brand name. Be careful not to use a brand name when you are not really referring to the specific brand. For instance, do not refer to Xerox copies if you are really talking about photocopies in general. The following are examples of brand names:

Snickers	candy bar
Pepsi	cola/soft drink
Kraft	various food products
Hormel meats	meat products
Land O Lakes butter	butter

14

whiskas   cat food (If you were to look at the can,
                       you would notice that whiskas, although
                       a brand name, is not capitalized.)

Capitalization in Correspondence

Each word in the salutation of a letter begins with a capital letter.

Dear Annie, (A comma follows an informal salutation.)

Dear Ms. Penwright: (A colon follows a formal salutation.)

Only the first word is capitalized in the complimentary close.

Yours truly,

Note that in the address for a letter, courtesy and professionals titles are capitalized.

Ms. Joan MacWorthy

Human Resources Manager

XYZ Corporation

111 Fun Lane

Writesville, WV 25555

SUMMARY

Capital letters are needed at the beginning of all sentences, including those that are directly quoted and those that are not. Proper nouns are usually capitalized. This means that specific names of persons, places, pets, institutions, companies, organizations, committees, boards, departments, and events should be capitalized. Titles of published works, television programs, movies, compact discs, and songs should be capitalized. Capitalize specific names of deities, religions, nationalities, and ethnic groups. When writing or typing specific days of the week, months of the year, or holidays, capitalize them. Specific names of languages and course titles should be capitalized. Courtesy titles are capitalized as well. A professional title is capitalized when it precedes a person's name, but not usually when it follows the name. Family titles, when not preceded by possessive pronouns, are capitalized. Capitalize abbreviations, certain letters of the alphabet, and brand names. All words in the salutation and the first word of a complimentary close in a letter must be capitalized. When unsure about capitalization, check a dictionary, company guidelines, or style sheets. If you still cannot find the word in question, determine the importance of whatever the word symbolizes. ■

14

14.1 END-OF-CHAPTER EXERCISES

Instructions: In the spaces provided, respond to the questions or statements. Answers will vary and will not be given in the Answers to Exercises at the end of the book.

1. What is your favorite brand of candy? _____

2. In which county or parish do you live? _____

3. In which city and state do you live? _____

4. What is your favorite holiday? _____

5. What is the name of the river closest to your home? _____

6. Write one of the compass points as a location. _____

7. Write one of the compass points as a direction. _____

8. Write the name of the high school you attended. _____

9. What is your favorite department store? _____

10. List an organization of which you are or would like to be a member. _____

11. Write the title of your favorite novel. _____

12. Write the title of a play you have read or seen. _____

13. Write the title of your favorite compact disc. _____

14. What is your favorite day of the week? _____

15. What is your favorite season? _____

16. What is your major? _____

17. You refer to yourself by using the first-person pronoun. Write it in the space provided. _____

18. Give the specific name of a class you are currently taking or your job title. _____

19. Write a salutation for a personal letter. Use the correct punctuation mark after the salutation. _____

20. Write a complimentary close. _____

14

Instructions: Correct all errors in capitalization. Draw a line through the misused letter and replace it with either a capital letter or a lowercase letter.

The Proposition

Matt parked his new ford taurus in the basement parking garage. A few minutes later, he rang annie's doorbell. Opening the door, Annie smiled and said, "what's your proposition, Matt? I can hardly wait to hear how i am involved."

Matt walked toward the sofa. "In another month," he said, "You'll be enjoying your Summer vacation. You usually travel, write about your travels, and sell your articles to various publishers. You mentioned that if you had photographs of professional quality you could sell even more articles."

"Yes, yes, go on." said Annie as she tied the shoelace of her left nike.

Smiling, Matt said, "Be patient, Annie. I've been hired as a photographer for *national geographic.* I'll be traveling all over the world—to africa, south america. you name it. I might float down the nile river one month and, the next, the yangtze."

"That's terrific! So, where do I fit in?" asked Annie.

"I want you to travel with me this Summer, Annie. I've talked with my supervisor at *national geographic,* and she would love to have you write for the magazine. I think we'd make a winning team," explained Matt.

Annie poured steaming earl grey tea into fine porcelain cups. Waiting for her response, Matt reached for the cup and saucer.

"I don't know, Matt. I usually spend independence day with my family, that is, my Aunts, Uncles, and cousins. Our annual family reunion is held during july, and grandmother Penwright is quite old. Still, I know what she would tell me. I'm tempted."

Seizing the opportunity, Matt said, "Come on, Annie. I'll brush up on my french. Where's your spirit of adventure?"

14

"Okay, Matt. I'll do it. We'll be business partners as we sail the atlantic and the pacific. I'll have marvelous tales to tell, and you'll have breathtaking scenes to photograph," said Annie.

As Matt left, he paused at the door and said with a sheepish grin, "Would you happen to have any taster's choice™?"

Thinking of those television commercials and a future filled with delightful surprises, they both laughed.

Chapter 15

Underlining Versus Quotation Marks, Numbers Versus Words

■ OBJECTIVES

In this chapter, you will learn to

- ••• underline or italicize and use quotation marks correctly to identify titles of works
- ••• underline or italicize specific names of ships, airplanes, spacecraft, and trains
- ••• underline or italicize words used as words and letters used as letters
- ••• underline or boldface words for emphasis
- ••• decide whether to use words or figures (numerals) when writing numbers

Underlining: A Message to the Typesetter

Before the advent of computers, writers used typewriters. They were not equipped to permit writers to italicize words. Writers had to resort to underlining the words they wanted the typesetter to italicize. You should know, then, that when you send a manuscript with underlined words to a typesetter, the typesetter will italicize all words you have underscored unless you have written specific instructions to leave the underlining intact. Most computer software programs today permit the writer to italicize words in the original manuscript, so if you want words italicized, you can italicize them.

Titles of Published Works, Television and Radio Programs, Movies, and Compact Discs

If a work, published or otherwise, is an entity in itself, its specific title or name should be underlined or italicized. If the work is part of a whole, such as a chapter within a book or a poem published in a book containing other works, then you use quotation marks around the title. The title of the book (an entity itself) would be either underlined or italicized. Some examples will make this clear.

Book	<u>Elements of Style</u>	or	*Elements of Style*
TV program	<u>Murder She Wrote</u>	or	*Murder She Wrote*
Radio program	<u>On the House</u>	or	*On the House*
Movie	<u>Sound of Music</u>	or	*Sound of Music*
Compact disc	<u>When Love Finds You</u>	or	*When Love Finds You*
Poem	"Fish"		(Note: You will often find titles of poems and the like italicized when listed in published works.)
Song	"South Side of Dixie"		(This song is included on the compact disc *When Love Finds You.*)

If the title of a publication begins with the word *the,* it must be underlined or italicized. Many titles do not begin with the word *the,* but when we refer to some of them, we often use *the* before the title. For example, *Charleston Daily Mail* is the title of a newspaper, but writers often write, "the *Charleston Daily Mail.*" In such cases, when the word *the* is not actually part of the title, it should not be italicized. What you must do, then, is check the exact title to be sure you italicize only the words in the title itself.

Titles of famous paintings are also italicized: VanGogh's *Sunflowers.*

Titles of sacred works and titles of divisions in those works do not need underlining, italics, or quotation marks: the Bible, the Talmud, Revelations, and the Vedas.

Names of Ships, Airplanes, Spacecraft, and Trains

Underline names of ships, airplanes, spacecraft, and trains.

Ship	the <u>Titanic</u>	or	the *Titanic* (Although *the* is not part of the name and should not be be italicized, it usually precedes the name when referred to in spoken or written form.)
Airplane	the <u>Spirit of St. Louis</u>	or	the *Spirit of St. Louis*
Spacecraft	the <u>Enterprise</u>	or	the *Enterprise*
Train	the <u>Orient Express</u>	or	the *Orient Express*

Words Used as Words

When you use a word as a word rather than using the word to convey its meaning, it should be either underlined or italicized. Look at the following examples:

Annie changed all the <u>he</u>'s to <u>she</u>'s.

or

Annie changed all the *he*'s to *she*'s.

Letters, when used as letters, can be treated in the same way.

Annie taught the <u>abc</u>'s of writing.

or

Annie taught the *abc*'s of writing.

Underlining or Boldfacing for Emphasis

You can use either italics (underlining) or boldface to emphasize words or phrases, but use one or the other consistently in a single document. Also, use emphasis sparingly so that it does not lose its ability to emphasize.

<u>Avoid</u> the <u>overuse</u> of underlining and boldfacing for emphasis. Use underlining or boldfacing **sparingly** for emphasis.

Numbers: Words or Figures

Some stylists will tell you that if a number requires more than two words, you should use figures (numerals). Others will tell you that only numbers from one through nine should be written as words. You can find support, then, for either method. You must decide which method you prefer, or you can ask your instructor which method he or she prefers.

With a few exceptions, I write as words all numbers from one to ten. There are some steadfast rules relating to numbers that are consistent in most handbooks of writing. For example, always write out numbers if they begin a sentence. Use figures when writing dates (September 14, 1997).

Money is usually written in figures unless it is more than a million; then it is written as follows: $5.6 million. Less than a dollar can be written in words (twenty-five cents).

Here is an example.

Twenty-five years earlier, when the independent bank manager was only **ten,** he celebrated his birthday on July **4, 1971.** His favorite gift was **$1,971,** although he appreciated the **fifty cents** his friend had given him.

15

Sometimes, it is better to reword a sentence than to begin it with a large number. Notice how much easier the second sentence is to read.

One thousand seven hundred dollars and fifty cents is required as a down payment.

A down payment of $1,700.50 is required.

Be consistent when you write numbers within a passage.

The basket contained 6 melons, 12 oranges, and 24 apples.

Page, chapter, and volume numbers are written as figures.

Chapter 4, page 155
Hamlet, Act 3, Scene 2
Volume 4

Percentages are written as figures. In a technical document, the percentage sign after the figure (like many other technical symbols) is acceptable. Nontechnical writing, however, requires the word *percent* after the figure.

Nontechnical	Technical
25 percent	25%
31.1 percent	31.2%

Generally, use figures in addresses.

444 Hummingbird Way
Goldpage, WV 55551

Written Expressions of Time

If *o'clock* is written, numbers indicating the time must also be written as words. Just as there are varying styles in the writing of numbers as words or figures, there are also variations in the writing of time. Journalists, for example, do not use a colon and two zeros after the figure expressing the hour. Most writers in the humanities and in business do. You can use either capital letters or lowercase letters, although the trend is toward lowercase.

Journalistic Style	Standard Style
6 p.m.	6:00 p.m.
6:30 p.m.	6:30 p.m.

You will be happy to know that all agree on the following: *six o'clock.*

SUMMARY

In this chapter, you have learned that underlining tells the typesetter to italicize all underscored words unless otherwise noted. You have learned when to use underlining or italics and when to use quotation marks for all published works. You have learned that names of ships, airplanes, spacecraft, and trains should be underlined (or italicized). You have learned that you can emphasize words and phrases by either underlining or boldfacing them. You have learned how to choose either words or figures when writing numbers and how to express time correctly.   ■

15.1 END-OF-CHAPTER EXERCISES

Instructions: Write sentences in which you include information requested in each of the following. Also, capitalize words correctly (refer to Chapter 14 if you are not sure about capitalization). Answers will vary and will not be given in the Answers to Exercises at the end of the book.

1. the title of your favorite song

_____

_____

2. the title of your favorite compact disc

_____

_____

3. the time you usually get up in the morning

_____

_____

4. the title of your favorite movie

_____

_____

5. the amount of money you paid for the last purchase you made

_____

_____

6. the amount you plan to pay for your next car

_____

_____

7. the name of your favorite television program

_____

_____

8. title of a poem contained in a book

_____

_____

9. title of a novel

_____

_____

10. title of a spaceship (may be fictional)

_____

_____

11. title of a newspaper

_____

_____

12. title of a column in a consumer magazine

_____

_____

13. a series (each containing numbers)

_____

_____

14. your address

_____

_____

15. emphasis of a word

_____

_____

Instructions: Underline for italics and insert quotation marks as necessary. If the sentence is correct, be happy and move to the next sentence.

16. The Death of the Ball-Turret Gunner is a gripping poem by Randall Jarrell.

17. It is in a book titled American Poetry.

18. The Koran is a sacred text.

19. Newsweek is a consumer magazine.

20. My Turn is a column in Newsweek, and it is written by freelancers.

21. Many financiers read The Wall Street Journal every day.

22. Reapers is a poem by Jean Toomer.

23. Amazing Grace is a hymn familiar to many people.

24. Home Improvement is a popular television program.

25. Salvation, an essay by Langston Hughes, is included in many anthologies.

26. The Great Gatsby, the novel, was the basis for a movie of the same title.

27. Annie enjoys reading the New York Times.

28. The President of the United States travels on Air Force One.

29. The word the is an article.

30. Charles Lindburgh made the first solo transatlantic flight in The Spirit of St. Louis.

31. ER is a popular television program.

32. Garrison Keillor hosted the enjoyable radio show A Prairie Home Companion.

33. No Time to Kill, a CD, contains the country song A Good Run of Bad Luck.

34. José regularly watches Lois and Clark on television.

35. Out of Africa is an excellent movie.

15

Epilogue

You were promised in Chapter 1 that you would be given a second chance to write about your attitude toward the study of grammar rules as they relate to writing skills. You have learned rules to help you write precisely, correctly, and effectively. This time, instead of writing just one paragraph, you will write an essay. It will contain a **thesis statement,** that is, a sentence that contains the main idea of your essay.

Instructions: Write an essay of approximately 500 words. In the first sentence, state your attitude toward grammar. Give at least three reasons to support your first sentence. Each reason may require a paragraph that includes details and perhaps a few examples. If you write sample sentences or words as words, underline them. End your essay with a sense of finality by restating in slightly different language your attitude toward rules for writers. The title has been written for you.

My Attitude Toward Grammar

_____

_____

_____

_____

_____

_____

_____

_____

_____

_____

_____

Glossary of Terms for Writers

absolute phrase See *phrase.*

abstract noun A noun that cannot be perceived by the five senses. An example is *loyalty.*

active voice See *voice.*

adjective A part of speech that describes or modifies nouns and pronouns. *Sweet, tall,* and *good* are examples.

adverb A part of speech that describes or modifies verbs, adjectives, or other adverbs. *Sweetly, well,* and *not* are examples.

adverbial conjunction See *conjunctive adverb.*

ambiguous pronoun A pronoun that does not refer clearly to its antecedent. *Annie told Jane she was ambitious.*

antecedent A noun or pronoun to which the pronoun refers. The pronoun and its antecedent must agree in number, person, and gender.

apostrophe A mark used to indicate possession and contractions. For consistency, the apostrophe is sometimes used to pluralize numbers, letters, or words used as words.

appositive A word or phrase that renames, explains, or identifies the word or phrase preceding the appositive. John, *my brother,* is here.

articles Three words—*a, an,* and *the*—that are often classified as adjectives. They usually precede common nouns. *A* and *an* are indefinite or unspecified articles. *The* is a definite or specified article.

auxiliary or helping verb A verb that helps to form future and all perfect tenses of verbs. *Has, have, had, is, are, am,* and *been* are examples.

biased language Language that can be offensive to certain groups in certain environments. To refer to a woman as a girl is an example.

brackets Punctuation marks used to indicate the writer is inserting explanatory words into directly quoted material. *He wrote, "I enjoy the writing of [Eudora] Welty."*

capitalization The use of an uppercase letter. Capital letters are used for the beginnings of sentences, proper nouns, professional and courtesy titles, and certain words of titles. Capitalization is used for certain words in salutations, complimentary closes, and addresses. The pronoun *I* is also capitalized.

case See *pronoun case.*

clause A group of words that contains both a subject and a predicate; it may be independent or dependent.

cliché An expression that has become trite from overuse.

collective noun A subclass of the noun that names groups, such as *team, jury,* and *choir.*

colon A punctuation mark used after the salutation in a business letter. It is also used to introduce a list when followed by an independent clause. The colon sometimes introduces an explanation.

comma A punctuation mark used within a sentence to indicate a separation, an interruption, or a pause.

comma splice An error in usage of the comma. A comma splice occurs when a comma is used *without* a conjunction to separate two or more independent clauses.

common noun The names of persons, places, things, qualities, ideas, or animals that are in a general class. *Man* and *dog* are examples.

comparative degree See *comparison.*

comparison The forms of adjectives and adverbs used to show degrees in comparisons. *Positive* is the dictionary listing (sweet, sweetly); *comparative* is the form used to compare only two (sweeter, more sweetly), and *superlative* is the form used to compare three or more (sweetest, most sweetly).

complement A word, phrase, or clause that completes the action of a verb (verb complement) or completes an object (object complement). *They named him Bob.*

complex sentence A group of words with only one independent clause and one or more dependent clauses.

compound–complex sentence A group of words containing at least two independent clauses and at least one dependent clause (possibly more).

compound sentence A group of words with two or more independent clauses.

conciseness Writing that is succinct, that says much in as few words as possible.

concrete language Language that appeals to the five senses. Examples are *cold, sweet, aroma, blue,* and *squeaking.*

concrete noun A noun that names something that can be perceived by the five senses. Examples are *wind* and *city.*

conjugation See *verb conjugation.*

conjunction A word that connects or links words and groups of words in a sentence.

conjunctive adverb A word that describes the relation between two main clauses. Examples are *furthermore, however,* and *therefore.*

connotation The implied meanings of a word.

coordinate conjunction One of the seven words connecting two or more words, phrases, or clauses that are similar in grammatical structure. Coordinate conjunctions link such items as *-ing* verbs with *-ing* verbs, nouns with nouns, phrases with phrases, and clauses with clauses. An acronym made up of the first letter of each coordinate conjunction is FANBOYS (*for, and, nor, but, or, yet, so*).

coordinate modifiers Two or more modifiers that describe the same word. Coordinate adjectives or modifiers are separated with commas.

correlative conjunctions Paired conjunctions that provide coordination or alternatives. They are, then, coordinate or disjunctive. Examples are *not only . . . but also* and *either . . . or.* Parallel structure is used with these conjunctions.

count noun A noun that can be counted. Examples are *book* and *pencil.*

dangling modifier A word, phrase, or clause that modifies an element in the sentence the writer has not intended it to modify. The word the reader intended the modifier to modify may or may not be included in the sentence. In the following sentence, *Mary,* the intended word to be modified, is missing: *Falling, her knee was fractured.* In this example, *Mary* is in the sentence but in the wrong place: *Falling, her knee was fractured as Mary ran.* A dangling modifier is an error.

dash A punctuation mark used for emphasis or for an abrupt shift in thought. The dash is also used to set off an appositive or a series of adjectives following the word they modify. *The house—dark, damp, and dreary—is owned by Count Drack.*

demonstrative pronoun A pronoun that points or demonstrates. There only four in the English language: *this, these, that,* and *those.*

denotation The dictionary definition of a word.

dependent clause A group of words containing both a subject and a predicate and introduced by a coordinate conjunction. A dependent or subordinate clause can never stand alone as a sentence; it depends on the independent clause to complete a thought.

diction Word choices in speaking or writing.

direct object A word that receives the action from the verb.

double negative An error that occurs when a negative word is repeated unnecessarily. **X** *I don't have no homework.* A corrected version follows: *I don't have any homework.*

ellipses Three or four spaced dots used to indicate omission of words from directly quoted material. An entire line of dots may be used when a great deal of material has been omitted.

end marks Punctuation marks that end sentences. The end marks are the period, exclamation point, and question mark.

essay A comparatively short piece of nonfiction writing that focuses on a single topic and reflects the author's view.

euphemism The substitution of a less offensive term for one that is harsh or offensive. The use of euphemisms is often regarded with disdain, especially if their use is an attempt to hide facts. An example of a euphemism is *passed away,* a term that often replaces *died.*

fractured cliché A cliché that has been changed slightly to make it fresh again.

fragment See *sentence fragment.*

fused sentence See *run-on sentence.*

gender The classification of masculine (he), feminine (she), or neuter (it) by the form of a word.

gerund A type of verbal that functions as a noun. It can be either in a subject or object slot. *Running* is good exercise (subject). I like *running* (object).

grammar A set of rules and the study of those rules that govern the selection and combination of words to form sentences according to standard usage.

homonym One of two or more words with similar sounds or spellings but different meanings.

hyphen A mark used in compound words. The hyphen is also used in adjectives that precede nouns and function as a single unit. Examples are *four-year-old* and *gray-haired* man.

indefinite pronoun Refers to a general class rather than specific persons, places, things, ideas, or animals. Examples are *all, any, some,* and *anyone.*

independent clause A group of words with both a subject and predicate that expresses a complete thought. An independent clause may stand alone as a sentence or be combined with other clauses.

indirect object A word or phrase indirectly receiving action from the verb. The indirect object is usually the beneficiary.

infinitive A type of verbal that can function as a noun, adjective, or an adverb. The infinitive is formed with the base form of the verb and is preceded by *to.* Examples are *to think* and *to be.*

intensive pronoun Pronouns that intensify or emphasize. These are all *-self* pronouns: *myself, ourselves, itself.*

interjection A word or exclamation that expresses emotion, mild or strong. Examples are *wow, aha,* and *oh.*

interrogative pronoun A pronoun that introduces a question. *Who screamed?*

intransitive verb A verb that has no object and is not followed by a predicate noun or predicate adjective. *Mary slept well.*

irregular verb Any verb that forms its past and past participle in any way other than by adding *-d* or *-ed.* Examples are *cost, cost, cost* and *go, went, gone.*

italic print or typeface A style of print or typeface that slants to the *right.* It is used for emphasis or for titles. Examples are titles of publications, plays, television and radio programs, cassette discs, movies, airplanes, trains, and ships.

jargon Technical vocabulary in a particular field or discipline. It also means nonsensical and incoherent language.

linking verb A verb that is followed by a predicate adjective or a predicate noun. Examples are forms of the verb *be* and *seems, appears, becomes,* and *grows.* The five senses are also linking verbs. *The food smells delicious. He appears angry. I feel bad.*

literary present tense Refers to tense used in writing that focuses on literature. The present tense is used consistently when referring to events that happen in fiction. *In Shakespeare's Twelfth Night, Viola is disguised as a page throughout most of the play.*

metaphor An implied comparison. One thing is figuratively and imaginatively called something else. *All the world is a stage.*

misplaced modifier A modifier misplaced in a sentence, thus causing confusion as to which word is supposed to be modified. **X** *The Whistle Top Buffet almost stayed open until midnight.*

mixed metaphor A metaphor in which illogical comparisons are made. *He is up a tree without a paddle.*

modifier A term used for any word or word group that describes, limits, or qualifies another word or word group. Adjectives and adverbs are modifiers, as are phrases that function as one of those parts of speech.

mood The form of a verb that indicates mood. There are three moods: indicative, which is used for statements or questions; imperative, which is used for commands and requests; and the subjunctive, which is used to express a wish or statement that is contrary to fact (*he wishes he were there*).

noncount noun A noun that cannot be counted, cannot be pluralized. Examples are *sugar* and *gasoline.* The noncount noun is sometimes referred to as the *mass noun.*

nonrestrictive element   A part of a sentence that is not essential to the meaning of another part of the sentence. Nonrestrictive or nonessential words are set off with commas.

noun   A part of speech that names a person, place, thing, idea, or animal.

number   The distinction between singular and plural as shown by an inflection or change in form. Verbs, nouns, and pronouns all have number. In irregular nouns, such as *deer,* there is no inflection or *s* to indicate plural number, and the number must be decided by the context. Pronouns change form. For example, *I* (singular) becomes *we* (plural).

object complement   See *complement.*

objective case   See *pronoun case.*

object of preposition   The object of a preposition shows relationship to some other word in the sentence.

object of verb   A word, phrase, or clause that receives direct or indirect action from the verb.

paragraph   A block of prose, often indented, that contains one controlling idea.

parallelism   The repetition of the same grammatical structures. Parallelism or parallel structure should be used with coordinate and correlative conjunctions. *College students spend their time working, playing, and resting.*

parentheses   A pair of punctuation marks used to enclose explanatory additions or to enclose a number repeated beside the word: *twenty-five (25).*

parenthetical element   A word or words that interrupt the main thought in a sentence. It can be set off with commas, parentheses, or dashes.

participle   A type of verbal that functions as an adjective.

The *jogging* woman laughed.

passive voice   See *voice.*

person (point of view)   The pronoun used to indicate point of view. The first person is the speaker or writer (*I, my, our, us*); the second person is the person to whom the speaking or writing is directed (*you, yours*), and the third person is the person, place, thing, idea, or animal spoken or written about (*he, they, it*).

personal pronoun   A pronoun that directly replaces or refers to a specific person, place, thing, idea, or animal. Examples are *I, you,* and *they.*

phrase   A related group of words that does not contain both a subject and a predicate. It functions as a part of speech. Types of phrases follow:

> **absolute phrase**   *The traffic having snarled,* Mary became frustrated.
>
> **appositive phrase**   Annie, *a writer,* is smart.
>
> **gerund phrase**   *Writing every day* is smart.
>
> **infinitive phrase**   *To write every day* is smart.
>
> **participial phrase**   *Running the race,* he fell.
>
> **prepositional phrase**   He ran *down the stairs.*
>
> **verb phrase**   I *have been writing* every day.

point of view   See *person (point of view).*

positive degree   See *comparison.*

possessive case   See *pronoun case.*

predicate   The verb and all its modifiers, objects, and complements.

predicate adjective   An adjective that follows a linking verb, such as *is,* and modifies the subject. *Annie is intelligent.*

predicate noun or nominative   A noun or pronoun that follows a linking verb, such as *is,* and renames the subject. *Annie is a writer.*

prefix   One or more letters attached to the beginning of a base or root word to change its meaning.

preposition   A part of speech that relates a noun or pronoun to some other word in the sentence. It often implies direction or gives a sense of time or place, figurative or literal. Examples are *to, at,* and *under.*

progressive verb form   A verb that ends in *-ing.* To be the main verb of a sentence, the progressive form of a verb must have helping verbs.

pronoun   A part of speech that replaces or refers to nouns and other pronouns. Examples are *he, its,* and *who.*

pronoun–antecedent agreement   The agreement of a pronoun with its antecedent (the word to which it refers) in number, person, and gender.

pronoun case   Refers to pronoun form or function in a sentence. The pronoun has only three cases: subjective, objective, and possessive. Subjects (*I, he, they*) are in the subjective case; objects (*me, him, them*) are in the objective case, and possessive pronouns (*my, his, their*) are in the possessive case.

proper noun   The names of specific persons, places, things, or animals. *Annie* and *Chicago* are examples.

quotation marks   A pair of punctuation marks used to set off direct quotations of exact words spoken or written and to set off titles of works within books, on cassette discs or tapes. Quotation marks can be used to set off words used as words.

reciprocal pronoun   Refers to a pronoun that reciprocates. *Each other* and *one another* are the only reciprocal pronouns in the English language.

redundancy   The use of more words than are necessary for clarity. Needless repetition and unnecessary qualifiers are types of redundancies. **X** *The very dead corpse is quite still.*

reflexive pronoun   Refers to a pronoun that reflects on the speaker or writer. These are the *-self* pronouns: *myself, himself, themselves.*

regular verb   A verb that forms its past and past participle by adding *-d* or *-ed.*

relative pronoun   A pronoun that introduces a dependent clause and relates to a word (the antecedent) in the independent clause. Examples are *who* and *that.*

restrictive element   A modifier that identifies the word it modifies and is, therefore, necessary or restricted to the sentence. It is not set off with commas.

run-on sentence   Two or more independent clauses written together without any punctuation marks or conjunctions separating the clauses. A run-on or fused sentence is an error. **X** *Annie went home then she prepared notes for a lecture.*

semicolon   A punctuation mark used to separate two or more independent clauses or a series of word groups with internal punctuation that call for a stronger punctuation mark to separate each word group.

sentence   A group of words that expresses a complete thought. A sentence begins with a capital letter and ends with an end mark.

sentence fragment   A group of words written as a sentence but not expressing a complete thought. A sentence fragment may be written deliberately or accidentally (an error).

simile   An open, figurative comparison of two unlike things. Either *as* or *like* is used in a simile. *The children were as noisy as thunder. Their shoulders drooped like the leaves of a May apple.*

simple sentence   A group of words with only one independent clause, that is, one subject–predicate combination.

slang expression   Expressions created by a particular generation or group. Such coinages or expressions are usually short-lived. *Slam back a cool one* is an example.

squinting modifier   A word or phrase that comes between two words or phrases, either of which could be described by the modifier. A squinting modifier confuses the reader. *The man who walked slowly waved his hand.*

subject   The "actor" of a sentence. The person, place, thing, idea, or animal about which or whom the clause (independent or dependent) is written.

subjective case   See *pronoun case.*

subject–verb agreement   The agreement of subject and verb in number and person.

subjunctive mood   See *mood.*

subordinate clause   See *dependent clause.*

subordinate conjunction   A word that introduces a clause that cannot stand alone as a sentence. This conjunction subordinates its clause to the main clause in a sentence. A few examples are *while, although,* and *unless.*

suffix   One or more letters attached to the end of a base or root word to change its part of speech, meaning, number, or tense.

superlative degree   See *comparison.*

synonyms   Two or more words that have similar definitions. Examples are *small* and *petite.*

tense   The time (real or grammatical) that the verb expresses. Verbs have six tenses, although helping verbs are needed to indicate all tenses except the present and past: **present tense** (dogs *bark*), **past tense** (dogs *barked*), **future tense** (dogs *will bark*), **present perfect tense** (dogs *have barked*), **past perfect tense** (dogs *had barked*), and **future perfect tense** (dogs *will have barked*).

tense sequence   The use of logical consistency in verb tenses. Such logic may or may not relate to actual time. For example, present tense also means an action that recurs or is ongoing.

thesis statement   A statement (not a question) that contains the controlling idea of an essay. Although only one sentence, the thesis statement should be developed sufficiently to provide the writer guidance throughout the essay.

topic or main sentence   The sentence in a paragraph that contains the topic or main idea of the paragraph.

transitional expression   A word or words that offer logical connections between single words, phrases, clauses, sentences, and paragraphs. They show similarities, contrasts, and additions, as well as sequence of items and time. They are used for examples, intensification, and cause and effect. Transitional expressions guide the reader smoothly through prose.

transitive verb   A verb with an object that receives action. Only sentences with transitive verbs can indicate active or passive voice.

usage   The usual, habitual way in which language is actually spoken or written by members in any given community or culture.

verb   A part of speech that expresses action (be it ever so weak) or establishes a state of being. It is the heartbeat of every sentence.

verbal   An umbrella term for gerund, infinitive, and participle. A verbal is derived from a verb but can function as a noun, adjective, or adverb.

verbal phrase   An infinitive, gerund, or participle (all verbals) with its modifiers, complements, and any other words belonging to it.

verb conjugation   A table that includes number, person, and the forms of a verb in its six tenses.

voice   The verb form that indicates active or passive voice. Active voice is indicated when the subject precedes the verb, and the verb is followed by a direct object. In passive voice, the direct object is brought to the front of the sentence and becomes the subject. *John wrote the report* (active voice). *The report was written by John* (passive voice).

wordiness   The use of unnecessary words. Needless repetition, redundancies, and the excessive use of qualifiers all contribute to wordiness.

Answers to Exercises

1. fewer ■ **2.** affect ■ **3.** ensure ■ **4.** eager ■ **5.** implied ■ **6.** there ■ **7.** supposed to ■ **8.** a lot ■ **9.** You're ■ **10.** unique ■ **11.** noun, preposition ■ **12.** noun, pronoun ■ **13.** adjective, conjunction ■ **14.** adverb. conjunction ■ **15.** preposition, adjective ■ **16.** verb, noun ■ **17.** pronoun, pronoun ■ **18.** conjunction, pronoun ■ **19.** adverb, adjective ■ **20.** adjective, pronoun ■ **21.** preposition, noun ■ **22.** conjunction, conjunction ■ **23.** preposition, verb ■ **24.** noun, adjective ■ **25.** conjunction, verb ■ **26.** well ■ **27.** me ■ **28.** I ■ **29.** run ■ **30.** gone ■ **31.** written ■ **32.** I ■ **33.** the food ■ **34.** whom ■ **35.** he ■ **36.** himself ■ **37.** his or her ■ **38.** lay ■ **39.** lying ■ **40.** were ■ **41.** its ■ **42.** bad ■ **43.** seen ■ **44.** an ■ **45.** taller ■ **46.** Matt's ■ **47.** an ■ **48.** those ■ **49.** comprised ■ **50.** its ■ **51.** Annie fractured her knee. ■ **52.** likes ■ **53.** meet ■ **54.** has ■ **55.** were ■ **56.** want ■ **57.** misspelled ■ **58.** all right ■ **59.** received ■ **60.** writing ■ **61.** Annie enjoys gardening; however, she has little time. ■ **62.** Annie enjoys gardening; she has little time, however. ■ **63.** She teaches at a local bank and at the college, and Matt works at the bank and learns at the college. ■ **64.** Annie writes, gardens, and jogs. ■ **65.** Annie and Matt's favorite meeting place is the Whistle Top Buffet. ■ **66.** It is located in Goldpage. ■ **67.** They discuss nouns, verbs, and adjectives when they meet. ■ **68.** During the long tutoring sessions, Matt learns a great deal. ■ **69.** Matt, who wants to succeed, works diligently. ■ **70.** Anyone who works diligently can succeed. ■ **71.** Because Matt works hard, he will become a confident writer. ■ **72.** Matt's efforts will pay great dividends. ■ **73.** Everyone's writing will improve. ■ **74.** Matt is a talented photographer; therefore, he hopes to become a professional photographer. ■ **75.** Annie's and Matt's talents will play a leading role in their destinies.

2.3 CHAPTER 2

The following explanations will provide you with any information you could not find when working on your assignment.

1. a lot/alot   To the strict grammarian, **a lot** means a parcel of real estate. Today, however, linguists are more flexible. They recognize that many people use **a lot** to mean a great deal or very much. Whether you use the two words to mean a parcel of land or to mean a great deal (for informal writing), you should write **a lot** as two words—never as one word. **Alot** is always an error.

2. burst/bursted   This is a word that does not change its spelling when it moves from present to past tense. Look at the following sentences: (*a*) My balloons **burst** at every party. (*b*) My balloons **burst** last week. (*c*) All my balloons have **burst.** Do not use **bursted** when something has **burst** in the past.

3. reason is that/reason is because   **The reason** I enjoy learning about language **is that** I can write with increased self-confidence. Never use **the reason is because;** it is as redundant as *dead corpse.*

4. centered on/centered around   You cannot **center around** something, but you can **center on** something.

5, 6. presently/currently   **Presently** means soon or in a short time. A second definition—now or currently—is given in most dictionaries. The precise writer will use **presently** to mean soon. **Currently** means at the present time or now.

7. in regard to/in regards to   Omit the *s* at the end of regard.

8, 9. moral/morale   **Moral** means a lesson or principle. The **moral** of the story is clear. The accent is placed on the first part of this word when it is spoken. To have a high **morale** is to be of high spirit, to feel good about yourself and your environment. The accent is placed on the end of this word when it is spoken.

10, 11. continual/continuous   **Continual** means ongoing with interruptions. **Continuous** means ongoing without interruptions. The s on the end of this word flows without interruption.

12, 13. a/an   The article **a** should be used before a word that begins with a consonant *sound.* Note the following examples: *a book, a card, a dollar, a history book, a historic occurrence, a humble man,* a *European tour.*

An should be used before a word beginning with a vowel *sound.* Look at the following examples: *an honest person, an herb, an ego, an igloo, an hour.*

As you can see, the *sound* that begins the word following **a** or **an,** not necessarily the first letter, determines whether you use **a** or **an.**

14, 15. your/you're   **Your** means belonging to you. Do not confuse

your with **you're,** which is a contraction for *you are.* Read the following sentence: **You're** learning a great deal, and as you learn, **your** writing skills will continue to improve.

16, 17, 18. to/too/two   **To** implies direction or is used before an action word (verb). **Too** means very or also. **Two** examples of **to** plus an action word (called an infinitive) follow:

- **to** learn
- **to** be

19. cannot/can not   **Cannot** is one word.

20, 21. as/like   Caution: Avoid using **like** when you mean **as. Like** should be used in two instances. Read the following three sentences. The first is incorrect, as indicated by the *X;* the second and third are correct.

X (*a*) The woman acts **like** she knows everything. (NO, NO, NO.)
  (*b*) The woman acts **as** if she knows everything. (YES, YES, YES.)
  (c) The students listened intently, **as** students should. See the following two examples for using **like.**

I **like** you.
Like is a verb in the preceding sentence.
Matt looks **like** his father.
Like is a preposition in the latter sentence .

Do not be concerned if you do not know the meanings of *verb* and *preposition* at this time. You can look at the examples and understand the ways in which you should use **like.**

22, 23. interdepartmental/intradepartmental   If you think of the word *interstate* and what it means, you should never confuse these two words. When you travel on interstate highways, you can travel from one state to another. If you use envelopes marked **"Interdepartmental,"** you are using envelopes that can be sent from one department to another. **Intradepartmental** then, means within the department.

2.4   **CHAPTER 2**

---

1. healthful **3.** Eager **5.** comprised **7.** hanged **9.** effect **11.** recur **13.** their **15.** pored **17.** supposed to **19.** You're **21. Regardless** of her status as a purchased slave, Phillis Wheatley became a published poet. **23.** The speaker often **implies** that Latin abbreviations and foreign phrases dropped into written works (like famous names dropped into conversations) can be a **nauseous** practice. **25.** Franklin Roosevelt was a **unique** leader; he was, for example, given unprecedented power in peacetime. **27.** Reading both fiction and nonfiction **complements** learning in the classroom and succeeding in life. **29. Almost** everybody knows that George Washington was the first President of the United States and, therefore, known as the father of our country. **31.** Pablo Picasso, a Spanish artist, was known for his cubistic and abstract works. (This sentence was correctly written.) **33.** The Malthusian theory **implies** that we may all starve one day. **35.** The reason is **that** you deserve the best.

3.1 CHAPTER 3

Note: Answers may vary. The following are suggestions.

1. unusual **3.** frugal **5.** firm **7.** thin **9.** linger

3.2 CHAPTER 3

Answers will vary. The following are examples.

1. Jenny attends class regularly, is always on time, and completes every assignment. **3.** John, my friend, works on a horse ranch in Kentucky; he is the only real cowboy I know. **5.** Pink in the middle, the ribeye was juicy and tender. **7.** The test contained ten pages, and each page had two long essay questions. **9.** Driving on I-77, I was startled by the sounds of ambulance sirens, fire trucks, squeaking brakes, and loud engines.

3.3 CHAPTER 3

The Advantages of Concise Prose   Writing concisely has several advantages. We can more easily make a point when we avoid unnecessary words and information. Our reader can more easily find and understand our main point. Streamlining prose can save the reader's time and eliminate frustration for the writer *and* reader.

3.4 CHAPTER 3

1. first **3.** new *or* innovation **5.** remains **7.** fact **9.** certain **11.** because **13.** result **15.** unique

3.5 CHAPTER 3

The following rewritten sentences are suggestions; yours may be different.

1. Criminal Justice is a unique field of study. **3.** In 1964, the Supreme Court decided that accused persons must be read their rights. **5.** The professor lectured on *surveillance*. **7.** Reporters use the word *alleged* when referring to accused persons. **9.** Investigators can appear calloused if they interview a critically injured victim too soon, but they can appear negligent if they wait too long.

3.6 CHAPTER 3

The following revised paragraphs will be different from those you have rewritten. Again, you might want to compare your versions with those of your peers.

Paragraph A   Crime Pays   Crime pays if you write about it. Many of the novels on the bestsellers' lists are crime novels. The following authors prove that writing about crime can be lucrative: James Lee Burke, Mary Higgins Clark, Patricia Cornwell, Elmore Leonard, Ed McBain, and James Patterson. These novelists' books have provided them with comfortable lifestyles. They have proved that writing concisely, correctly, and creatively can earn for the writer money, prestige, and fame. Each successful author, however, has already learned the basic rules that govern our language. Also, each successful writer of crime novels must conduct thorough research to ensure accuracy of facts. Done well, writing about crime pays.

Paragraph B   A Cappella and Other Types of Caps in Humor Writing Humor writing is in great demand because people need to laugh. Richard Lederer, Andy Rooney, and Art Buchwald are writers who have proved that if you can make people laugh, you can make money. Writers of humor, however, perform a high balancing act on a "write" rope. What is funny to one reader may not be funny to another. Successful writers of humor have learned to perform the delicate balancing act. For example, Lederer has quoted many of his former high school students, and the results are hilarious. The anonymous quotations offend no one. Lederer's quoted definitions remind me of the time one of my fellow students defined *a cappella* as part cap and part umbrella. Perhaps, I could write a book of humorous quotations because humor writing pays.

Paragraph C   A Naked Audience and Other Speech-Making Tips To most people, only death is more frightening than public speaking. Even many college students are terrified to speak in front of their peers. Some public speaking gurus have advised nervous speakers to pretend their audience is naked. That never worked for me; indeed, I found such pretense to be disconcerting. My first tip, then, is to ignore that advice. Next, know your subject thoroughly. What you do not know about your topic, you must research until you find sufficient information to make you confident. You are now ready to type notes on index cards. Number each card and include the subtopic in large print at the top. You will not read your speech, but the notes will serve as a guide so you do not omit important points. Now, stand in front of a mirror and practice. You can also videotape your speech. When the day arrives, dress appropriately, but when you are in front of your audience, forget about your looks. If you are enthusiastic about your topic, your fully dressed audience will be enthusiastic, too.

3.9 CHAPTER 3

1. In the event of a disastrous chemical explosion, we must have escape routes. **3.** Large companies have been decreasing the number of employees for several years. **5.** Brainstorming can be part of the writing process. **7.** Making contacts with influential persons is a vital part of job searching. **9.** Although couched in clever language, the student's argument was flawed.

3.10 CHAPTER 3

1. as fit as a fiddle **3.** count their chickens before they hatch **5.** an ounce of prevention is worth a pound of cure **7.** burn the midnight oil **9.** true blue

3.11 CHAPTER 3

1. He is in excellent health. **3.** Too many persons working on one job can sometimes ensure failure. **5.** Do not cause trouble. **7.** Every person gets a chance sooner or later. **9.** Children hear and understand more than we think they do.

3.13 CHAPTER 3

1. chair, chairperson **3.** flight attendant **5.** letter carrier **7.** weather forecaster or meteorologist, depending on amount of education in field **9.** humanity **11.** poor driver of either sex **13.** husband and wife, man and woman **15.** sewage lid, sewage cover **17.** Novelists use *perps* as a short-ened form of *perpetrators*. Either term refers to persons who break the law. **19.** Annie wants to contact Maria. **21.** Annie and José drank a cool beverage. **23.** Ms. Perez, a police officer in our neighborhood, just received a promotion. **25.** The use of excessive repetition of consonant sounds should be avoided. **27.** The doctor told her patient that he must have his gallbladder removed. **29.** The editor of the student newspaper wants the best person for the job. **31.** Although *jargon* has several meanings, Ms. Gomez, the departmental secretary, views it as specialized or technical language in a particular profession. **33.** At that time, I wondered what we had done. **35.** The working mother enjoys sharing her time with her daughter on the weekends.

4.2   CHAPTER 4

Proper nouns are boldfaced; common nouns are underlined.

1. Charleston is the <u>capital</u> of **West Virginia**. **3. Matt** works at the **Goldpage National Bank** and attends the local <u>college</u>. **5. Saturday** is their favorite <u>day</u> because they can relax. **7.** One fall <u>evening</u>, **Annie** told **Matt** that **Appalachia** would be the next nationwide <u>fad</u>. **9. Annie** loved to predict the <u>future</u> and play with <u>language</u>. **11.** She recently told him to capitalize all proper <u>nouns</u> and each <u>word</u> beginning a <u>sentence</u>. **13.** <u>Loyalty</u> is an admirable <u>trait</u>, and the <u>professor</u> has <u>loyalty</u>. **15.** Annie's <u>editor</u> lives in **New York**.

4.3   CHAPTER 4

1. class **3.** council **5.** jury **7.** public **9.** crowd, mob

4.4   CHAPTER 4

1. Matt's red car has <u>fewer</u> gallons of gasoline now. **3.** Since Annie accepted Matt's invitation to dinner, she has had <u>fewer</u> hours for writing. **5.** She has <u>less</u> sand in her hourglass.

4.5   CHAPTER 4

Your list of nouns should include all the underlined words in the following sentences.

1. In the <u>Whistle Top Buffet</u>, <u>Annie</u> leaned across the <u>table</u>, smiled, and said, "Remember, <u>Matt</u>, that abstract <u>nouns</u> are most appropriate when they are used in the <u>thesis</u> of an <u>essay</u>." **3.** <u>Matt</u> listened closely, for he wanted to succeed in his college <u>classes</u>. "Tell me more," said <u>Matt</u>. **5.** <u>Matt</u> promised and asked, "Will I learn about <u>pronouns</u> later?" **7.** Again, leaning toward <u>Matt</u> to emphasize her <u>point</u>, she said, "Always anchor your abstract <u>language</u> with concrete <u>examples</u>. Your <u>writing</u> will improve." **9.** <u>Matt</u> said, "So you're talking about concrete <u>language</u> versus abstract <u>language</u>. It's more than just noun <u>choices</u>." **11.** <u>Matt</u> frowned, "Oh, I know that." **13.** "Yes," replied <u>Matt</u>, "will you go with me?" **15.** "You bet," replied <u>Matt</u> as he motioned to the <u>waiter</u>. **17.** Dark <u>clouds</u> rolled in the <u>sky</u>, giving <u>promise</u> of an autumn <u>storm</u>. **19.** The <u>temperature</u> had dropped during the past <u>hour</u>.

1. Matt likes to talk with Annie because **he** learns so much about the language. antecedent—Matt; pronoun—he. **3.** As a **student** at the college, **he** is committed to becoming an excellent writer. antecedent—student; pronoun—he. **5. Matt** and **Annie** met on a sunny July day when **they** attended a picnic. antecedents—Matt/Annie; pronoun—they. **7.** Annie asked **Matt** to the picnic, and **he** accepted. antecedent—Matt; pronoun—he. **9. "Matt,"** said Annie, "a singular antecedent requires a singular pronoun. **You** cannot mix singular with plural." antecedents—Matt; pronoun—You. **11. Matt** and his **brother** attend a writing class each week, and **both** are earning high grades. antecedent—Matt, brother; pronoun—both. **13. Mark** forgot to write **his** name in **his** book. antecedent—Mark; pronoun—his, his. **15. Mark** wrote **his** name in **his** new book. antecedent—Mark; pronoun—his, his.

1. The brown-headed *cowbird* is fascinating; *its* song is a thin whistle. **3.** The *cowbird* lays *its* eggs in the nest of another species. **5.** *Cowbirds* beg for food, and *their* begging is noisy. **7.** The *hummingbird* has a long slender bill, and *it* can use that bill in the same way a person uses a straw. **9.** Although the *hummingbird* is barely larger than my thumb, *it* can travel thousands of miles. **11.** The tiny *bird* flies south in the fall, but *it* returns to the same bird feeder in the spring. **13.** The sweet-eating *ant* loves the sugar water, and some people rub cooking oil outside the feeder to keep *it* away. **15.** The male and female *bluebirds* mate for life, and together *they* build a nest and feed *their* young. **17.** After several days of hard work, the *female* laid her eggs; *she* waited patiently for the eggs to hatch. **19.** During a heavy rainstorm, the male *phoebe* perched on the branch of a nearby chestnut tree; despite the downpour, *he* would not relinquish *his* watch over *his* family. (This was correct.)

The words in brackets in the following sentences cause problems.

1. The diners stared at [Annie, Annie's editor, and] <u>him</u>. **3.** Matt would drive [Annie's editor and] <u>her</u> to the marketing workshop. **5.** [Annie's editor and] <u>she</u> would learn a great deal. **7.** During the break, the trainer told [Annie and] <u>them</u> that many would-be poets make a living in advertising careers. **9.** <u>We</u> [trainees] learned that appearance and reality are often different. **11.** [The editor, and] <u>he</u> learned that one company's test market of its new product indicated the price had to be raised. **13.** Ms. Wise emphasized to the group, including [Annie and] <u>me</u>, the importance of attractive packaging. **15.** [Annie and] <u>we</u> also learned that excellent products have not sold well because of poor advertising campaigns.

5.4 CHAPTER 5

1. <u>they</u> **3.** <u>them</u> **5.** <u>she</u> **7.** <u>we</u> **9.** <u>they</u> **11.** <u>I</u> **13.** <u>she</u> **15.** <u>her</u>

5.5 CHAPTER 5

1. Between you and <u>me</u>, Matt is learning a great deal. **3.** The people elected John Broadgrin, Matt Murray, and <u>me</u> to represent them. **5.** <u>Whom</u> did the accountant believe? **7.** <u>Who</u> is calling? **9.** John, whose name we misspelled, is angry at Matt and <u>me</u>. **11.** Richard Burden, Annie's cat, does not have an ounce of body fat on him, for <u>he</u> and a few other cats have been working out at Naughtiness. **13.** Smiling sweetly, Annie asked "<u>Whom</u> do you like as a tutor?" **15.** <u>Whose</u> book is lost?

5.7 CHAPTER 5

1. *All people* must be careful about their use of language. Everybody must be careful about *his or her* use of language. **3.** Somebody forgot *his or her* books. **5.** Neither of the women wore *her* hiking boots. **7.** Each of the men liked *his* instructor. **9.** Nobody in the class has written *his or her* second draft. Nobody in the class has written *the* second draft.

5.8 CHAPTER 5

1. Who **3.** whom **5.** who **7.** whomever **9.** Whoever **11.** whoever **13.** whom **15.** who

5.9 CHAPTER 5

1. <u>who</u> **3.** <u>who</u> **5.** <u>which</u> **7.** <u>who's</u> **9.** <u>who</u> **11.** <u>whom</u> **13.** <u>that</u> **15.** <u>who</u>

5.10 CHAPTER 5

1. those **3.** those **5.** that **7.** this **9.** this **11.** those **13.** One Boomer **15.** those days

5.11 CHAPTER 5

The corrections are boldfaced.

An Appalachian Uncle   When I was a child, my Uncle Alfred was influential in my life. He **himself** had not even gone through elementary school, much less college. Still, he placed a high value on education. One cold winter day, the snow was two feet deep. I did not want to go to school, but my uncle insisted. He upset my mother and **me** when he told her I should go despite the weather. My uncle and mother **themselves** discussed the matter on the phone. Soon, I was on my way to my first-grade class. Years later, as I reached for my college diploma, my mother, father, and uncle sat on the first row. We were proud of **ourselves.** They were proud because they had not let me give up. I was proud because they were my family. During my school years, I had learned much. Education is not an end in itself; it is an ongoing process. I knew it would enrich the lives of my classmates and **me.** My parents and **I** are still grateful to my Uncle Alfred, my uncle from the hills of Appalachia.

5.12 CHAPTER 5

Your sentences may be slightly different.

1. Some people say you will have bad luck if a black cat crosses your path. **3.** Annie dropped the paperweight on the glass-topped desk and broke the paperweight. **5.** It has been a terrible winter. (This was correct.) **7.** Garcia and John are entertaining because they like poetry and drama. **9.** When Annie added a page to her book, the page contained many references to wildlife.

5.13 CHAPTER 5

Answers that are boldfaced may vary.

1. The United States Congress refers to our nation's governing body, which is located in Washington, D. C.; each state is represented in Washington by **its** members of Congress. **3.** Each legislature comprises two bodies, a senate and a house of delegates; legislators' offices are located in the state's capitol. **5.** The governor of each state gives a state-of-the-state address in which **he or she** discusses accomplishments of the preceding year and budget allocations for the next year. **7.** Governors meet once a year; **their annual meeting** focuses on the governors' main concerns. **9. Most people know** *writing* has one *t*, but written has two *t*'s; at least, they should know that. **11.** The man **who** was called a politician became angry. **13.** The senator introduced a bill to increase punishment for persons convicted of driving under the influence of alcohol (DUI), and **introducing the bill** was a good idea. **15.** The three branches of government are the legislative, the judicial, and the executive; legislators, **whom** the people elect, write the bills that become laws. **17.** You and **I** are expected to obey those laws. **19.** Members of a state supreme court belong to the judicial branch; the three branches provide a system of checks and balances for **us** citizens. **21.** West Virginia's capital is Charleston, and **West Virginia** is not part of Virginia. **23.** Each of the states has **its** own brand of politics. **25.** United States citizens have the privilege of voting for their representatives, and if **they** do not vote, **they** are not a part of the democratic process. Your *sentences may be different from the ones given.* **27.** The members of Congress were in caucus; they arrived early to attend the caucus. **29.** The musician's opus has already become a classic; the audience was pleased to hear classical music. **31.** The two diners discussed the meaning of *circumlocution* with each other, and one said, "Circumlocution occurs when a dog goes around and around in a circle before it lies down." **33.** Ordering prime rib a la carte, the two diners argued with each other over the definition of *Cameroon*; one said, "Cameroon is not a cookie, but it is an African country." **35.** Matt himself knows that keeping abreast of topical issues is an important part of his ongoing education. **37.** Back at the Whistle Top Buffet, the two diners accused each other of being quixotic. **39.** Don Quixote himself is quixotic; that is, he tries to reach impossible goals and becomes the target of ridicule. **41.** Proper names from which words are derived are known as eponyms; eponyms are fascinating. **43.** Hearing a mort, Degas knew a deer had been fatally shot. **45.** Samuel Clemens himself chose the pseudonym *Mark Twain*; *pseudo-* means false, and *-nym* means name. **47.** Send copies of the memo to **whomever** you wish. **49.** With **whom** did you say Matt had talked? **51. Whom** did the manager believe? **53.** Matt played with Bob, his five-year-old nephew, and he laughed at **Bob. 55.** Annie was to meet Matt and **him** at the Whistle Top Buffet. **57.** Matt and **she** looked at the report in stony silence. **59. We** ourselves learned that the whole comprises the parts. **61.** The clever squirrel jumped from **its** nest onto the squirrel-proof bird feeder. **63.** I watched a squirrel as it hung upside down from a metal feeder; **I** could see the squirrel eat as it hung by its back feet. **65.** Between you and **him,** you should create a popular book on wildlife. **67.** Rose Marie, **whom** I was telling you about, has been promoted; she is now an editor. **69.** Rose Marie, **who** will serve as Annie's editor, is a grammarian. **71.** Everyone in the woods during hunting season should wear **his or her** bright orange clothing. **73. Many people** say that when a person walks under a ladder, he or she will have bad luck. **75.** Grammar and success are somehow connected; do not try to spell *grammar* **and** *success* backwards because they do not spell anything.

6.1 CHAPTER 6

1. visited **3.** flew **5.** appreciated **7.** searched **9.** seemed **11.** scuttled **13.** have enjoyed **15.** meet **17.** have met **19.** has talked

6.2 CHAPTER 6

1. covered **3.** heard **5.** awoke or awaked **7.** were **9.** lay **11.** began **13.** startled **15.** opened **17.** asked **19.** known

6.4 CHAPTER 6

1. be **3.** were **5.** were **7.** get **9.** were

6.5 CHAPTER 6

1. linking **3.** transitive **5.** linking **7.** transitive **9.** intransitive **11.** transitive **13.** intransitive **15.** transitive

6.6 CHAPTER 6

Your sentences may be slightly different.

1. Before killing a mouse, a cat first tantalizes it. **3.** A cat will never chase an artificial rabbit around a track. **5.** Cats will not usually perform tricks for treats. **7.** A cat never ignores another cat. **9.** A cat uses a silent meow as an attention-getter. **11.** Cats use litter boxes. **13.** Cats use catnip-treated scratching pads. **15.** Cats demonstrate their intelligence and independence in a number of ways.

6.7 CHAPTER 6

1. were **3.** were **5.** correct **7.** were **9.** be

The following verb forms should be included and underlined in your sentences.

11. has become **13.** has run **15.** has eaten **17.** have gone **19.** lay **21.** has written **23.** have seen **25.** has frozen **27.** were **29.** used **31.** saw **33.** become **35.** drunk **37.** lying **39.** hanged

7.1 CHAPTER 7

1. the, quaint **3.** eager, Annie's, exciting, writing **5.** the, smiling, the, tallest, the **7.** Organized, ambitious **9.** anxious, the, first **11.** the, last, an, expensive, a, confident **13.** The, hard, important, the, nervous, little **15.** the, grueling, delicious

 CHAPTER 7

A. only two persons, places, things, ideas, or animals. **B.** three or more persons, places, things, ideas, or animals. **1.** brighter **3.** more bravely **5.** most efficient **7.** more beautifully **9.** more intelligent

7.4 CHAPTER 7

1. well, important **3.** Third **5.** best **7.** more **9.** lesser **11.** calm **13.** Thus **15.** delicious

7.5 CHAPTER 7

1. too, already **3.** well, a lot **5.** well **7.** an **9.** those **11.** a **13.** most **15.** an **17.** The student who was rapidly writing walked to the front of the room. **19.** He danced nearly all night. **21.** Its hours run from noon to nearly midnight. Its hours run from nearly noon to midnight. **23.** The WTB's competition stays open almost until midnight. **25.** The Whistle Top has perfect hours for its diners.

How to Become an Effective Writer   Many people say that they could write a book based on **their** lives. Someday, they plan to write "that book." Most people, however, have not learned the rules necessary for successful writing. They believe they can already write **well** enough. More **important,** many who know they **easily** make mistakes believe those mistakes do not matter. **Their** writing, then, is often riddled with mistakes that have euphemistically been called surface errors. The problem with so-called surface errors is that they can block the message **a** writer is trying to convey.

These potential writers could write more **effectively** if they understood that editors have neither the time nor the inclination to clean up grammar, replace misused words, and correct faulty punctuation. **These** kinds of mistakes **only** get manuscripts rejected **more quickly** than anything else, boring prose excluded.

First, you must learn the basics. In recent years, the basics have been downplayed. Many still feel that teaching rules is **almost** tantamount to destroying creativity. Writing, however, is more than creating, although it is that, **too.** Writing is **a** skill that demands knowledge and **an** apprenticeship.

Second, to become a writer, you must make a commitment. You must decide if you want to succeed in life or if you want **only** to slide by. **Only** you can decide if you want your work published or if you want to receive rejection slip after rejection slip. **Only** you can make **a** commitment to do **well** in life and climb the ladder of success.

Third, and just as **important,** you must be a reader. If you are moved by **a** powerful sentence, you have the potential to become a writer. If you savor words that have been carefully chosen and skillfully combined, if you can be touched by a **well**-turned phrase, then you, my friend, do have the potential to become **a** writer in the true sense of the word. Continue to be **an** eager learner. As you begin to feel **good** about yourself, I wish you **well.**

8.1 CHAPTER 8

1. Although grammar has gone _out_ of **style,** effective business writing still demands knowledge and application _of_ the grammar **rules. 3.** Matt has learned that to move _up_ the **ladder** _at_ the **bank,** he must learn to apply the rules _of_ **grammar** and **punctuation** _to_ his **writing. 5.** _After_ much **consideration,** she agreed. **7.** Matt sometimes writes _with_ a **pencil,** sometimes _with_ a **pen,** and sometimes _on_ a **computer. 9.** It allows him to make corrections _with_ just a few **taps** _on_ certain **keys. 11.** Annie is a best-selling writer, but Matt thinks she is a bit _of_ a **snob** _about_ **usage. 13.** Annie had promised to bring an autographed copy _of_ her latest **book** _on_ **language. 15.** He knew that most successful employees _at_ the **bank** could speak two dialects: the one they spoke _during_ **childhood** and the one they learned as adults.

8.2 CHAPTER 8

1. During the lunch hour (noun) for our meeting **3.** for one hour (adverb) **5.** between you and me (adjective) **7.** in the Administration Building (adverb) **9.** of prepositions (adjective) from the objective case **11.** to life (adverb) by the use of sensory language **13.** on Annie's comments (adverb) **15.** in the same place (adverb)

8.3 CHAPTER 8

1. To write effectively is important. infinitive; noun **3.** Annie enjoys writing every day. gerund; noun **5.** Annie researched to prepare for her lecture on Greek culture. infinitive; adverb **7.** Her first lecture focused on the Greeks' dividing and classifying their language. gerund; noun **9.** Aristophanes, the Greek playwright, was famous for reflecting human foibles in his comedies. gerund; noun **11.** Maintaining a sense of humor is essential for both individuals and nations. gerund; noun

13. <u>Using humor</u>, the playwright enlightened his audience. participial; adjective **15.** He excelled in <u>writing comedy</u>. gerund; noun

8.4 CHAPTER 8

1. subject **3.** object of the verb **5.** adverb (modifies *researched*) **7.** object of preposition **9.** object of preposition **11.** subject **13.** adjective (modifies *playwright*) **15.** object of preposition

8.5 CHAPTER 8

1. participial; adjective; Jaguar **3.** infinitive; adverb; left **5.** prepositional; adjective; car **7.** infinitive; noun **9.** participial; adjective; she **11.** absolute; the entire sentence **13.** participial; adjective; he **15.** participial; adjective; Tom **17.** infinitive; adjective; plans **19.** infinitive; adverb; went

Your rewritten versions may vary slightly.

21. correct **23.** To clean the windshield, Matt drove to the nearest service station. **25.** While leaving the service station, Matt remembered that he needed to purchase gasoline. **27.** His car had a clean windshield and a tank full of gas; Matt was ready to drive to class. **29.** As he warmed to his topic, however, his essay began to take on a life of its own. **31.** To produce an engaging essay, he had to be sure each sentence focused on the topic. **33.** Writing the first draft, Matt was not concerned about surface errors. **35.** When proofreading and editing the final version, he would correct all errors. **67.** All things considered (absolute) **69.** While lying in bed (participial) **71.** Resting on top of the file cabinet (participial) **73.** in the late Hemingway's house (prepositional); in Key West, Florida (prepositional) **75.** Being biographical in nature (participial); on his hometown (prepositional) **77.** After writing *Look Homeward Angel* (participial); to his editor (prepositional) **79.** Within a short time (prepositional); after that (prepositional) **81.** During Wolfe's writing career (prepositional) **83.** during his childhood (prepositional) **85.** Sharing tourists with the elegant Biltmore Estate (participial) **87.** To have the opportunity to purchase his books and copies of his letters (infinitive) **89.** Touring Statesville (participial) **91.** Drawn to Europe and back to the States again and again (participial) **93.** To feed her family (infinitive) **95.** of his own (prepositional); into another room (prepositional)

9.1 CHAPTER 9

1. <u>birds</u> fly **3.** <u>female</u> searches **5.** <u>chickadee</u> has become **7.** <u>Corn</u> and <u>thistle</u> attract **9.** <u>animal</u> and <u>eater</u> is [the squirrel]

9.2 CHAPTER 9

1. wants **3.** objects **5.** is **7.** is **9.** have **11.** creates **13.** are **15.** wants **17.** grades **19.** is

9.3 CHAPTER 9

1. have **3.** has **5.** has **7.** is **9.** is **11.** focuses **13.** is **15.** lives

9.4 CHAPTER 9

Gwendolyn Brooks: A Living Poem Gwendolyn Brooks, one of the most talented of American poets, **likes** to be referred to as black rather than African-American. The first black writer to receive the Pulitzer Prize, she is now Poet Laureate Gwendolyn Brooks of Illinois. Carl Sandburg was the first to serve in this position. Brooks **has** followed him. A series of awards **has** come her way, including the Shelley Memorial Award and two Guggenheim Fellowships. There **were** also the American Academy of Arts and Letters Award and the Anisfield-Wolf Award, to mention only a few. Named in her honor **are** the Gwendolyn Brooks Junior High School and the Gwendolyn Brooks Cultural Center. Indeed, the number of awards she **has** received **is** too numerous to mention. She and her husband **live** in Chicago. The poet, as well as her daughter, **is** talented. Among Brooks' many publications **are** an autobiography, one novel, several books of poetry, and writing manuals. Although Linguistics **is** not her specialization, her poetry and prose **let** the reader know she is nonetheless a sculptor of language. A large number of people who **love** poetry **are** among her fans. What is more, the number of her fans **continues** to increase as they become acquainted with her works. One of her latest books **has** a cover resembling a notebook that an elementary student might use. Enclosed in a marbleized black and white cover, *Children Coming Home* **is** about the size of a school notebook.

Brooks, like other fine poets, skillfully **uses** sensory language. "Kitchenette Building," one of her many poems, **penetrates** to the core of naked reality. An appeal to our five senses and this naked reality **are** sharply delineated. When the battle between the dream world and real life **begins,** the necessity of day-to-day survival "**grays**" away any chance for dreams to emerge as victors. The first lines of this poem **set** a universal theme in motion. "We" **conveys** an image of all people, through no fault or plan of their own, who **are** forced to live in a substandard environment. Imagery, which is etched in desolation and hopelessness, **pervades** the poem. In the last stanza, the dream, along with any hopes of a dream, **has** vanished. Brooks, like the best of other poets, **succeeds** in making us sense, see, smell, hear, and taste quiet desperation. The reality of being left without dreams **has** been made concrete in this poem.

Gwendolyn Brooks has, indeed, earned the continuing series of awards that **has** come her way. It is no wonder that her life itself has been referred to as a living poem.

10.1 | CHAPTER 10

1. The Milky Way is a galaxy, and it contains approximately 100,000 million stars. **3.** A light-year represents the distance required for light to travel in one year, but such a distance is still beyond our comprehension. **5.** The Sun is a star, and it is located 30,000 light-years from the center of the galaxy. **7.** Some galaxies are much farther from Earth than the Milky Way, so their light requires 10 billion years to reach Earth. **9.** Our Solar System contains the Sun and also boasts nine planets. (Sentence was correct.)

10.2 | CHAPTER 10

1. Mercury is located closer to the Sun than any other planet in our Solar System, **and** Pluto is located farthest from the Sun. **3.** Pluto is farther from the Sun than any of the other planets, **and** it travels almost 248 years to complete its journey around the Sun. **5.** The Hubble Space Telescope was named after Edwin Hubble, **and** it is the largest telescope ever launched into space. **7.** This distance allows the telescope to clear Earth's atmosphere, **so** the Hubble provides a clearer picture of the universe than is provided by Earth-bound telescopes. **9.** Nothing can live on Venus, **for** its surface temperature is 900°F. **11.** Planets in science fiction often have more than one moon, **and** some planets in our Solar System have more than one moon. **13.** Writers of excellent science fiction research carefully, **so** many planets in their works have more than one moon. **15.** These forecasts are viewed by many people as mere superstition, **but** others read their astrological forecasts every day.

10.3 | CHAPTER 10

1. Because reading is a prerequisite to effective writing, writers of engaging prose are also readers. **3.** You cannot become an effective writer unless you learn the rules of writing. (Sentence was correctly written.) **5.** So that he would understand comma usage, Matt practiced applying the rules to actual writing. **7.** While he edited his essays, Matt sometimes had to look up a rule for comma placement. **9.** After Matt polishes an essay, he has a real sense of accomplishment.

10.4   CHAPTER 10

1. <u>I know the town</u> [where Annie was born]. **3.** <u>We cannot apply the</u> <u>rules of writing</u> [until we have learned them]. **5.** <u>I can write with</u> <u>increased self-confidence</u> [when I use commas correctly]. **7.** <u>My self-</u> <u>esteem really soared</u> [when I received my first check for a published essay]. **9.** <u>I can now write at home in the evenings and receive money</u> <u>for my efforts</u> [because I have both knowledge and a computer].

10.5   CHAPTER 10

Answers may vary slightly.

1. Because I want to impress my instructor, I attend every class. **3.** The instructor knows I am a serious student because I complete every assignment. **5.** I often study late at night, although I work and go to college during the day. **7.** When I receive an *A* on a writing assignment, I become encouraged again. **9.** After I graduate, my chance to receive excellent instruction will be gone. **11.** Unless I understand the importance of this time in college, my time could be wasted. **13.** Since I have learned that logical thinking is a requirement for clear writing, I think now before writing. **15.** It is easier to write a rough draft when I follow steps in the writing process. **17.** Before I learned the recursive nature of writing, writing was difficult for me. **19.** Once I formulate a preliminary thesis statement, I am ready to write the rough draft.

10.6   CHAPTER 10

1. Students can either learn the rules or suffer the consequences. **3.** Both writing in a vacuum and writing without knowledge lead to failure. **5.** She made her students understand that effective writing required both the knowledge of rules for writing and the application of rules to writing. **7.** Whether you submit your essay or rewrite it matters not to me. **9.** Not only was Annie attractive, but also she was intelligent.

10.7   CHAPTER 10

1. compound **3.** complex **5.** compound–complex **7.** simple **9.** complex

10.8   CHAPTER 10

Proofreading Tips   As soon as we have written our last draft**, we** should proofread carefully. There are so many kinds of errors to look for**, for**

example, misspelled words, comma splices, run-ons, fragments, and errors in grammar. Reading the last sentence first and continuing to read backwards, **we** can more easily find word groups that are not really sentences. Also, if we begin reading the last word, then the second to last, and so on, **we** can isolate word**s. Then** we can more readily catch misspelled words. After all, computer spell-checks do not catch every misspelling. **They** will, for example, accept *their* when we meant to write *there.* We should also ask someone else to read our writing, if possible. **Another** proofreader will not have fallen in love with our prose. We do tend to love our own writing**. It** is, after all, our baby. Regardless of its deformities**, we** think it is beautiful. Because we want to find all our **errors before** our reader sees them**, we** must learn to proofread carefully. This means we must proofread small amounts of writing at one **time so** that we do not become too tired to catch our mistakes. Also, it is a good idea to put our work in "cold storage" for as long as possible, retrieve it, and proofread it again. Proofreading and correcting all errors, we can be assured of receiving a high grade**, at** least, if the content is compelling. Knowing the steps in the writing process is important**, especially** knowing those steps involving proof-reading and editing.

10.9 | CHAPTER 10

Your rewritten version may vary slightly.

1. Because Matt learned a great deal about science fiction from his discussions with Annie, his interest in the genre increased, and he continued to learn. **3.** Frank Herbert wrote excellent science fiction. He wrote *Dune,* for example. **5.** However, *Dune* is much more than a story about the physical world. It is a story about the human mind, including its strengths and its weaknesses. **7.** The obese character leans over a globe of his world, placing one hand over the entire globe. **9.** "I Have No Mouth, and I Must Scream" is a chilling science fiction story by Harlan Ellison. Its main character is a computer that overpowers humankind. **11.** Wanting at least to scream, the character has no mouth. He is doomed to silent and eternal entrapment. **13.** Never a genre that highlights only technology, science fiction explores the human condition. **15.** Containing all the themes of mainstream fiction, science fiction has much to teach us. **17.** An organization of fine science fiction authors, the Science Fiction Writers of America was founded in 1965. **19.** Many science fiction writers of this century have distinguished themselves. Included in a long list of such writers are Isaac Asimov, Ray Bradbury, Edgar Rice Burroughs, Ursula LeGuin, Theodore Sturgeon, A. E. van Vogt, Roger Zelazny, and, of course, Frank Herbert.

10.11 CHAPTER 10

Your rewritten version may vary slightly.

Dear Jill,

Your request that I offer advice on advertising for your new gourmet restaurant was a welcome **one because** you and Jack have been helpful to me in the past.

You should choose a color for the paper of your brochure that is beautiful yet elegantly understated**, for** instance, a tint that might resemble the color of a gallon of white paint with only four drops of rich brown added. Ah, yes, that would do it. The color of the paper would dictate the color of the printer's ink. **It,** of course, would have to be chocolate brown.

The cover of your brochure might feature an artist's sketch of the famous old **home that** will house your restaurant. The name of your restaurant, Top of the Hill, could complete the cover.

The language must appeal to a certain group. **For** example, it should have some snob appeal. After all, a connoisseur has acquired a taste that is discriminating**. Then,** you should include the words *discriminating taste* in your brochure. Also, you can banty about a few choice words**, for** example, *bon appetit, elegant,* and *dining pleasure.* Scratch that last one**. It** has become a cliché. *Palate* is still **good if** it is combined with the right words.

Jill, short of writing your brochure for you, **I'll** just mention a few tips with respect to the magical world of advertising. The language can provide a powerful tool**. It** can seduce, titillate, excite, and thereby bring customers—nay, clients—through your doors. Like the subtle color of your brochure that the customer never notices**, the** language itself will not be noticed consciously for what it is really doing**. For** instance, the diction suggested in the beginning of this letter appeals to the reader's desire to be in a class apart. You can also appeal to your clients' other desires**. They** want to be happy and healthy. They want to belong, so choose words that appeal to those desires, *highest standards, exclusive clientele, superb service,* and *ambiance,* for example.

Sculpted like a work of art**, language** can serve your marketing purpose. You must, however, include some basic **information amid** the fluff of advertising. Containing the name, address, and phone number of your restaurant, the time and days your establishment is open, meals served, and a mention that reservations are required**, your** brochure will launch your new business. Do not mention prices. **If** clients need to ask about prices, they cannot afford you.

If you couch the above information in persuasive language that is enfolded between the covers of a tasteful **brochure, your** new restaurant will soon become the famous Top of the Hill. If I can be of further help, Jill, **just** let me know.

Best wishes,

Annie

11.1 CHAPTER 11

1. Annie was invited to participate in a panel discussion for a local organization, and she wrote a letter in which she accepted the invitation. **3.** On the day of the dinner meeting, she arrived early. **5.** She, of course, had no speech prepared. **7.** Self-assured and knowledgeable, she would move to Plan B. **9.** Armed with hurriedly scribbled notes, her letter, and lots of speaking experience, she approached the lectern. **11.** Yes, she had reason to be concerned, for she had been prepared for a panel discussion. **13.** Next, she aimed a confident smile at her audience. (Sentence was correct.) **15.** After thanking the program chairperson for inviting her, she shared parts of her letter. **17.** Not knowing what this will do to your nervous system, I must confess that I am not an organized person. **19.** I may be organized, but I regard perseverance and commitment to be as important as organizational skills. **21.** I might have spent Monday evening with Amy Tan, Tuesday evening with Richard Rodriguez, Wednesday with Mary E. Mebane, Thursday with Russell Baker, Friday with Cherokee Paul McDonald, and Saturday with Annie Dillard. **23.** On Sundays, I did countless chores, for I no longer had the luxury of procrastinating. **25.** Setting priorities and learning to juggle became an everyday part of my life. **27.** I adjusted to frozen dinners, stacks of laundry, and dustbunnies on the floor. (Sentence was correct.) **29.** During those long sessions of reading, I encountered the prose of Annie Dillard.

11.2 CHAPTER 11

Commas for Clarity When we write, commas must be used to set off mild interjections, such as *oh* or *well.* Of course, we should use such interjections sparingly. Writing that is clear, concise, complete, and concrete is easy to read and understand. Commas may not do much to make writing concise, complete, and concrete, but they certainly do help to make writing clear. We know, for example, that commas should be used in long numbers like 6, 324, 940. Also, they should be used between city and state. Examples are New York, New York, and Charleston, West Virginia. (Yes, there is another Charleston.) A comma should also be used between the date of the month and the year. An example follows: July 4, 1997. If you write a personal letter, you must use a comma after the salutation. A business letter, of course, requires a colon after the salutation. All in all, commas are handy little squiggles, and each one guides the reader along the road to understanding meaning in any piece of writing. You do agree, don't you? Since they help us writers to make our meaning clear, we should use them with care.

11.3 ┃ CHAPTER 11

1. Annie said, "Matt, remember that you must use commas to set off names of person you are addressing directly." **3.** "How does it feel to have your latest essay published?" asked Matt. **5.** Matt asked, "Was that really the title of your essay?" **7.** Annie said, "Not to change the subject, Matt, but have I told you about the time I was asked to participate in a panel discussion?" **9.** She said, "It could have been a disaster." **11.** Standing in the parking lot, Matt asked, "Is that fire shooting from the roof?" **13.** He said, "This reminds me of the maxim about 'the best-laid plans of mice and men,' Annie." **15.** "Oh, it wasn't a panel discussion; I learned when I arrived at the club that I had to make a speech, not serve on a panel," said Annie as she laughed.

11.4 ┃ CHAPTER 11

1. "Commas and periods should be placed inside the closing quotation marks," said the trainer. **3.** Matt said, "Annie, I especially enjoy your teaching at the bank." **5.** "Can you tell me why the exclamation point and question mark are placed sometimes inside and sometimes outside the closing quotation marks?" asked Annie. **7.** Did she say, "You get only one in a lifetime"? **9.** The author's quotation is worth mentioning: "Grammer [sic] is an easy word to misspell."

11.5 ┃ CHAPTER 11

1. Annie's mother, Mrs. Penwright, wrote an essay on high school reunions; it was written in first person. **3.** She had no electricity; the house was dark. **5.** Suddenly, the lights came on; she could hear the hum of the refrigerator. **7.** Mrs. Penwright smelled smoke and saw fire; it was time to take action. **9.** Aiming the hose at the roof of her brick house, she turned the water on full force. (Sentence was correct.) **11.** It was Annie; she said that she and her friends were coming to help fight the fire. **13.** All of them went to the garage and collected the following: rakes, hoes, shovels, and weedeaters. **15.** Firefighters could not get close enough to do anything; nevertheless, they were ready to work as soon as they could. **17.** Annie saw many frightened animals that night: deer, rabbits, squirrels, raccoons, skunks, opossums, and groundhogs. **19.** Looking out the windows, they saw miles of smoldering embers and blackened, leafless trees silhouetted against a full autumn moon; miraculously, no one had been seriously injured.

11.6 CHAPTER 11

Sometimes, dashes and parentheses can be used interchangeably, depending on your intention to emphasize or de-emphasize.

1. A knock at the door (it interrupted the silence) startled the diners. **3.** The firefighter (a 20-year-old woman) was invited to eat. **5.** The woman—tired, hungry, and sleepy—was obviously courageous. **7.** José (his face was smudged with black smoke) looked tired. **9.** José (despite his smudged face) was handsome. **11.** Nonetheless, at least two-thirds of the forest had been destroyed. **13.** Her name (this was learned during the introductions) was Thelma Martinique. **15.** The conversation eventually turned to Mrs. Penwright's well-written essay, and José asked if he could share a copy with his sister-in-law.

11.7 CHAPTER 11

All corrections are boldfaced.

High School Reunions My high school reunion will be held in a few **weeks. It** will be my fortieth. **Although I** have never attended before, I have decided to attend this **highly touted** celebration. Each time that I received a **well-written** notice in the **past, I** tossed it in the trash because I thought I should wait. I thought my looks would improve if I **waited. I** would be **beautiful, thin, and** young looking. **Alas, Father** Time continues to scratch a **deep-lined** surface on my face. My lips and eyes continue to **shrink, but** everything else gets bigger. I really should have attended earlier when I looked like Liz Taylor in *National Velvet.* Now, I just look like National Velvet, the horse. Of **course, I'm** sure everyone else will have aged more than **I. That's** the real advantage of attending reunions.

My husband thinks that (I don't know where he got such an idea) I was an outstanding **student—beautiful,** brilliant, and popular. I'll be **hard-pressed** to explain to him why no one at the reunion will even remember my name.

You must wonder why I have chosen to attend this **time, given** my Delta Dawn looks and unpopular status. The years **do, indeed,** leave a philosophic mind. At last, I know my classmates will look beyond such superficial characteristics (right!) as beauty and popular status. I have a successful marriage of **thirty-four** years. **I** have a career that is often gratify**ing (sometimes** not, but that's another **story) and** a business that grows steadily.

Father Time isn't winning all the **battles. I** may not be svelte and beautiful, but I still love life. For a **57-year-old,** I'm doing all right. I'll see you at the **reunion. Please** remember my name, for, Tom Penwright, my husband will be with me.

1. One of Mrs. Penwright's recent essays "A Pocketful of Love" was published in a prestigious periodical. (Sentence was correct.)
3. Describing her grandmother, the author **says, "My** grandmother was remarkable in many ways." **5.** She wore her gray hair wound into a circle at the top of her **head; it** looked like a silver crown that belied her small income and simple homespun life. **7.** Work was her **life. Even** when she sat down to rest, she was snapping beans or making the long magic curl of an apple peeling fall into a shallow pan. **9.** As time pas**sed, we** both grew older. **11.** Tiny stitch**es—thes**e were ha**nd-sew**n stitch**es—secur**ed a large pocket to the front of each of her several aprons.
13. Actually, I never saw everything in her pocket; however, I can still see her hand reaching into it to give me a surprise. **15.** Whenever my childish heart was broken or my knee was skinn**ed,** she would again reach into that bulging pocket and pull out a bit of happiness in the form of gum or candy. **17.** My grandmother was always able to distinguish between my need and my gree**d when** I asked for a piece of candy. **19.** As I gained some of her insight**, I** began to understand just how little she had to use or to save. **21.** She lived in a time when a woman's place was in the ho**me; she** accepted that most of the time. **23.** Neverth**eless, her** feet remained on practical ground. **25.** She had something speci**al—so**mething that would transcend death, live beyond the grave, and endure through the **ages. S**he had a pocketful of love.

Your rewritten version will probably be somewhat different. The flexibility of our rich language can make your paragraph different from anyone else's version. Still, if you have inserted transitions, you will have improved the original paragraph.

Transitions in Writing   Transitions are important devices for writers **because they** serve as guides to **both** the writer and reader. **For example,** transitions offer logical connections between words, phrases, clauses, and sentences. **Indeed, they can** transform short, choppy sentences into smooth-flowing prose. Transitions **also** provide logical connections between sentences. **In addition,** they can move the reader from one paragraph to the next by connecting paragraphs. **In that way,** transitions help the reader glide from one major idea to the next. **Moreover,** they are used to show similarities, contrasts, and additions. Transitions are **further** used for sequence of both items and time, **as well as** for examples, intensification, and cause and effect. **They** can

even signal conclusions. **These marvelous writing tools** provide **otherwise** choppy prose with rhythm, logic, and **certainly** smoothness.

12.2 CHAPTER 12

The Devil Made Me Do It   First, I want to ask you a few questions. Are you <u>a leader</u> or <u>a follower</u>? Are you <u>a dreamer</u> or <u>a doer</u>, <u>a whiner</u> or <u>a winner</u>? Are you <u>a protester against authority</u> or <u>a provider of fresh ideas</u>? [All the underlined words in this paragraph are parallel because of the coordinate conjunction *or.*]

Before you answer these questions, travel with me on an armchair journey all the way back to the Great Depression in the early 1930s. Most people in West Virginia, my home state, <u>were poor</u>, <u>had been poor</u>, and <u>would continue to be poor</u>. [Repetition of the forms of the verb *be* followed by the adjective *poor* is effective here.] Poverty during those bleak, gray days was <u>so severe</u>, <u>so widespread</u> that you might think crime was rampant. [Repetition is effective.] It was not. Despite the poverty, people seldom locked their doors.

Today, crime <u>is repeatedly blamed</u> on poverty, but the experiences of West Virginians during a time of abject poverty <u>do not support</u> such an oft-repeated <u>assertion</u>—an <u>assertion</u> that has become a myth. [The two underlined phrases are parallel because of *and. Assertion* is repeated to reinforce the lack of proof in the blame.] People from both <u>poor</u> and <u>wealthy</u> backgrounds commit crimes. [Adjectives are parallel because of *and.*]

The big myth I am shattering is the myth that people commit dastardly acts <u>because of the system or because of their parents or because of their unfair teachers or because of society as a whole</u>. [Repetition of the "because phrase" is required when *or* is used. *Or* is used to replace commas to emphasize the long list of excuses used for criminals and others who break the law.] We <u>have</u> ready excuses for almost any negative behavior, and the excuses <u>make</u> the perpetrator feel purged, exonerated. [The transitive verbs are connected by *and.*] The rest of us are burdened with guilt for others' actions: those of us <u>who have obeyed the laws</u>, <u>who have worked hard</u>, <u>who have been good students, good parents, and good citizens</u>. [This is effective use of repetition.] We have <u>worked</u> and <u>planned</u> and <u>made</u> wise decisions, but we have nonetheless been targeted as the bad guys. [Parallelism is required because of *and,* which replaced commas for effectiveness.]

It is time we put a halt to this devil-made-me-do-it mentality. If I decide to <u>take that first drink</u>, <u>smoke that first cigarette</u>, or <u>experiment with that popular drug</u> of the day, that decision is <u>mine</u> and <u>mine</u> alone. [Parallelism and repetition of <u>mine</u> used for emphasis.] If I blame society for the consequences, I am <u>a whiner</u>, <u>a mimic</u>. [Parallel structure is used for reinforcement. Also, *and,* although deleted, would connect the underlined elements.]

Think about it. When you make decisions to avoid addictive and destructive behavior, you are paving the way to becoming <u>a winner—not a whiner</u>, <u>a leader—not a follower</u>, <u>a thinker—not a mimic</u>. [Here, the elements are strictly parallel, even the dashes.]

Despite your supportive teachers and professors, you cannot succeed unless you make a commitment to learning, unless you study, unless you read, unless you complete the assignments. [Obviously, the repetition of the "unless clauses" pounds home the message.] It is, then, not <u>who your parents are</u>, but <u>who you are</u>; it is not <u>who your friends are</u>, but <u>who you are</u>. It is not <u>where you live</u> or <u>where you attend college</u>. [The "who clauses" and the "where clauses" continue to bring the message home.] Peer pressure cannot make you commit any act you do not wish to commit. <u>You alone</u> must take responsibility for your decisions. <u>You</u> will live with their rewards or their consequences. [This is effective repetition.]

12.3 CHAPTER 12

Your answers may vary slightly.

1. Sentence was correct. **3.** The rhythm created by repetition and parallelism in writing is similar to the rhythm in life. **5.** Not only does Annie use parallel structure in her prose, but also she uses repetition. **7.** Life's rhythm can be found in the cycle of seasons, in the cadence of heartbeats, in the repetition of day and night, and even in the routines of all living creatures. **9.** Neither Matt nor Annie was a naturalist. **11.** He was not so much trying to communicate as he was trying to impress. **13.** Under Annie's guidance, the man gradually wrote prose that was clear, rhythmic, and powerful.

13.1 CHAPTER 13

1. approaches **3.** editors-in-chief **5.** judgment **7.** accommodations **9.** deer **11.** Memories **13.** familiar **15.** conscience **17.** opossum **19.** separated **21.** traveling **23.** Their **25.** canceled

13.2 CHAPTER 13

The Picnic It seemed a lifetime ago **since** Matt had become acquainted with Annie at the bank's picnic. **Its** picnic had been held in July of that **memorable** year. The two of them had sat on adjoining **benches.** They watched various species of **fishes** swimming in the blue lake. Two large red **foxes** darted through the woods on the opposite side of the lake. Suddenly, a green snake slithered beneath Annie's bench. Not afraid of nonpoisonous snakes, Annie laughed and told Matt she was glad no **mongooses** could threaten **their** native snakes. During the next hour, Matt discovered that Annie was an **alumna** of his college.

Not yet working on his M.B.A., Matt remembered saying, "**You're** an alumna of my college." This comment led to a discussion of the college cafeteria's food, especially **its** mashed **potatoes.** They both agreed that the taste must surely have been **similar** to wallpaper paste. So engrossed in their conversation were Matt and Annie, they did not see the many **passers-by,** three young **deer,** or the four **sheep** that were grazing on a nearby hill. Only when a **woman** exclaimed that three **trout** had swum to the surface of the water did they once again notice **their** surroundings.

Yes, Matt remembered well **their** first conversation. That was even before he had **received** his undergraduate degree. That was before Annie had worked with several **editors-in-chief.** That was the **beginning** of a long friendship. That was a lifetime ago. Remembering **their** many sessions in which he had learned valuable **writing** tips, Matt was now ready to call Annie. He was planning to end another sentence with proposition.

13.3 CHAPTER 13

1. New Year's Day is a time for beginnings. **3.** A decade's beginning presents an even greater challenge to set goals. **5.** Mrs. Marsha Jones' journal contained many references to her experiences in Annie's writing classes. **7.** The two women's essays won high praise from Annie. **9.** Marsha wrote about her own experiences. **11.** The women lived only a stone's throw from the college. **13.** The Joneses' house was near Annie's luxurious apartment building. **15.** Marsha often wrote about today's society with its many problems and its many opportunities for solutions. **17.** She wrote about the spirit of love that could create its own juncture where all people could meet and live in harmony. **19.** During one session, Annie told the class about the time a woman had wanted to take credit for Annie's writing.

13.4 CHAPTER 13

1. The sentences that follow are excerpts from a new book by one of Annie's former students; its title is *The Book of Esther: Mother Tongue.* **3.** The nurse, according to my mother, had an additional degree in Psychology. **5.** Laughing at her comments, I said, "You surely mean *inflammation,* don't you, Mom?" **7.** My mother creates her own words and, therefore, often needs an interpreter; I'm usually it. **9.** The doctor's repeated question about her symptoms did not surprise me. **11.** Despite her creative language, my mother understands people's behavior and motivations better than anyone I know. **13.** Her advice only irritated me because naturally I knew more than she ever could. **15.** A daughter's hairstyle should never be discussed between mother and daughter. **17.** I said that I liked my hair's length but might get a perm. **19.** "It's been four months, Mom," said I with a sigh. **21.** Later, during a writing conference that Mother attended with me, she said, "Let's leave. I'm not one bit 'insterned' in this." **23.** This kind of blending takes nothing short of brilliance, all of which proves that people whose dialects are "different" can be brilliant. **25.** Cushions are "cooshions," according to my mother's pronunciation. **27.** Not a linguistic snob, I know that my mother is wise, wonderful, and witty, which is why I like writing about her. **29.** Annie Dillard's mother inspired Annie because of her mother's expertise with language. **31.** shining, library **33.** hours' **35.** José's **37.** wasn't, its **39.** complements **41.** chosen, convenience **43.** disastrous, retrieved **45.** mom and dad's **47.** car's **49.** others'

14.1 CHAPTER 14

The Proposition   Matt parked his new **F**ord **T**aurus in the basement parking garage. A few minutes later, he rang **A**nnie's doorbell. Opening the door, Annie smiled and said, "**W**hat's your proposition, Matt? I can hardly wait to hear how **I** am involved."

Matt walked toward the sofa. "In another month," he said, "**y**ou'll be enjoying your **s**ummer vacation. You usually travel, write about your travels, and sell your articles to various publishers. You mentioned that if you had photographs of professional quality you could sell even more articles."

"Yes, yes, go on." said Annie as she tied the shoelace of her left **N**ike.

Smiling, Matt said, "Be patient, Annie. I've been hired as a photographer for *National Geographic.* I'll be traveling all over the world—to Africa, **S**outh **A**merica. You name it. I might float down the **N**ile **R**iver one month and, the next, the **Y**angtze."

"That's terrific! So, where do I fit in?" asked Annie.

"I want you to travel with me this **s**ummer, Annie. I've talked with my supervisor at *National Geographic,* and she would love to have you write for the magazine. I think we'd make a winning team," explained Matt.

Annie poured steaming **E**arl **G**rey tea into fine porcelain cups. Waiting for her response, Matt reached for the cup and saucer.

"I don't know, Matt. I usually spend **I**ndependence **D**ay with my family, that is, my **a**unts, **u**ncles, and cousins. Our annual family reunion is held during **J**uly, and **G**randmother Penwright is quite old. Still, I know what she would tell me. I'm tempted."

Seizing the opportunity, Matt said, "Come on, Annie. I'll brush up on my **F**rench. Where's your spirit of adventure?"

"Okay, Matt. I'll do it. We'll be business partners as we sail the **A**tlantic and the **P**acific. I'll have marvelous tales to tell, and you'll have breathtaking scenes to photograph," said Annie.

As Matt left, he paused at the door and said with a sheepish grin, "Would you happen to have any **T**aster's **C**hoice™?"

Thinking of those television commercials and a future filled with delightful surprises, they both laughed.

15.1 CHAPTER 15

17. It is in a book titled <u>American Poetry</u>. **19.** <u>Newsweek</u> is a consumer magazine. **21.** Many financiers read <u>The Wall Street Journal</u> every day. **23.** "Amazing Grace" is a hymn familiar to many people. **25.** "Salvation," an essay by Langston Hughes, is included in many anthologies. **27.** Annie enjoys reading the <u>New York Times</u>. **29.** The word <u>the</u> is an article. **31.** <u>ER</u> is a popular television program. **33.** <u>No Time to Kill</u>, a CD, contains the country song "A Good Run of Bad Luck." **35.** <u>Out of Africa</u> is an excellent movie.

Index

363